THE PRINCETON REVIEW: WHO WE ARE

A HISTORY OF RESULTS

The Princeton Review has rapidly expanded from just 15 SAT course students in 1981 to more than 70,000 course students of all test types in 1996. We are now the nation's most popular standardized test preparation company across four channels of distribution: courses, books, software, and online services. Small classes, personal attention, a unique approach, and great results are some of the key characteristics for which The Princeton Review is famous.

A CHAMPION OF STUDENTS' RIGHTS/ FOSTERING CHANGE

The Princeton Review has always been an aggressive advocate of students' rights, promoting open and fair testing. Our presence fosters accountability (and intelligence) in the unjust world of standardized testing. Our history of involvement in controversial testing issues gives hope to present and future students everywhere.

GUIDING PEOPLE THROUGH TRANSITIONS

The phenomenal success of our SAT course led to an overwhelming demand for other courses. The Princeton Review's exclusive methods are now helping high school and graduate school students crack all major standardized tests. We also offer a broad range of basic skill-building courses, as well as professional and career programs.

CRACKING THE SYSTEM

The Princeton Review began its Publishing Division in 1985 and made history from the start with *Cracking the SAT*. Our library, now 100 titles strong, includes a series of student, career, and professional books, each designed to help guide people through critical stages in their lives.

LEADING THE EDUCATIONAL SOFTWARE REVOLUTION

In 1994 we entered the retail software market, and within one year our Inside the SAT title took over as the "Best of Breed" product in test preparation software. Currently, we have an award-winning line of six titles, recognized by publications such as Home PC, The New York Times, Fortune, and The Washington Post.

HELPING OTHERS

The Princeton Review Foundation, a nonprofit organization, was established in 1987 to address the test prep needs of underprivileged students. Through a nationwide network of programs, The Princeton Review Foundation helps financially disadvantaged students in inner-city public school and provides free assistance to students in disputes with test companies.

ENDLESS STUDENT SUPPORT

The Princeton Review offers students a wealth of free and unique resources. Through our special student programs and our informative and comprehensive internet site, students can gather information about tests, admissions, internships, and career programs. We also work with a wide range of companies to obtain discounts on various products and services for our course students.

THE
PRINCETON
REVIEW

800 2-REVIEW

World Wide Web: http://www.review.com
E-mail: info.tpr@review.com

COURSES • BOOKS • SOFTWARE • ONLINE

BOOKS IN THE PRINCETON REVIEW SERIES

THE PRINCETON REVIEW

Cracking the AP:
U.S. History Exam

By Tom Meltzer

1997-98 EDITION
RANDOM HOUSE, INC.
NEW YORK 1997

Princeton Review Publishing, L.L.C.
2315 Broadway
New York, NY 10024
E-mail: info@review.com

ISSN: 1076-5395
ISBN: 0-679-76925-0

AP is a registered trademark of The College Board.

Editor: Amy Zavatto
Designer: Illeny Maaza
Production Editor: Rich Klin

Manufactured in the United States of America on partially recycled paper.

9 8 7 6 5 4 3 2 1
First Edition

ACKNOWLEDGMENTS

First and foremost, thanks to Jean Hofheimer Bennett, a high school history teacher in Weston, Connecticut, whom I had the great fortune of meeting via e-mail and, later, in person. Jean provided me with a steady stream of ideas, answers to questions, critiques, and encouragement, and it is an understatement to say that this book would not have been possible without her assistance.

I solicited suggestions for this book by e-mailing all the history teachers, professors, and AP exam graders listed at the College Board's AP History Web Site. The following people generously provided their insights even after I warned them that this acknowledgment would be their only payment: Theodore C. DeLaney, assistant professor of history at Washington & Lee University; Dr. Keith Edgerton, Montana State University—Billings; Chuck Quirk, University of Northern Iowa; Pamela Riney-Kehrberg, department of history at Illinois State University; Marion Roydhouse, associate professor of history at Philadelphia College of Textiles and Science; John R. Struck, Thomas Jefferson High School of Science and Technology, in Virginia; and Darril Wilburn, Bardstown High School in New York. Thanks again for your help. Having been out of school for a while, I had forgotten how giving teachers can be; you all reminded me.

I scavenged the other *Cracking the System* books in search of good ideas for this one, and I found many. Thanks to all the *Cracking* authors, particularly Grace Roegner Freedman, Geoff Martz, Laurice Pearson, John Katzman, and Adam Robinson. Thanks also to the Princeton Review publishing staff for their patience on this project, particularly to my editors, Celeste Sollod and Amy Zavatto, and head honcho Jeannie Yoon. Also pitching in with major assists was the production staff: Greta Englert, Effie Hadjiioannou, Rich Klin, Illeny Maaza, and John Pak.

Thanks finally to my family, to Lisa, and to Paul, Steve, Neil, and Pete for listening to me ramble on about American history for the past six months, and for being good friends.

CONTENTS

INTRODUCTION

WHAT IS THE PRINCETON REVIEW?

The Princeton Review is an international test preparation company with branches in all the major U.S. cities and several abroad. In 1981, John Katzman started teaching an SAT prep course in his parents' living room. Within five years Katzman (in partnership with fellow test-guru Adam Robinson) had established the largest SAT coaching program in the country.

The Princeton Review's phenomenal success in improving students' scores on standardized tests was (and is) due to a simple, innovative, and radically effective philosophy. Study the test, not what the test *claims* to test. This approach has led to the development of techniques for taking standardized tests based on the principles the test writers themselves use to write the tests.

The Princeton Review has found that its methods work not just for cracking the SAT, but for any standardized test. We've already successfully applied our system to the GMAT, LSAT, MCAT, and GRE, to name just a few. Although in some ways the AP United States History Test is a very different test from those mentioned above, in the end, a standardized test is a standardized test. This book uses our time-tested principle: Crack the system based on how the test is written.

We also publish books and CD-ROMs on an enormous variety of education and career-related topics. If you're interested check out our website at http://www.review.com.

part 1

HOW TO CRACK THE SYSTEM

1

ABOUT THE ADVANCED PLACEMENT PROGRAM

WHAT IS THE ADVANCED PLACEMENT PROGRAM?

The fact that you are reading this book means that you probably already know something about the Advanced Placement (AP) program. After all, how many people pick up a test preparation guide for a little light reading? So, you probably already know that the AP courses at your high school are supposed to be the toughest available, and also that at the end of the school year you can take an AP exam that may allow you to earn college credit for your work in the course. However, you probably don't know the following: Who decides what constitutes an AP course? Are AP courses the same at every high school? Who writes and grades the AP exam? This section of the book answers these and other related questions.

The Advanced Placement program is coordinated by an organization called **The College Board**. The College Board oversees college admissions examinations. It also publishes test and course materials from previous years, holds seminars on college admissions, and sponsors educational research. Its membership is made up of college administrators, educators, and admissions officers, as well as high school administrators, guidance counselors, and teachers.

The College Board appoints a **development committee** for each of the 29 subjects in which AP exams are available. Each committee meets to decide what should be covered in an AP course and what should be on the AP exam. The history committee is made up of three high school history teachers and three college history teachers. Its decisions are included in a publication called *Advanced Placement Course Description: History*, which is available from The College Board (the book you are now reading includes all the pertinent information from that publication, so you don't need it. If you do want to take a look at this booklet, ask your history teacher if he or she has a copy; most history departments should have copies of all the important College Board AP publications. Since those publications are available for sale to the general public, there's no reason your teacher should refuse to let you see them.).

The history development committee does two important jobs: it updates the course description to reflect recent events and trends in historical analysis; and, it writes the AP History exam. The committee very rarely makes major changes to the course or the test format. Here are some of its recent changes: In 1996 it shortened the multiple-choice section (yeah!). In 1994 it decided to require two free-response essays rather than one, as it previously had (boo!). In 1982 the committee shortened the Document-Based Question from 20+ documents to approximately nine, but it also added the requirement that students include outside information in their essays (yeah? boo? sigh!). When the committee finishes writing each year's exam, it hands it over to the **Educational Testing Service** (ETS), which prints up and administers the exam. Yes, they are the same folks who administer the SATs and many other admissions exams.

Most AP History teachers have a copy of the development committee's course requirements, which includes an outline of everything a thorough history course should cover (as well as suggested drills, reading assignments, paper topics, etc.). However, no one forces teachers to teach AP History in a particular way; the committee's requirements are actually more like suggestions. If you discuss your AP History course with a friend taking the same course at a different school, you will likely find that his or her course is noticeably different from yours (especially if you are using different textbooks). Don't worry about these differences: there is no one *right way* to teach history. Different teachers will interpret the meaning and importance of events differently. In that way, your AP History course is similar to a college course. In most other ways, it will probably be easier than a typical college course, although much harder than a typical high school course. The course is usually most difficult if you have a really good teacher (who wants to push you to reach your highest potential) or a really bad teacher (who simply is not isn't up to the material).

SHOULD YOU TAKE AP CLASSES? SHOULD YOU TAKE AP EXAMS?

There's an obvious downside to taking AP classes: they're more difficult than regular classes. Compared with regular classes, AP classes mean more detailed lectures, more homework, more research papers, more tests, and, possibly, a lower grade. So, why take an AP course?

First, if you're looking to go to college, you want as many AP courses on your transcript as you can comfortably handle. These classes indicate to your prospective schools that you're serious about studying. Many admissions offices will give your AP grade a one-level "bump": that is, they will consider your "C" as a "B." (That's how some high school students end up with GPAs above 4.0: they get almost all As, including their AP courses) College admissions officers are more favorably disposed to students who take AP courses.

Second, AP courses help you develop skills you will need in college. A good AP teacher will assign research papers and essay tests; require you to study primary source material, maps, census data, and lots of other resources beyond your textbook; encourage discussion of course material; and lecture in such a way that you have to take good notes in order to pass the course. All of these aspects of AP courses will help prepare you for your college courses.

Third, AP courses are supposed to prepare you for AP exams, which can be quite helpful in getting your college degree. Many schools award college credit for good grades on the AP. Since college credits cost money, each of your successes on an AP exam could save you and/or your parents a lot of money. Some schools will admit you as a sophomore if you get high enough marks on three (or more; it varies from school to school) AP exams. In a best case scenario, then, the AP's can help you skip a year of college (and save a year's tuition). It is important to note that you do *not have to take an AP course* to take an AP exam. If you feel that you are up to speed in a subject, you should take the AP exam regardless of the course you took. Remember also that it is the individual college, and not The College Board, that decides whether to grant advanced placement for AP scores; the schools themselves also determine what is considered a satisfactory grade. (AP exams are graded on a scale of 1 to 5, with 5 being the highest possible score.) Before committing to an AP exam, contact your prospective schools and find out their AP policy. You could also check the school's course catalogue: almost all schools print their AP policies in their catalogues, which are usually available on microfiche at the larger libraries in your area. Ask the reference librarian for assistance.

Taking AP tests can help your college application in other ways as well. The College Board confers a number of awards to students who excel on three or more AP exams. The **AP Scholar Awards** are given to students who exceed an average grade of 3 on three or more exams; more prestigious awards are given to students who take more tests and receive higher grades. These awards are noted on the score reports that are sent to your prospective colleges.

How Do I Sign Up for the Exam? What Should I Expect on Test Day?

If you want to take one or more AP exams, the first thing you should do is go see your guidance counselor. He or she will direct you to the **AP Coordinator** for your school. The AP Coordinator is usually a teacher or a counselor; he or she is the one in charge of collecting your money and telling you when and where the exam will be held. If for some reason you can't take the test through your school—for example, if you're the only student who wants to take an AP exam, and so your school has not designated a coordinator–you can still take the test through another school. To find out which schools in your area offer the test, call The College Board's AP Services office at (609) 771-7300, or write them by March 1 at: P.O. Box 6671, Princeton, NJ 08541-6671.

It costs $73 to take each exam, with a few exceptions for half-year courses (some of which are offered at a "two for $73" rate). This fee is expensive, but still much cheaper than a college course. Your school keeps $7 for administrative fees, and The College Board suggests that the school refund that money to you if you and your family have financial difficulties. You may also apply to The College Board for a $22 fee reduction based on financial need. If for some reason you need to take the test at a different time you may be charged an additional fee of $30. Your AP Coordinator will collect the fees. The College Board does not accept money from you directly.

Here is The College Board's Suggested Timetable for Those Preparing to Take an AP Test:

- **January**—Go see your history teacher and your guidance counselor to discuss whether you should take the exam. If you decide to take the test, go see the AP coordinator and pay your fees. If you need to make special arrangements because of a disability, do so at this time. If your school does not offer AP exams, contact The College Board and ask for the location of the closest school offering the tests.

- **Mid-February**—If you need to take the exam at another school and you still have not yet made plans to do so, DO IT NOW!

- **May 5–9 and May 12–16**—AP exams are administered.

- **Early and Mid-June**—AP exams are graded. If you want your score report sent to colleges other than those you provided with your test registration, or if you want to cancel your test scores, you have until **June 15** to contact The College Board with your request. (There's more about canceling your test scores below, under the heading *Special Circumstances*.)

- **Early July**—Your prospective colleges start to receive your grades.

- **Early to Mid-July**—You receive your grades.

The AP U.S. History exam will be offered at **8 A.M.** on **Friday, May 9, 1997**. The test may start a little earlier or later at your school, but not much: College Board rules prohibit starting before 6 A.M. or after 10 A.M. On test day, you will need to bring:

- two number-two pencils (for the multiple choice section). Make sure you have an eraser.

- a dark-blue or black pen (with which to write your essays).

- a watch (in case there's no clock in your testing room). Do not bring a watch with an alarm or a calculator: It will be confiscated by the proctor.

- a photo ID if you are taking the AP at a school other than your own.

HERE ARE SOME THINGS YOU MAY **NOT** BRING TO THE EXAM:

- textbooks, notebooks, a dictionary, or a pocket encyclopedia. In short, no books!

- laptop computers.

- cameras (to prevent you from photographing the exam and giving the pictures to someone like me).

- portable stereos or radios.

The AP U.S. History exam consists of three sections. First, you will fill out a bunch of forms, which takes 10 to 15 minutes. Then, you will take an 80-question multiple -choice section, for which you are given 55 minutes. Afterwards, you will be given a break of approximately 15 minutes. This break is the only one you get during the test. Then there is the Document-Based Question (DBQ), which consists of a 15-minute reading period, followed by a 45-minute writing period. Finally, there are two free-response essay questions; you have 70 minutes to complete both. We will discuss each of these sections in detail in the following chapters.

SPECIAL CIRCUMSTANCES

Special conditions for students with disabilities—Students who seek special testing conditions to accommodate disabilities should have either a current Individualized Education Program (IEP) on file at their school OR a signed letter from an appropriate professional (doctor, psychologist, reading specialist, etc.) describing the disability and verifying the need for different testing arrangements. Qualified students have several options: Students with poor or no vision may take large-type tests and Braille tests. Poor-sighted students may also use a reader or amanuensis. Qualified students also have the right to take the exam at a different, more accommodating location. Take note: You must present documentation of your disability in order for your score report to indicate "Certified Disability." Otherwise, your test report will simply indicate a "Nonstandard Administration," which is the same indication given on the test of a non-disabled student who takes the exam untimed. As an untimed exam may give the appearance of an advantage, admissions officers are not always sympathetic to the "Nonstandard Administration" report. So, contact your AP Coordinator as soon as possible, but no later than April 1 about arranging your test. Make sure your documentation is in order long before test day, and, if possible, take the test under standard conditions.

Problems on test day—On rare occasions, The College Board writes a lousy question. Sometimes ETS misprints a question, misprints a page of the exam (or leaves it blank!), or makes some other such error. If, during the test, you believe that one or more of the questions on the test don't work, you should contact The College Board as soon as possible after the test. Provide the test title, the question number, and a description of what you think was wrong with the question. Honestly, this is extremely unlikely to happen in the History exam—such errors are almost invariably on tests in math or science. If you see a misprint, you should report it immediately to the proctor, and then, after the exam, to The College Board. The phone number, address, and e-mail address to use appear at the end of this chapter.

More common are problems in test administration. Maybe your proctor gave the directions incorrectly. For you, that should be no big deal, as you will know all the directions well before test day (because you read this book!). The big problem is if your proctor mistimes the exam, particularly if he or she gives you too little time (you *could* report an error if your proctor gave you too *much* time, but why would you want to?). In the case of a timing error, notify the school's AP Coordinator immediately. If the coordinator does not help (maybe he or she is the proctor who screwed up the timing), go see the principal. If you wait too long, you may be forced to retake the exam. Even worse, you may get stuck with the score you got on the mistimed exam.

That covers what happens when The College Board, ETS, or your proctor screws up. What about when you screw up? If you think (or know) that you blew the exam, you have until June 15 to contact The College Board and cancel your score. June 15 is also the date by which you have to contact The College Board if you want to: withhold your grades from certain colleges; or, add schools to the list of those receiving your grades. Unless you're reasonably certain you got a "1" on an AP exam, you probably shouldn't cancel your grade.

Finally, here's a list of things that will get you thrown out of the test, have your scores canceled, and raise serious suspicion that you are a cheater:

- leafing through the exam booklet before the exam begins
- trying to give answers to or receive answers from someone else during the exam
- working on the wrong section of the exam
- continuing to work on the exam after you have been instructed to stop
- tearing a page out of your test booklet, or trying to sneak the entire exam out of the test site
- looking in a textbook, notebook, encyclopedia, etc., during the exam or during the break

- failing to obey any other testing regulation

- behaving disruptively by screaming, whooping, dancing, singing, smacking your lips with pleasure or disgust, throwing things, pacing around the room, performing auto-surgery, etc.

FINALLY...

Most of the information in this chapter appears in a College Board publication called *Advanced Placement: Bulletin for Students and Parents*. It's free and you should be able to get a copy of it from your guidance counselor. If not, write to:

AP Services
P.O. Box 6671
Princeton, NJ 08541-6671

Their phone number is (609) 771-7300, and their e-mail address is **apexams@ets.org**. Students who are deaf or hard of hearing can call the teletypewriter (TTY) at (609) 882-4118. If you have access to the Internet, you can visit The College Board's home page for the AP U.S. History exam at **http://cbweb1.collegeboard.org/ap/history/html/indx001.html**. It includes sample test questions and updated information about the 1997 exam. It also contains some test-taking suggestions that you should ignore; the good suggestions have been incorporated into this book. Those suggestions that we at the Princeton Review think are not so good are not included here.

2 BEING A GOOD TEST TAKER

Very few students stop to think about how to improve their test-taking skills. Most assume that if they study hard, they will test well; and if they do not study, they will do poorly. Most students continue to believe this even after experience teaches them otherwise. Have you ever studied really hard for an exam, then blown it on test day? Have you ever aced an exam you thought you weren't well prepared for? Most students have had one, if not both, of these experiences. The lesson should be clear: Factors other than your level of preparation influence your final test score.

This section will provide you with some insights that will help you perform better on the AP U.S. History exam and on other exams as well.

TEST ANXIETY

Everybody (with the possible exception of people on sedatives) experiences anxiety before and during an exam. To a certain extent, test anxiety *can* be helpful. Some people find that they perform more quickly and efficiently under stress. If you have ever pulled an all-nighter to write a paper and ended up doing good work, you know the feeling.

However, *too much* stress is definitely a bad thing. Hyperventilating during the test, for example, almost always leads to a lower score. If you find that you stress out during exams, here are a few preemptive actions you can take:

- **Take a reality check**. Apprise your situation before the test begins. If you have studied hard, remind yourself that you are well-prepared. Remember that many others taking the test are not as well-prepared, and (in your classes, at least) you are being graded against them, so you have an advantage. If you didn't study, accept the fact that you will probably not ace the test. Make sure you get to every question you know something about. Don't stress out or fixate on how much you don't know. Your job is to score as high as you can by maximizing the benefits of what you do know. In either scenario, it is best to think of a test as if it were a game. How can you get the most points in the time allotted to you? Always answer questions you can answer easily and quickly before you answer those that will take more time. When confronted with a choice, answer those questions that are worth more points rather than those that are worth less.

- **Learn to relax**. Slow, deep breathing works for almost everyone. Take a few seconds, close your eyes, and take a few, slow, deep breaths, and concentrate on nothing but your inhalation and exhalation. This is a basic form of meditation, and it should help you to clear your mind of stress and, as a result, concentrate better on the test. If you have ever taken yoga classes, you probably know some other good relaxation techniques. Use them when you can (obviously, anything that requires leaving your seat and, say, assuming a handstand position won't be allowed by any but the most free-spirited proctors).

- **Eliminate as many surprises as you can**. Make sure you know where the test will be given, when it starts, what type of questions are going to be asked, and how long the test will take. You don't want to be worrying about any of these things on test day or, even worse, after the test has already begun.

The best way to avoid stress is to study both the test material and the test itself. Congratulations! By buying or reading this book, you are taking a major step toward a stress-free AP U.S. History exam.

PACING

A big part of scoring well on an exam is working at a consistent pace. The worst mistake made by inexperienced or unsavvy test takers is that they spend too long on a single question. They come to a question that stumps them, and, rather than just skip it, they panic and stall. Time stands still when you're working on a question you cannot answer, and it is not unusual for students to waste five minutes on a single question because they are too stubborn to cut their losses.

Don't make that mistake. Tests are like marathons, and you do best on them when you work through them at a steady pace. You can always come back to a question you don't know. When you do, very often you will find that your previous mental block is gone, and you will wonder why the question perplexed you the first time around (as you gleefully move on to the next question). Even if you still don't know the answer, you will not have wasted valuable time you could have spent on easier questions.

This is particularly true on multiple-choice tests like Part A of the AP U.S. History test or the SAT. On these tests, questions are worth the same value toward your final score. Remember, when all the questions on a test are of equally value, no one question is that important. You should always skip questions that give you trouble until you have answered every question that you know the answer to.

Finally, you should set a realistic goal for your final score. Depending on the score you need, it may be in your best interest *not* to try to answer every question. In trying to do too much, you can easily hurt your score with careless mistakes. Check with the schools to which you are applying. Do you need a "3" to earn credit for the test? If you get a **raw score** of 48 (out of 80) on the multiple choice exam *and* do as well on the essays, you will get a "3." Your raw score is determined by adding up the number of questions you answer correctly, then subtracting the number of questions you answer incorrectly. In other words, you could answer 60 questions, get 51 right and 9 wrong, and *leave 20 blank* and still be on pace for a "3." Only students who need a "5" should try to answer every question on the multiple-choice section; everyone else should go slower and spend more time on each question in order to avoid careless mistakes.

Because The College Board has not recently released its grading statistics, the following is an approximation of how to pace yourself on the AP test:

If you want to get a:	Answer this many:	And leave this many blank:
2	≈45	≈35
3	≈60	≈20
4	≈70	≈10
5	as many as you can	as few as possible

We will talk more about pacing on the multiple-choice section in the next chapter.

IN THE WEEKS BEFORE THE TEST...

There are a few things you should start doing any time after January 1 (but certainly before May 1). One of them is to read this book. Here are some others:

- **Ask your teacher for copies of old AP U.S. History exams**. The College Board releases copies of at least one, and sometimes two, old exams. The College Board also publishes a book that contains every DBQ that has appeared on the test since 1974 and another that contains all the free-response questions asked during the last five years. Your school history department probably has copies of all of these. Look at them, and, for practice, do one or more of the DBQs and one or more sets of free-response essays. Hand them to your teacher; he or she will probably be happy to review your work with you. NOTE: Practice only on DBQs written after 1982 and free-response questions written after 1994 (because those are the years when The College Board changed the question formats).

- **Commit a little time every night to test preparation**. A little studying every night is much better than a lot of cramming in the week before the exam. Starting in late March or early April, try to set aside 30 to 45 minutes three or four times a week to review this book, the textbook you use in class, your notes on your teacher's lectures, and any other class materials. If you have Internet access, you can spend a few (but not a lot) of those nights surfing the Web for history sites—there are thousands of them. (A list of some of the ones I like appears at the end of this book.)

IN THE FINAL WEEK BEFORE THE EXAM...

In a best case scenario, you should not cram for the test. However, cramming is better than not studying at all. If it's one week before the test and you haven't started studying yet, you should cram. If, on the other hand, you have been preparing, you should:

- **Maintain your usual routine**. Try not to go to bed a lot later or a lot earlier than usual. Don't start a new diet or a new exercise program. Don't get emotionally involved with a dangerous psychopath who will put your pet rabbit in a pot of boiling water in your kitchen. In other words, stay the course.

- **Do a general history review**. Stop concentrating on details this week. Focus instead on "big picture" issues, such as political, social, and economic trends. In other words, stop asking yourself questions like "What was the Gadsden Purchase?" and start asking yourself questions like "What other issues (besides slavery) divided the North and South during the first half of the nineteenth century?"

- **Read all the directions for the exam**. They're all in this book. Don't waste valuable time during the exam reading instructions. Know what you're supposed to do on each section of the test long before test day.

ON TEST DAY...

- **Start the day with a reasonable, but not huge, breakfast**. You'll need energy for the exam. Have a nice breakfast, but nothing so big that it will put you to sleep. Beware of coffee, tea, or anything else that will send you to the rest room during the test.

- **Bring everything you need**. Those things would be: two or more number-two pencils (for the multiple-choice section), an eraser, a dark-blue or black pen (for the essay sections), and a watch. Do not bring a watch with an alarm or one that beeps; it will be taken from you.

- **Wear comfortable clothing.**

- **Bring a snack**. A piece of fruit or a candy bar during the break can give you a much-needed energy boost. A kind proctor might even let you munch on a noise-less snack (e.g., a banana or a candy bar) during the test, but don't count on it.

FINALLY...

Learn everything you can about the exam. The more you know, the less you will be surprised by during the test, and the easier and quicker the exam will go. To learn everything you need to know about the AP U.S. History test, read on. The following chapters will tell you all about the exam's multiple choice section and the two essay sections of the exam.

SUMMARY

- Start studying for the test a month or more in advance. Just 30 to 45 minutes a few nights a week will make a huge difference.

- Ask your teacher for copies of old AP U.S. History exams. Write some practice essays and review them with your teacher.

- Don't change your regular routine in the week leading up to the test. Do, however, refocus your studies from details to "big picture" questions.

- On test day, wear something comfortable. Have a nice breakfast. Bring pencils, a pen, and a watch to the test. Bring a snack.

- Beat test anxiety. Prepare for the test so that there will be few surprises on test day. Take deep, slow breaths to relax during the test.

- Maintain a steady pace throughout the exam. Don't get hung up on any one question. Set a target score and pace yourself to achieve your goal.

3

CRACKING
THE MULTIPLE-CHOICE
SECTION

THE BASICS

The directions for the multiple-choice section of the AP U.S. History exam are pretty simple. They read:

Directions: Each of the following questions or incomplete statements below is followed by five suggested answers or completions. Select the one that is best in each case and then blacken the corresponding space on the answer sheet.

In short, you are being asked to do what you have done on lots of other multiple-choice exams. Pick the right answer, then fill in the appropriate bubble on a separate answer sheet. You will *not* be given credit for answers you record in your test booklet (e.g., by circling them) but not on your answer sheet. The section consists of 80 questions. You will be given 55 minutes to work on the section.

The College Board provides a breakdown by era and by general subject matter of the exam's questions by era and by general subject matter. This breakdown will *not* appear in your test booklet. It comes from the preparatory material The College Board publishes. Here it is:

Breakdown by Era		
Era	Percent of Questions	Number of Questions
1600 to 1789	17	13 to 14
1790 to 1914	50	40
1915 to present	33	26 or 27

Breakdown by General Subject Matter		
Subject	Percent of Questions	Number of Questions
Political institutions and behavior and public policy	35	28
Social change	35	28
Diplomacy and international relations	15	12
Economic change	10	8
Cultural and intellectual developments	5	4

As you can see, the test shows a decided bias toward the period between the ratification of the Constitution and the beginning of the First World War; it also emphasizes political and social activities, while caring relatively little about economic and cultural trends. Remember this as you study.

You should note that you will see *at most* two or three multiple-choice questions about the period following 1972. The test writers understand that many classes fall behind and don't ever get to the 1970s, 1980s, and 1990s. None of the essay questions will deal exclusively with the post-1970 era, although one essay question *may* touch on the period (you will almost certainly be able to do well on that essay without mentioning the 1970s at all). In short, if you don't study the post-1970 period, you're final score will be, at most, minimally affected.

TYPES OF QUESTIONS

The majority of questions on the multiple-choice section of the test are pretty straightforward. They ask questions such as:

3. Roger Williams was exiled from the Salem Bay settlement because he

   (A) endangered the colony by negotiating with neighboring Native Americans
   (B) championed the abolition of private property
   (C) questioned Parliament's authority to tax the colonists
   (D) disputed the authenticity of the Mayflower Compact
   (E) argued for the separation of church and state

Sometimes, The College Board makes the questions a little trickier. One way it does this is by phrasing a question in such a way that four answers are correct and one is incorrect. We call these questions "NOT/EXCEPT" questions because they usually contain one of those words (in capital letters, so they're harder to miss). Here is an example:

6. The New Deal included programs for achieving all of the following goals EXCEPT

   (A) developing an interstate highway system
   (B) stabilizing agricultural prices
   (C) insuring bank deposits
   (D) eliminating industrial overproduction
   (E) providing employment for the unemployed

Once or twice during the multiple-choice section, you will be asked to interpret an illustration, often a map or a political cartoon. These are usually pretty easy. The key is *not* to try to read too much between the lines.

Here is an example:

Hanna: That Man Clay was an Ass.
It's Better to be President than to be right!

45. The political cartoon above implies that

(A) McKinley was the first president to favor big
    business interests openly
(B) by the 1890s, Henry Clay's political
    approach had lost favor with the
    electorate
(C) McKinley's presidential campaign was
    masterminded by Marcus Hanna
(D) Marcus Hanna single-handedly controlled
    all three branches of the federal
    government
(E) McKinley was too young to be an effective
    president

Finally, there will be one or two questions on your test asking you to interpret a graph or chart. Again, these are usually very straightforward, and the most important thing for you to do is *not* to overinterpret the data. The correct answer will be indisputably supported by the information in the chart.

Here's an example:

Average, Highest, and Lowest Approval Ratings, by percentage of all eligible voters, for American Presidents, 1953 to 1974

	Average	High	Low
Eisenhower	65	79	48
Kennedy	70	83	56
Johnson	55	79	35
Nixon	49	67	24

Source: Gallup Polls

13. Which of the following conclusions can be drawn from the information presented in the chart above?

(A) Eisenhower was the most consistently popular president in the nation's history.
(B) Kennedy received greater Congressional support for his programs than did any other president during the period in question.
(C) Nixon's lowest approval rating was the result of the Watergate scandal.
(D) The difference between Johnson's highest and lowest approval ratings was the greatest for any president during the period in question.
(E) Eisenhower and Johnson were equally well-liked by all Americans.

Answers to these and other drill questions appear at the end of this chapter.

No Military History and No Trivial Pursuit

Here's some good news. The AP U.S. History exam doesn't ask about military history. You will never see a question on the AP exam like the one below:

XX. Union general Ulysses S. Grant was intent on capturing Vicksburg, Mississippi, because

    (A) Vicksburg was the munitions capitol of the Confederacy
    (B) whoever controlled the city could control transportation along the Mississippi River
    (C) Grant hoped to use the city as a supply depot for Union troops stationed throughout the South
    (D) the city was poorly defended, and the Union desperately needed a victory for morale purposes
    (E) Vicksburg was controlled by Indians hostile to the Union

Although Grant's siege of Vicksburg in 1863 marked an important moment in the Civil War, you won't be asked about it on the test. The AP U.S. History test does not ask about important battles, military strategy, or advances in weapons technology. When it asks about war, the questions concern the political or social implications of a war rather than the details of warfare. (The correct answer, by the way, is (B). If you tried it and got it wrong, so what? It won't be on the test.)

Also, AP U.S. History questions never test rote memorization *only*. While you have to know your facts to do well on this test, the questions always ask for information in the context of larger historical trends. Therefore, you will never see a question like this one:

YY. The treaty that ended the War of 1812 was called

    (A) The Anglo-American Treaty
    (B) The Treaty of Versailles
    (C) The War of 1812 Treaty
    (D) The Jay Treaty
    (E) The Treaty of Ghent

Chronological Order and the Order of Difficulty

More good news: The folks who write the AP U.S. History exam organize the multiple-choice section in a predictable way. Here are two things you can count on:

- Questions will be organized in groups of 8 to 12. Each group of questions will be presented in chronological order. The first question in a group, for example, may ask about the Townshend Acts (1767); the second, about the feud between Hamilton and Jefferson (1790s); the third, about the War of 1812; and so on. You will notice a sharp break in chronology when you move from one group of questions to another. When you see a question about Martin Luther King Jr. followed by a question about the Chesapeake Bay colonies, for example, you will know that you have moved on to a new grouping.

and

- Each group of questions will be a little bit more difficult than the group that preceded it. The questions generally go in order of difficulty, with the easiest questions appearing at the beginning of the multiple-choice test and the most difficult questions appearing at the end. Think of the first 20 questions as easy, questions 21 through 60 as being of medium difficulty, and 61 through 80 as difficult.

Remember that easy questions have easy answers. Do not choose an obscure or trivial answer for an easy question. Remember also that all questions are worth an equal amount toward your final score. Therefore, it is important that you go slowly enough in the beginning so that you do not make careless mistakes on the easier questions. The points you lose early in the test will be much harder to make up later on, when the questions get more difficult.

You can use this information to your advantage. Ask yourself how you can use this information as you look at the following three questions (the answers have been purposely omitted):

17. Which of the following characterizes the way in which the colonists' reaction to the Stamp Act of 1764 differed from their reaction to the Sugar Act of 1763?

18. The XYZ affair resulted in a change in public opinion toward which foreign nation?

19. In the 1803 Supreme Court decision *Marbury v. Madison*, Chief Justice John Marshall established the principle that...

Here's what you might have figured out:. Since the test goes in order of difficulty, and since these are questions 17, 18, and 19 out of 80, these three questions are relatively easy. When you actually do these questions, that should give you confidence. Second, you should have realized that the XYZ affair took place some time between 1764 and 1803. If you had forgotten about the XYZ affair, this information should help you find the correct answer, or at least eliminate a few incorrect answers. Now let's look at those three questions *with* the answer choices:

17. Which of the following characterizes the way in which the colonists' reaction to the Stamp Act of 1764 differed from their reaction to the Sugar Act of 1763?

(A) The colonists accepted the validity of the Sugar Act, but not the Stamp Act.
(B) The colonists objected more strenuously to the Sugar Act because it included a prohibition against slavery.
(C) Opponents of the Sugar Act included British troops and Native Americans; only settlers opposed the Stamp Act.
(D) Opposition to the Stamp Act was better organized and more widely supported in the colonies.
(E) Protests against the Sugar Act were often violent; Stamp Act protests adhered to the principle of non-violent civil disobedience.

18. The XYZ affair resulted in a change in public opinion toward which foreign nation?

(A) Germany
(B) France
(C) Mexico
(D) Russia
(E) Spain

19. In the 1803 Supreme Court decision *Marbury v. Madison*, Chief Justice John Marshall established the principle that

(A) the Supreme Court has the right to review the constitutionality of Congressional legislation
(B) a criminal defendant must be provided with a defense lawyer, at the state's expense, if he or she cannot afford a lawyer
(C) the president may withhold information from Congress by claiming executive privilege
(D) "separate but equal" facilities for people of different racial backgrounds are unconstitutional
(E) British impressment of American sailors violated international law

Here's How to Crack It

Because you know that these are relatively easy questions, you can eliminate any answers that would require you to know something trivial. Furthermore, the correct answers will affirm a basic principle of American history during the era in question, while the incorrect answers should contain information that clearly identifies them as incorrect.

Consider **question 17**. We know that, as the Revolution approached, the colonists grew more resentful of English rule, not less. Answer choices (B), (C), and (D) all indicate that opposition to the Sugar Act of 1763 was more widespread than was opposition to the Stamp Act of 1764. Those answers are wrong, because they contradict the trend of growing resentment to English rule. Now look at answer choice (E). Is non-violent civil disobedience associated with the colonial era? No. Non-violent civil disobedience is associated with Thoreau (mid-1800s) and Martin Luther King Jr. (1950s and 1960s). The correct answer is (A).

Now let's look at question 18. Chronological order tells us that the XYZ affair occurred sometime between 1764 and 1803. Did the U.S. have close ties to Germany during this period? No. Nor did the U.S. have any relations with Russia. Who did the U.S. have close ties to? France, who came to the colonists' assistance during the Revolutionary War. Even if you had forgotten the XYZ affair, your knowledge of chronological order and the order of difficulty should have told you that France, the most obvious choice, was the answer to this relatively easy question.

Question 19 asks about the famous Supreme Court case that established the principle of judicial review. Had you remembered that, you could have chosen the answer choice that best defined that concept. If you had forgotten, you should have been able to eliminate answer choice (B) because the expansion of the rights of the accused is a much later development; (D) because desegregation is also a much later development; and (E), because the Supreme Court doesn't rule on international law. The correct answer, (A), would be the better guess (between (A) and (C)) because it directly relates to the Supreme Court, and is thus the more obvious answer (remembering, again, that this is an easy question).

THE BIG PICTURE

In the explanations for questions 17 through 19 above, we hinted at one of the most important characteristics of AP U.S. History multiple-choice questions. The questions and answers are designed to illustrate **basic principles** of American history. Multiple-choice questions will NOT ask about exceptions to historical trends; the test ignores these, because the test writers are trying to find out whether you have mastered the important generalizations that can be drawn from history. They do not want to know whether you have memorized your textbook (they already know that you haven't).

Therefore, you should always keep the **big picture** in mind as you take this exam. Even if you cannot remember the specific event or concept being tested, you should be able to answer the question by remembering the general social and political trends of the era.

Let's look at a couple of illustrative examples:

53. During the Harding and Coolidge administrations, the Federal Trade Commission

   (A) greatly increased the number of court cases it brought against unethical businesses
   (B) controlled the rationing of food, rubber, and gasoline
   (C) generally worked to assist businesses, rather than to regulate them
   (D) was permanently eliminated
   (E) saw its regulatory powers expanded

Here's How to Crack It

At first glance, this questions appears to require you to remember the history of the Federal Trade Commission. It's not that tricky, though. To answer this question correctly, you really only need to remember the big picture. What was the attitude of the Harding and Coolidge administrations toward business? Harding and Coolidge were president after the Progressive era and World War I both ended; the country grew more conservative during their administrations, and both pursued policies favorable to business. Because pro-business governments weaken regulations, you should have been able to eliminate answer choices (A) and (E). Now let's look at the remaining answer choices. Was there rationing during the 1920s? No, rationing occurred during World War II, in the early 1940s. Eliminate answer choice (B). How about answer choice (D)? Is there still a Federal Trade Commission today? Yes; therefore, the FTC wasn't "permanently eliminated." Eliminate answer choice (D). The correct answer is (C), which illustrates a "big picture" principle; the 1920s were a pro-business era.

Let's try one more question:

68. "[This state Assembly declares] that it views the
power of the Federal Government as resulting
from the compact to which the states are parties,
as limited by plain sense and intention of the
instrument constituting that compact... and that,
in case of a deliberate, palpable, and dangerous
exercise of other powers, not granted by the said
compact, the states...have the right, and are duty
bound, to interpose, for arresting the progress of
the evil, and for maintaining...the authorities,
rights, and liberties, pertaining to them."

The quotation above appears in

(A) the Halfway Covenant
(B) The Wealth of Nations
(C) Common Sense
(D) Virginia Resolutions of 1798
(E) The Liberator

Here's How to Crack It

The first thing you should notice is that this is questions number 68, so it's pretty difficult. Of course, you probably could have figured that out by reading the quotation, which is one long, difficult sentence filled with archaic language and syntax. However, if you key in on the big picture, this question isn't all that hard, provided you've prepared for the exam. The central concept of the quotation is that the states have the right to try to stop the federal government when it tries to exercise too much power (particularly when it exceeds the constitutional limitations on it). Sounds familiar? It's the doctrine of *nullification*. If you remembered that the source of the doctrine of nullification was the Virginia and Kentucky Resolutions, you would already be on your way to the next question. If not, look at the other answer choices. *The Halfway Covenant* concerns the baptism of Puritans; *The Wealth of Nations* is a treatise on capitalism; *Common Sense* was written before there even *were* states, let alone state assemblies; and *The Liberator* was an abolitionist newspaper. Looking at the big picture, you should realize that only the *Virginia Resolutions* and *The Liberator* could conceivably be right. If you don't know, guess. A 50-50 shot is pretty good on question 68. (Only about 30 percent of students taking the test will get this question right.)

THE GUESSING PENALTY AND PROCESS OF ELIMINATION

Did the suggestion that you should guess take you by surprise? Lots of students think that they should never guess on an exam. But even The College Board will tell you that that's not true. This passage appears on the first page of the AP U.S. History exam:

"Many candidates wonder whether or not to guess the answers to questions about which they are not certain. In this section of the examination, as a correction for haphazard guessing, one-fourth of the number of questions you answer incorrectly will be subtracted from the number of questions you answer correctly. It is improbable, therefore, that mere guessing will improve your score significantly; it may even lower your score, and it does take time. If, however, you are not sure of the best answer but have some knowledge of the questions and are able to eliminate one or more answer choices as wrong, your chance of getting the right answer is improved, and it may be to your advantage to answer such a question."

The only thing wrong with this advice is that it understates the value of guessing once you have eliminated one or more answer choices. Statistically speaking, guessing after you have eliminated one or more incorrect answer choices *will* improve your final score on the multiple choice section.

Here's why. Suppose you guess randomly on five questions. Probability tells you that you should get one correct and four incorrect. Your raw score for those five questions would be +1 for the correct answer and –1 for your four incorrect answers $-4 \times {}^1/{}_4 = -1$. Your guesses would net exactly 0 points. That's the exact same score you would have received if you had skipped all five questions! There is, then, no guessing penalty. Random guesses cancel each other out, unless you are either very lucky or very unlucky.

However, you will rarely be faced with a question on which you can't eliminate at least one of the answer choices. In many cases, you will be able to eliminate two or even three incorrect answers. Whenever you get this far but can get no further, you **must** guess from among the remaining answer choices.

Consider this scenario. Billy and Cal are both taking the AP U.S. History exam. Each one knows the answers to 48 of the 80 multiple-choice questions. Each has time to look at most of the other questions——let's say, 24 of the remaining 32——and in each case, each could eliminate two incorrect answers but could go no further. Billy doesn't guess on those 24 questions, and he ends up with a raw score of 48. He's right on pace for a final score of "3." Cal, on the other hand, guesses on all 24. Because he is guessing from among three answer choices, he will probably get one out of every three correct. He winds up with +8 for his correct answers and $16 \times {}^1/{}_4 = -4$ for his incorrect answers. Cal's raw score of 52 gives him a boost toward the final score of "4" that he is shooting for.

Had Billy and Cal been able to eliminate three answer choices on each of the 24 questions, the results would have been even more dramatic. Billy, who didn't guess, would have gotten that same raw score, 48. Cal, however, would have gotten 12 of the 24 correct for a +12, while losing only $-12({}^1/{}_4) = -3$ for his incorrect answers. His final raw score of 57 would have sent him well on his way to that "4."

Does this mean you should take a guess on every question on the test? No. Because you have only a limited amount of time to spend on the multiple-choice section, you have to maximize that time. The first thing you want to do is make sure you have answered every question to which you know the answer. Only then do you want to guess on questions to which you don't know the answer. However, once you have worked on a question, eliminated some answers, and convinced yourself that you cannot eliminate any other incorrect answers, you should guess and move on to the next question.

If it seems that we are focusing more on eliminating incorrect answers than on finding the correct answers, it is because that is the most efficient way to take a multiple-choice exam. Use **process of elimination** to whittle down the answer choices down to one on all but the easiest questions (on easy questions, the correct answer will be obvious), because incorrect answers are much easier to identify than the correct one is. When you look for the correct answer among the answer choices, you have a tendency to try to justify how each answer *might* be correct. You'll adopt a forgiving attitude in a situation in which tough assertiveness is rewarded. Eliminate incorrect answers. Terminate them with extreme prejudice. If you have done your job well, only the correct answer will be left standing at the end.

This all probably sounds pretty aggressive and testosterone-laced to you. It is. The main reason men generally score higher than women on standardized, multiple-choice tests is that they take them more aggressively. (But if you are female, and you follow our advice, you will not fall prey to this gender typing.) By all means, sift through the answer choices, toss incorrect answers into the bin, guess without remorse, and prowl the test searching for questions you can answer—all with the tenacity and ruthlessness of a shark. Okay, maybe that overstates the case a *little*, but you get the point. This test rewards male-pattern, assertive test-taking. So, guess if you don't know the answer but can eliminate at least one answer choice.

COMMON SENSE CAN HELP

Sometimes an answer on the multiple-choice section contradicts common sense. Eliminate those answers. Common sense works on the AP U.S. History exam. Which of the answer choices to the question below don't make common sense?

26. Which of the following best explains the most important effect tobacco cultivation had on the development of the Chesapeake Bay settlements during the seventeenth century?

    (A) Because tobacco cultivation requires large tracts of fertile land, it led to rapid expansionism in the region.
    (B) The immediate commercial success of tobacco forced the settlers to defend against attacks by Spanish and French settlers, who wanted to take control of the tobacco trade.
    (C) Tobacco provided the settlers a lucrative crop to trade with nearby Native American tribes.
    (D) Dependence on tobacco as their only cash crop brought the settlements to financial ruin in the early 1600s.
    (E) British customs houses established in the region to regulate tobacco trade led to widespread resentment of the British by the colonists.

Here's How to Crack It

Common sense should allow you to eliminate answer choice (C) immediately. Nearby Native American tribes lived on farmland similar to that held by the Chesapeake Bay settlers; why would they trade for something they could have easily grown themselves? Now let's consider the other answer choices. Did the Spanish or the French attack the Maryland/Virginia region during the seventeenth century? It would have been a pretty big deal if they had, right? You would remember if there had been a war for the control of Virginia in the 1600s, wouldn't you? You don't remember because it didn't happen; eliminate answer choice (B). Answer choice (D) gets it all wrong; in the early 1600s, tobacco cultivation *saved* the Chesapeake Bay settlements from financial ruin, as tobacco proved an immediately popular product in England. Answer choice (E) is anachronistic. The period of colonial resentment toward England was still one hundred years away during the seventeenth century. The correct answer is (A).

CONTEXT CLUES

Some questions contain context clues or vocabulary words that will either lead you to the correct answer or at least help you eliminate an incorrect answer. Look at the question below:

60. The confiscation act of 1861 authorized the Union to

    (A) divert commercial production in the North toward the war effort
    (B) negotiate a settlement to the Civil War with ambassadors from the Confederacy
    (C) liberate those slaves used by the Confederacy "for insurrectionary purposes"
    (D) stop merchant ships headed for Europe and seize their cargo
    (E) arrest those advocating secession and hold them without a writ of habeas corpus

Here's How to Crack It

If you don't remember the exact purpose of the confiscation act of 1861, the word "*confiscation*" might give you enough of a context clue to answer this question correctly anyway. Which answer choices have nothing to do with confiscation? Clearly, (B). How about (E)? You might think that arresting someone is the same as confiscating the person, but it's not. The dictionary definition of "*confiscation*" is "the seizure of private property." Answer choice (A) seems pretty unlikely, too. It indicates that the government used industry for the war effort, not that it confiscated the factories. Answer choice (D) looks good, except when you ask yourself: For what purpose would the Union be stopping ships headed *away* from the Confederacy? This answer would much more likely be correct if it discussed the confiscation of property headed *for* the Confederacy. The correct answer, choice (C), is a little tricky since we don't normally think of human beings as private property. Slaves, however, were exactly that: The private property of slave holders. In order to liberate them, the Union had to "confiscate" them.

DRILL

Here is a group of five questions that could have come from the multiple-choice section of the AP U.S. History exam. As you work through them, try to apply everything you have learned in this chapter. Use the chronological ordering of the questions to eliminate impossible answers. Make sure you keep the big picture in mind as you consider the answer choices. Use process of elimination. If you can get rid of one or more answer choices and can go no further, guess and move on. Use common sense and context clues. The answers and explanations of how to attack these questions follow the drill. Good luck!

33. Between 1836 and 1844, a gag rule prevented Congress from

    (A) increasing tariffs
    (B) admitting new states to the Union
    (C) declaring war
    (D) overriding a presidential veto
    (E) considering abolitionist petitions

34. The Wilmot Proviso was most firmly supported by which national political party?

    (A) Federalist
    (B) Whig
    (C) Free Soil
    (D) Know-Nothing
    (E) Populist

35. The Reconstruction plan approved by Congress included all of the following provisions EXCEPT

    (A) the imposition of martial law in the South
    (B) the implementation of black codes to govern the behavior of freedmen in the South
    (C) a requirement that each Southern state ratify the Fourteenth Amendment before being readmitted to the Union
    (D) the establishment of a government bureau to help relocate, feed, and employ newly liberated blacks
    (E) a mandate that all Southern states rewrite their constitutions and submit them to Congress for approval

36. Theodore Roosevelt's policy toward Cuba reflected his belief that

(A) any domestic instability in Latin America could justify American intervention
(B) it was in the United States' best interest to foster democracies in the region, even if those democracies were hostile to the United States
(C) the United States should avoid all foreign entanglements
(D) a multinational governing board made up of the United States and all Latin American countries should confer on all crises in the Western Hemisphere
(E) the Monroe Doctrine was outdated and should be discarded

37. Which of the following best characterizes the purpose of English mercantilist policy in the colonies?

(A) develop the colonies' industrial base
(B) exploit colonial resources for the benefit of England
(C) foster democracy and self-government in the New World
(D) establish British military bases in the New World
(E) create a new nation to which those who were persecuted at home, such as the Puritans, could be sent

Here's How to Crack It

The five questions in the drill are of medium difficulty. On average, between 50 and 70 percent of those taking the test will get each one right. As we discuss how to take your best guess on the following questions, it should go without saying that, if you know the correct answer to the question, you should simply select it and move on.

Chronological order should have told you that the drill began in the middle of one grouping of questions, and that question 37 started a new grouping. You probably noticed that the group that ended with question 36 only made it up to the first decade of the 1900s. That's okay; not every grouping will begin with the colonial era, and not every grouping will end with a question about relatively modern times.

Question 33 begins with a good context clue: the phrase *"gag order."* If you know that a gag order prevents discussion of a particular subject, you should have been reasonably certain that (E) was the correct answer. You should also have been thinking about the "big picture" as you worked on this question. Which of these answer choices discusses an important issue of the era? Tariffs were important earlier in the 1830s, so answer choice (A) might seem a reasonable answer. However, tariffs were a "big picture" issue only in 1831 and 1832, when the "tariff of abominations" led to the nullification crisis. This question addresses a period five years later, so (A) is, in fact, an unlikely answer choice. Common sense should tell you that Congress didn't stop admitting states during this period, nor was it about to deny itself the right to declare war or override a presidential veto; both of these privileges are guaranteed to Congress by the Constitution. The answer has to be (E). Slavery is *the* "big picture" issue of the era.

If you've forgotten what the Wilmot Proviso was, you can use chronological ordering to pinpoint its relevance to some time between 1836 (the earliest period mentioned in question 33) and Reconstruction (mentioned in question 35). You should have concluded, then, that it probably had something to do with the Civil War or the events leading up to the war. From that information, you should have eliminated both the Federalists and the Populists, since neither party existed during the period. Look at the remaining three choices: the Whigs, the Know Nothings, and the Free Soilers. Remember, the national Whig party was split on the slavery issue; the Know-Nothings were a single-issue party, and that issue was the opposition to immigration; and, the Free Soilers were also a single-issue party, but their issue was slavery. Your best guess, the Free Soilers (C), is the correct answer.

Question 35 asks you to play "one of these things is not like the other." Even if you don't remember that the black codes placed burdensome restrictions on the behavior of the freedmen, you should have realized that answer choices (A), (C), (D), and (E) were all similar in that they all clearly indicated a punitive approach toward the South. That would have made (B), the correct answer, your best guess.

Question 36 is an easy one if you remember the "big picture" regarding Roosevelt and his foreign policy. Theodore Roosevelt's administration is associated with imperialism and interventionism, particularly (but not exclusively) in Latin America. That should have led you to choose answer choice (A), the correct answer. Notice that answer choice (E) is a nice distracter; if you remembered that there was a Roosevelt Corollary to the Monroe Doctrine, you might have been tempted to choose this. The Corollary, however, was Roosevelt's improvement to the Monroe Doctrine, not a rejection of something he thought was already a pretty good idea.

Question 37 asks about English mercantilism, indicating that the test has returned to the colonial period and that you have moved up to a slightly more difficult set of questions. Again, think "big picture." What did the British want from the colonies? Wealth! By the way, you will very rarely go wrong if you attribute the actions of people and nations to their desire to acquire greater wealth. The correct answer is (B).

Finally, here are the answers to the questions that appear in the first part of this chapter. 3: (E); 6: (A); 45: (C); 13: (D); XX: (B); YY: (E); 17: (D); 18: (B); 19: (A); 53: (C); 68: (D); 26: (A); 60: (C)

SUMMARY

- Don't overextend yourself. If all you need is a final score of "3," don't even try to finish the exam. Take your time and work on the first sixty questions only. If you are shooting for a "4," take your time and work on the first seventy questions only.

- Familiarize yourself with the different types of questions that will appear on the multiple-choice section. Be aware that you will see many questions about political and social history, some questions about international relations, and relatively few about economic and cultural trends. Tailor your studies accordingly.

- Look for "big picture" answers. Correct answers on the multiple-choice section confirm important trends in American history. The test will not ask you about weird exceptions that contradict those trends. It also will not ask you about military history. You will not be required to perform miraculous feats of memorization; however, you must be thoroughly familiar with all the basics of American history. (And there are a lot of them! See our history review later in the book.)

- Use the chronological ordering of questions to figure out which time period you are being asked about. Be aware that the questions are presented in groups of 8 to 12, that each group maintains chronological order, and that each group is a little more difficult than the one that precedes it.

- Use process of elimination on all but the easiest questions. Once you have worked on a question, eliminated some answers, and convinced yourself that you cannot eliminate any other incorrect answers, you should guess and move on to the next question.

- Use common sense. Look for context clues.

4

CRACKING
THE ESSAY QUESTIONS

There are two types of essay questions on the AP U.S. History exam. The first is the Document-Based Question (DBQ), which requires you to answer a question based on eight to ten primary source documents and whatever outside knowledge you have about the subject. The second is the free-response question, and it is more like a typical essay question on a history exam. You are given four questions, two about the period preceding the Civil War and two about the period following it. You are required to answer two of these essay questions, one from each group. We will discuss each of these question types in greater detail in the next two chapters. First, let's talk about the basics of writing a successful AP essay.

WHAT ARE THE AP ESSAY GRADERS LOOKING FOR?

To find out, we asked some AP graders. Here is what one said:

> "My most basic advice to students taking the AP U.S. History exam would be the same advice I give to college students facing an essay exam: ANSWER THE QUESTION, begin with a thesis, and follow a reasonable outline. Questions usually suggest a basic thesis statement, and a logical outline, so look for them and follow them. The less a writer confuses his or her reader, the better."
>
> —Pamela Riney-Kehrberg, Illinois State University

In other words, be straightforward. Do not try to fudge your way through the essay; the graders are all experts in history, and you will not be able to fool them into thinking you know more than you actually do.

It is also very important to focus on the phrasing of the question. Some students are so anxious to get going that they start writing as soon as they know the general subject of the question, and many of these students lose points because their essays do not answer the question being asked. Take, for example, an essay question that asks you to discuss the effects of the Depression on working-class citizens. The overanxious test taker might start rattling off everything he or she knows about the Depression: its causes, its effect on the presidential election of 1932, the New Deal programs that helped alleviate its effects, etc. No matter how well this essay is written, points are going to be lost for one simple reason—the writer did not answer the question!

Second, a good essay does more than rattle off facts. It reveals an understanding of the general principles or the "big picture" of American history. Professor Keith Edgerton at Montana State University in Billings grades AP essays. He says:

> "The best essays that I encountered were the ones that wove an understanding of content with some critical analysis. I am impressed with some originality of thought, too; so few students possess it these days. Students should be willing to take something of a chance with the essays and not simply provide recitation of the few 'facts' that they have memorized. Longer essays, though not necessarily better, are usually more thorough in their coverage rather than the quick, I-need-to-get-this-done-because-I'm-tired-and-sick-of-this-test essays. It is a cliché, to be sure, but there still is no substitute for hard work. It can be painful and awfully grinding sometimes to learn history well, and it seems that there are not many students who want to devote much time to it. It does not provide instant gratification and cannot be mastered quickly and it certainly does not happen in twenty-three minutes with appropriate commercial interruption. Students should read everything they can get their hands on and turn off the television. That is the best advice I can give."

If all this sounds intimidating, read on! There are a few simple things you can do to improve your grade on your AP essays.

REASONS TO BE CHEERFUL

AP graders know that you are given only 15 minutes to prepare and 45 minutes to write about the DBQ, and that you have only 70 minutes to plan and write both of your free-response essays. They also know that is not enough time to cover the subject matter tested by the question. The fact is, many very long books have been written about any subject that you might be asked about on the DBQ and the free-response questions. That is why The College Board's Advanced Placement Course Description: History states:

> "Answers to standard essay questions will be judged on the strength of the thesis developed, the quality of the historical argument, and the evidence offered in support of the thesis, *rather than on the factual information per se*. Unless a question asks otherwise, *students will not be penalized for omitting one or another specific illustration* [emphasis added]."

In other words, expressing good ideas and presenting valid evidence in support of those ideas are important. Making sure you mention every single relevant piece of historical information is not so important.

Remember that the graders are not given a lot of time to read your essays. One of them explains the grading experience this way:

> "[In 1995] there were about 545 graders drawn from colleges, universities, high schools, and prep schools. We had about seventy tables of readers. A table leader presides over each group. A typical schedules looks like this: 8:30 A.M. to 10:00 reading; 10:00 to 10:20 break; 10:20 to 12:00 reading; 12:00 to 1:00 lunch; 1:00 to 3:00 reading; 3:00 to 3:20 break; 3:20 to 5:00 reading. We read for six and a half days. Before grading the essays, we read sample packets selected by the table leaders, who arrive a few days before the rest of us. With the sample packets we try to establish standards using a 0-to-9 scale [or, for the DBQ, a 0-to-15 scale]. When the table leader believes we all have 'locked into' the standards, we commence reading. The table leader occasionally samples our finished product in order to ensure accuracy. Also, a computer correlates the essay scores with the grade received on the multiple-choice section. The AP authorities emphasize accuracy rather than speed. In the six and a half days I read 995 essays. I do not know how this rate relates to other readers... We look for responsiveness to the question. For the DBQ, we seek a clear thesis statement and supporting evidence."

> —Charles Quirk, University of Northern Iowa

Think about it. One hundred thousand students take this test. Each writes three essays. That's 300,000 essays! Professor Quirk averaged almost 150 essays a day—a little more than two minutes per essay. At that rate, readers cannot look for anything profound or subtle. What they can do is look for evidence that you have something reasonably intelligent to say and that you know how to say it. Furthermore, the graders read many god-awful essays. (Not everyone, remember, is preparing for this test as well as you are.) It is true that you can only get the best possible score if you have mastered the material. However, regardless of how well-prepared you are, you can improve your score if you follow the guidelines below. They will tell you how to avoid the mistakes all graders hate and how to use writing and organizational techniques they will love.

Before we get to those guidelines, a final word from Darril Wilburn, a high school history teacher in Bardstown, New York. We think it is inspirational:

> "On essay questions I stress two things: detail and staying positive. You must be able to substantiate your ideas and thoughts with detail (factual, of course). This will go very far in impressing the reader that you do indeed know what you are talking about… On staying positive, I ask the students not to think of the essay questions (or any part of the exam for that matter) as something you lose points on. Think of each question and each bit of detail and each morsel of fact as an addition to your score; do not think of everything you leave out as being a subtraction from your score. This helps you stay focused and keeps stress levels lower (unless, of course, you do not know anything; then you deserve to be nervous). You can also play a mind game with yourself: 'How many points can I gather on this question?' This also keeps stress low."

Focus on what you know, rather than on what you do not know. Turn the test into a game. In the immortal words of Johnny Mercer: "Accentuate the positive!"

THINGS THAT MAKE ANY ESSAY BETTER

There are two essential components to writing a successful in-class essay. First, plan what you are going to write before you start writing! Second, use a number of tried-and-true writing techniques that will make your essay appear better organized, better thought-out, and better written. This section is about those techniques.

Before You Start Writing

Read the question carefully. Then, brainstorm for one or two minutes. In your test booklet write down everything that comes to mind about the subject. (There is room in the margins and at the top and bottom of the pages.) Look at your notes and consider the results of your brainstorming session as you decide what point you will argue in your essay; that argument is going to be your thesis. Tailor your argument to your information, but by no means choose an argument that you know is wrong or that you disagree with. If you do either of these things, your essay will be awful. Finally, sort the results of your brainstorm. Some of what you wrote down will be "big picture" conclusions, some will be historical facts that can be used as evidence to support your conclusions, and some will be garbage.

Next, make an outline. You should plan to write five paragraphs for each of the three essay questions, and plan to go into special detail in each of the paragraphs on the DBQ. (Remember, you will have the documents and your outside knowledge to discuss on the DBQ. Plus, you will have more time.) Your first paragraph should contain your thesis statement. Your second, third, and fourth paragraphs should contain three arguments that support that statement, along with historical evidence to back those arguments. The fifth paragraph should contain your conclusion and will be where you specifically answer the question.

Before you start to write your outline, you will have to decide what type of argument you are going to make. Here are some of the classics:

Three Good Points

This is the simplest strategy. Look at the results of your brainstorming session and pick the three best points supporting your position. Make each of these points the subject of one paragraph. Make the weakest of the three points the subject of the second paragraph, and save the strongest point for the fourth paragraph. If your three points are interrelated and there is a natural sequence to arguing them, then by all means use that sequence, but otherwise, try to save your strongest point for last. Begin each paragraph by stating one of your three points, and then spend the rest of the paragraph supporting it. Use specific supporting examples whenever possible. Your first paragraph should state what you intend to argue; your final paragraph should explain why you have proven what you set out to prove.

The Chronological Argument

Many questions lend themselves to a chronological treatment. Questions about the development of a political, social, or economic trend can hardly be answered any other way. When you make a chronological argument, look for important transitions and use them to start new paragraphs. A five-paragraph essay about the events leading up to the Civil War, for example, might start with an introductory discussion of slavery and regional differences in the early nineteenth century. This is also where you will state your thesis. The second paragraph might then discuss the Missouri Compromise and other efforts to avoid the war. The third paragraph might mention the expansionism of the Polk era and how it forced the slavery issue, and then, the fourth paragraph might cover the collapse of the Missouri Compromise and how the events that followed—the Compromise of 1850, the Kansas-Nebraska Act, and the Dred Scott case—led the country into war. Your conclusion in this type of essay should restate the essay question and answer it. For example, if the question asks whether the war was inevitable, you should answer "yes" or "no" in this paragraph.

Similarities and Differences

Some questions, particularly on the free-response section, ask you to compare events, issues, and/or policies. Very often, the way the question is phrased will suggest the best organization for your essay. Take, for example, a question asking you to compare the impact of three events and issues on the United States' decision to enter World War II. This question pretty much requires you to start by setting the historical scene prior to the three events/issues you are about to discuss. Continue by devoting one paragraph to each of the three, and conclude by comparing and contrasting the relative importance of each. Again, be sure to answer the question in your final paragraph.

Other questions will provide options. If you are asked to compare the political philosophies of two presidents, you might open with a thesis stating the essential similarity or difference between the two. Then, you could devote one paragraph each to a summary of each president's philosophy. The fourth paragraph could point out the major similarities and differences between their philosophies. In the final paragraph you could draw your conclusion (e.g., "their similarities were more significant than their differences," or vice versa).

Or, using another angle altogether, you might start with a thesis, then discuss in the body of your essay three pertinent political issues and how each president stood on them, and wrap up with an overview of your argument for your conclusion.

The "Straw Dog" Argument

In this essay writing technique, choose a couple of arguments that someone taking the position opposite yours would take. State their arguments, and then tear them down. Remember that proving that your opposition is wrong does not mean that you have proved you are correct; that is why you should choose only a few opposing arguments to refute. Summarize your opponent's arguments in paragraph two, dismiss them in paragraph three, and use paragraph four to make the argument for your side. Or, use one paragraph to summarize and dismiss each of your opponent's arguments, and then make the case for your side in your concluding paragraph. Acknowledging both sides of an argument, even when you choose one over the other, is a good indicator that you understand that historical issues are complex and can be interpreted in more than one way—which teachers and graders like to see.

No matter which format you choose, remember to organize your essay so that the first paragraph addresses the question and states how you are going to answer it. (That is your thesis.) The second, third, and fourth paragraphs should each be organized around a single argument that supports your thesis, and each of these arguments must be supported by historical evidence. Your final paragraph then ties the essay up into a nice, neat package. Your concluding paragraph should also answer the question. And remember, stay positive!

As You Are Writing, Observe the Following Guidelines

- **Keep sentences as simple as possible.** Long sentences get convoluted very quickly and will give your graders a headache, putting them in a bad mood.

- **Throw in a few big words.** But don't overdo it, because it will look like you are showing off. Remember that good writing does not have to be complicated; some great ideas can be stated simply. NEVER use a word if you are unsure of its meaning or proper usage. A malapropism might give your graders a good laugh, but it will not earn you any points, and it will probably cost you.

- **Write clearly and neatly.** As long as we are discussing your graders' mood, here is an easy way to put them in a good one: Graders look at a lot of chicken scratch; it strains their eyes and makes them grumpy. Neatly written essays, in contrast, make them happy. When you cross out, do it neatly. If you are making any major edits— if you want to insert a paragraph in the middle of your essay, for example—make sure you indicate these changes clearly.

- **Define your terms.** Most questions require you to use terms that mean different things to different people. One person's "liberal" is another person's "conservative," and yet another person's "pinko radical." What one person considers "expansionism," another might call "colonialism" or "imperialism." The folks who grade the test want to know what you think these terms mean. When you use them, define them. Take particular care to define any such terms that appear in the question. Almost all official College Board materials stress this point, so do not forget. Be sure to define any term that you suspect can be defined in more than one way.

- **Use transition words to show where you are going.** When continuing an idea, use words such as furthermore, also, and in addition. When changing the flow of thought, use words such as however and yet. Transition words make your essay easier to understand by clarifying your intentions. Better yet, they indicate to the graders that you know how to make a coherent, persuasive argument.

- **Use structural indicators to organize your paragraphs.** Another way to clarify your intentions is to organize your essay around structural indicators. For example, if you are making a number of related points, number them ("First… Second… And last…"). If you are writing a compare/contrast essay, use the indicators "on the one hand" and "on the other hand."

- **Stick to your outline.** Unless you get an absolutely brilliant idea while you are writing, do not deviate from your outline. If you do, you will risk winding up with an incoherent essay.

- **Try to prove one "big picture" idea per paragraph.** Keep it simple. Each paragraph should make one point and then substantiate that point with historical evidence.

- **Back up your ideas with examples.** Yes, we have said it already, but it bears repeating: Do not just throw ideas out there and hope that you are right (unless you are absolutely desperate). You will score big points if you substantiate your claims with facts.

- **Try to fill the essay form.** An overly short essay will hurt you more than one that is overly long.

- **Make sure your first and last paragraphs directly address the question.** Nothing will cost you points faster than if the graders decide you did not answer the question. It is always a safe move to start your final paragraph by answering the question; if you have written a good essay, that answer will serve as a legitimate conclusion.

SUMMARY

- Read questions carefully. You must answer the question in order to get full credit.

- Do not start writing until you have brainstormed, chosen a thesis, and written an outline.

- Follow your outline. Stick to one important idea per paragraph. Support your ideas with historical evidence.

- Write clearly and neatly. Do not write in long, overly complex sentences. Toss in a couple of "big" words you know you will not misuse. When in doubt, stick to simple syntax and vocabulary.

- Use transition words to indicate continuity of thought and changes in the direction of your argument.

5

CRACKING THE DOCUMENT-BASED QUESTION (DBQ)

WHAT IS THE DBQ?

DBQ stands for "document-based question." The DBQ is an essay question that requires you to interpret *primary source* documents. (There are typically nine documents in a DBQ.) These documents will include many, if not all, of the following: newspaper articles and editorials, letters, diaries, speeches, excerpts from legislation, political cartoons, charts, and graphs. The documents will *not* include excerpts from current textbooks. Occasionally, one or two of the documents will be taken from something "classic" that you may have previously seen, but generally the documents will be new to you. However, they will discuss events and ideas with which you are familiar. All the documents will pertain to a single subject. The documents are usually between a quarter and a half page long, although occasionally you will see something longer.

The hour-long DBQ is the second part of the AP U.S. History test; it is administered immediately after the 5 to 10 minute break that follows the multiple-choice section. At the beginning of the DBQ, you will be handed a green booklet in which the essay question and documents are printed as well as a separate form on which to write your essay. The DBQ session begins with a 15-minute mandatory reading period, during which you are allowed to read the documents and take notes in the DBQ booklet. You may not start recording your essay on the essay form until the 45-minute writing period begins. However, if you finish taking notes and outlining your essay before the reading period is over, you should write a first draft of your opening paragraph in your DBQ booklet; then, when the writing period begins, you can transcribe it into your essay booklet and continue.

To give you an idea of what you can expect on your DBQ, let's look at what appeared on a recent test. The question asked students to decide whether liberal opponents, conservative opponents, or President Woodrow Wilson bore the responsibility for the Senate's defeat of the Treaty of Versailles. The nine documents included excerpts from the following:

- a speech by a conservative senator, denouncing the League of Nations

- an editorial from the then-liberal magazine *The New Republic*, criticizing the Treaty of Versailles

- a speech by President Wilson, defending the League of Nations

- a letter from Herbert Hoover to Wilson, urging him to compromise with the Senate

- an editorial cartoon from a newspaper, opposing the League of Nations

- an article by economist John Maynard Keynes, discussing the European victors' opposition to Wilson's Fourteen Points

- a 1920 speech by Wilson, asking voters to support the League of Nations

- a 1921 article by W.E.B. DuBois, criticizing Wilson for his handling of the treaty negotiations with the Senate

- a 1922 article by Jane Addams, discussing the necessity of the League of Nations

As you can see, a typical DBQ may contain documents you might have seen prior to the exam. (The first Wilson speech, for example, is famous.) However, the DBQ also includes documents you certainly have not seen before. Each of the documents, though, represents a political position you have studied. Many are written by famous people about whom you should know quite a bit (Keynes, Addams, DuBois, Hoover), even if you do not know precisely how they felt about the Treaty of Versailles before reading the documents. In other words, you will not be starting from square one, even when the documents are new to you.

IS THERE A "RIGHT" ANSWER TO EACH DBQ?

No. DBQs are worded in such a way that you can argue any number of positions. In the example above, the documents provide evidence for those who would blame the failure of the Treaty of Versailles on Wilson, liberals, conservatives, or some combination of the three. So long as you support your argument with evidence, you can argue whatever thesis you want.

Similarly, The College Board claims that there is no "checklist" of facts and ideas against which DBQs are graded. According to their official material:

Answers to standard essay questions will be judged on the strength of the thesis developed, the quality of the historical argument, and the evidence offered in support of the thesis, rather than on the factual information per se. Unless a question asks otherwise, students will not be penalized for omitting one or another specific illustration.

Graders are supposed to take into account the strength of your argument and the evidence you offer in support of it. In other words, if you forget to mention a good, illustrative historical event but manage to back your point up in some other way, you will not be penalized.

However, in order to earn the most credit for your essay, you must include *outside information*. You will notice that your DBQ contains a phrase that looks something like this:

USING THE DOCUMENTS AND YOUR KNOWLEDGE OF THE SUBJECT . . .

"Your knowledge of the subject" is the outside information. It includes historical facts and ideas that are relevant to the question but which are not mentioned in the DBQ documents. For example, in the Treaty of Versailles DBQ described above, any information offered about the writers' backgrounds would count as outside information, as would information about the war itself. Of course, to receive credit, that information would have to help explain who was responsible for the failure of the Treaty of Versailles in the United States. Some students make the mistake of throwing everything they know about a subject into their essays, whether or not it pertains to the question. That type of information receives partial credit, at best.

HOW IS THE DBQ SCORED?

The DBQ is graded on a 1 to 15 scale. Here's how those grades are assigned, according to The College Board:

Grade	Description of Essay
13 to 15	Well-developed, focused thesis; in-depth document analysis; numerous references to outside information; analysis of complexity of issue, acknowledgment of opposing viewpoints; well-written and well-organized.
10 to 12	Consistent thesis; analysis of several documents; reference to most documents and to numerous items of outside information; clearly written, logical but with flaws.
7 to 9	Partially developed thesis; describes documents but does not analyze them well; sketchy outside information; contains errors; does not necessarily address the entire question; acceptable writing.
4 to 6	Confused thesis; poor understanding of question; erroneous analysis of documents; ignores most documents; outside information sparse and often inaccurate; contains major errors; weak writing.
1 to 3	Awful.

GETTING STARTED ON THE DBQ: THE QUESTION

Start by reading the question. This direction may seem obvious, but it obviously is not, given how many students write essays on subjects that are only marginally related to the question being asked. Students miss the question because they get anxious during the exam. They panic. They think they are going too slowly. In an effort to speed up, they read half the question, say to themselves, "A-ha! I know what they're going to ask!" and stop reading. Do NOT make this mistake! The question is probably the shortest thing you have to read on the DBQ. Take your time; savor it. Explore its nuances. Essays that address the question fully earn huge bonuses; those essays that ignore parts of the question are doomed to a grade of 9 or lower.

Here's a sample question:

1. "Both the constituencies and the agenda of the Progressive movement of the early 1900s were more similar to those of the reform movements of the 1830s and 1840s than to those of the Populist movement of the 1890s."

Using the documents and your knowledge of the periods in question, assess the validity of the statement.

As you look the question over, you should ask yourself two questions:

- Do I have an opinion about this subject?

- What must I discuss in order to write a successful essay?

Of the two questions, the second is much more important. You can construct a position later, after you have gathered the information you want to include in your essay. First, you need to figure out what issues you must address and what data you will use in your discussion.

To begin with, you should notice that the question asks you to compare three movements—the Progressives, the Populists, and the reformers of the 1830s and 1840s. Your essay will obviously have to mention all three groups. Equally important, the question asks you to consider the constituencies and the agendas of these three groups in drawing your comparisons. Also, you must decide whether the Progressives were more similar to the Populists or to the reformers. Finally, you must include a discussion of the given documents and your outside knowledge in your essay.

Some people find it helpful to circle and underline key elements of an essay question. If you did that, your question probably looked something like this:

1. "Both the constituencies and the agenda of the Progressive movement of the early 1900s were more similar to those of the reform movements of the 1830s and 1840s than to those of the Populist movement of the 1890s."

Using the documents and your knowledge of the periods in question, assess the validity of the statement.

However you decide to approach the question, it is essential that you not rush. Read carefully to make sure that you understand what issues must be addressed in your essay. Then, determine how to organize the information you are going to collect from the documents and from memory for inclusion in the essay.

ORGANIZING YOUR ESSAY: GRIDS AND COLUMNS

Many DBQs ask you to draw comparisons. For those questions, you can always organize your thoughts about a DBQ in a grid. Drawing a grid particularly helps in seeing all sides of an argument, which is important because DBQ graders will reward you for acknowledging arguments other than your own. Consider the question above; here is how you could grid this question:

	Constituency	Agenda
Progressives		
Reformers		
Populists		

As you remember appropriate outside information and as you read the documents, take notes in the appropriate boxes. When it comes time to write your essay, you will find it easier to compare and contrast the three movements because your information will already be organized in a way that makes similarities and differences more obvious.

If you cannot draw a grid for a question, you can instead set up column headings. Because every DBQ can be argued from at least two different positions, you can always set up two (or more) columns, designating one for each position. Consider the DBQ about the Treaty of Versailles, which we discussed at the beginning of the chapter. You could create one column entitled "It was Wilson's fault," one entitled "It was the Senate's fault," a third entitled "It was both their faults," and even a fourth for information that you know belongs in your essay but which you cannot yet classify (give that the title "To be classified").

Good essays do not just flow out of your pen by accident. They happen when you know what you are going to say *before you start writing*. Although, given the time constraints, it is difficult (if not impossible) to prepare your entire DBQ essay before you begin writing, pre-organization and a good outline will get you much closer to that goal.

A Sample Question

Let's take a look at another question. Circle and/or underline the key elements of the question, then create a grid (or columns) in which to organize your information.

1. From the end of World War II through the Eisenhower administration, many Americans feared that communism threatened the existence of the United States. Using BOTH the documents AND your knowledge of the 1940s and 1950s, assess the validity of and the reasons for those fears.

Your question should look something like this:

1. From the end of World War II through the Eisenhower administration, many Americans feared that communism threatened the existence of the United States. Using BOTH the documents AND your knowledge of the postwar period through 1950s, assess the reasons for and the validity of those fears.

Your essay will have to address the "Red Scare," the widespread fear of a Communist takeover that Americans experienced during the early Cold War. You will, of course, have to include analysis of both the documents and outside information, and your essay should cover the years between the end of the war and the end of the Eisenhower administration. Last (and what most students miss), you must answer two questions: Why did Americans fear a Communist takeover? And, how valid were their fears?

Because the question does not ask you to draw any comparisons, you might want to organize your information in columns titled "Valid reason," "Not a valid reason," and "Maybe valid/maybe not." However, the question naturally lends itself to comparisons among the various perceived and real threats to the United States, which means that you could use a grid instead. Americans feared Communist attacks both from Communist nations and from subversives in the government. You could, therefore, draw a grid, giving your rows the headings "Threats from other countries" (e.g., the USSR and China), and "Threats from within the United States" (e.g., the Communist Party of the United States of America). This analysis would leave you with a grid that looks like the following:

	Valid	Not valid	Maybe/maybe not
Threats from other countries			
Threats from within the United States			

Once you have created your grid, begin collecting information for your essay. At this point, you are probably anxious to start reading the documents. Resist the temptation. You have one more important job to do before you start reading.

GATHER OUTSIDE INFORMATION

Most students read the DBQ documents first and then try to think of outside information to supplement their essays. This is a mistake. The reason? *The power of suggestion.* Once you have read the documents—a chore that can take six to eight minutes—those documents will be on your mind. If you wait until after you have read them to think of outside information, you will not be able to get the documents out of your head. Invariably, you will think of things you have already read about, rather than things you *have not* read about, which is precisely what outside information means.

Plus, reading and processing the documents is a big task. Once you have accomplished that, you will want to get started right away on organizing and writing your essay while the documents are fresh in your mind. You *do not* want to stop to think of outside information to include in your essay. And you certainly do not want to be trying to come up with outside information *while* you are writing your essay. So, do it *before* you read the documents.

Here's what you do. Look at your grid or columns and brainstorm. In a separate blank space in your green booklet (*not* in your grid/columns), write down everything you can think of that relates to the question. Spend two or three minutes on this task, then look at what you have written, cross out what you know you cannot use, and enter the rest into your grid/columns in the appropriate spaces.

Chances are that some of the "outside information" you think of will be mentioned in the documents, which means that it will not be outside information any more. That is no big deal. In fact, you should think of it as something good. If some of what you remembered shows up in the documents, that means you are on the right track toward answering the question!

This is what a brainstorming grid for the communism question might look like:

	Valid	Not valid	Maybe/maybe not
Threats from other countries	- Soviets develop H-bomb - U.S.-Soviet confrontations: containment, Greece, Marshall Plan, Truman Doctrine - Korean War heightens tensions - fall of Cuba		- Chinese revolution - fall of Hungary: Soviet aggression,or Soviets protecting border? - U.S. involvement in Vietnam - Guatemala's ties to USSR
Threats from within the United States	- there was an American Communist party - Though small, party was influential in powerful labor unions - some evidence of espionage: the Rosenbergs	- Rosenbergs' punishment too great for crime, shows U.S. paranoia - Red Scare:Loyalty Review Board; McCarthy's list of State Dept. subversives; blacklisting; bomb shelters. - post-War affluence made Americans more conservative	- Alger Hiss case

READ THE DOCUMENTS

After you have gathered outside information to include in your essay, you are ready to read the documents. As you read, keep the following things in mind:

- **The order in which documents appear is almost always helpful.** Very often, the documents in the DBQ appear in chronological order. When they do, it often indicates that the AP wants you to trace the historical development of the DBQ subject. On such questions, you do not have to write an essay that adheres strictly to chronological order, but chronology should play an important part in the development of your thesis. When the documents appear in an order other than chronological, they usually are organized so that you can easily compare and contrast different viewpoints on a particular event or issue. On these questions, one of your main goals should be to draw those comparisons.

- **Watch for inconsistencies within and among the documents.** The documents will not necessarily agree with one another. In fact, they are almost certain to present different viewpoints on issues, and almost as certain to present conflicting accounts of a historical event. Some documents might even contradict themselves! This is intentional. The AP is testing your ability to recognize these contradictions. You are expected to resolve these conflicts in your essay. To do so, you will have to identify the sources of the documents. (See below.)

- **Identify the sources of the documents.** Why do two accounts of the same event contradict each other? Why do two economists, looking at the same data, come up with dissimilar interpretations of their significance? It is because the people giving these accounts—the sources of the documents—have different perspectives. Identify the sources and explain why their opinions differ. As you explain these differences, look for the following differences between sources:
    - political ideology
    - class
    - race
    - religion
    - gender

Consider the question of whether communism posed a serious threat to the United States in the 1940s and 1950s. A Northeastern urban intellectual, a wealthy Midwestern industrialist, and an Asian immigrant on the West Coast would offer very different answers to that question. The graders will be looking specifically to see if you have tried to explain those differences.

- **Look for evidence that could refute your argument.** Once you have decided what your thesis will be, you will be looking through the documents for evidence to support your argument. Not all the documents will necessarily back you up. Some may appear to contradict your argument. Do not simply ignore those documents! As you read them, try to figure out how you might incorporate them into your argument. Again, let's consider the communism DBQ. Suppose you argue that Americans overreacted to the Communist threat. Now suppose that one of the documents presents evidence of subversive Communist activity in the United States. You might be tempted to pretend that the document does not exist. How ever, you will be better off if you incorporate the document into your essay: Acknowledge that America was not immune to Communist subversion but that the threat was nowhere near as great as most anti-Communists claimed. By doing this, you will be acknowledging that this historical issue, like all historical issues, is *complex*. This acknowledgment is good. AP essay graders are instructed to look for evidence that you understand that history has no simple answers, and to reward you for it.

As you read the documents, be aware that each one holds a few morsels of information for your essay. Do not fixate on any one document, and try to ignore as few as possible. Weston, Connecticut, history teacher Jean Bennett says:

"Don't panic if you are initially confused by a document. Remember, the AP puts each document in the DBQ to serve one or two purposes, rather than five. Think about it and try to figure out why they've included this document and you'll have a pretty good idea of why it's in the DBQ and how to fit it into your essay. Unless you are clueless (which is unlikely), you will be able to find a way to include each document in your essay: that's better than leaving it out entirely. And be confident: If you're in an AP History course, you're smart enough to figure out why the document has been included in the DBQ."

As you read the documents, take note of any "outside information" that the document reminds you of and enter it into your grid/columns. Again, as Bennett says:

"Don't panic if you can't think of any outside info after reading the question, because you will remember stuff after looking at the documents. Even though brainstorming first is best, if you freeze, then you should go to the documents and let the documents get you going on the outside info."

DRILL

Below is a "mini-DBQ" (it has only four documents, instead of the usual nine). Read through the documents, taking notes in the margins and blank spaces.

1. From the end of World War II through the Eisenhower administration, many Americans feared that communism threatened the existence of the United States. Using BOTH the documents AND your knowledge of the 1940s and 1950s, assess the validity of and the reasons for those fears.

Document A

Source: Decoded Telegram from a KGB agent, New York to Moscow. Intercepted by U.S. intelligence.

November 14, 1944

To VIKTOR,

LIBERAL has safely carried through the contracting of Kh' YuS. Kh' YuS is a good pal of METR's. We propose to pair them off and get them to photograph their own materials having given them a camera for this purpose . . . LIBERAL will receive the film from METR for passing on . . .

OSA has agreed to cooperate with us in drawing in ShMEL' . . . with a view to ENORMOUS. On summons from KALIER she is leaving on 22 November for the Camp 2 area . . .

_____
Notes:
VIKTOR = Lt. Gen. P. M. FITIN [KGB Moscow]
LIBERAL = Julius ROSENBERG
Kh' YuS = probably Joel BARR or Alfred SARANT
METR = probably Joel BARR or Alfred SARANT
OSA = Ruth GREENGLASS
ShMEL'/KALIER = David GREENGLASS
ENORMOUS = Atomic Energy Project
Camp 2 = LOS ALAMOS Laboratory, New Mexico

Document B

Source: Speech in Congress, Representative John F. Kennedy, January 1949

Mr. Speaker, over this weekend we have learned the extent of the disaster that has befallen China and the United States. The responsibility for the failure of our foreign policy in the Far East rests squarely with the White House and the State Department.

The continued insistence that aid would not be forthcoming unless a coalition government with the Communists was formed, was a crippling blow to the National Government.

So concerned were our diplomats and their advisers . . . with the imperfection of the democratic system in China . . . and the tales of corruption in high places that they lost sight of our tremendous stake in a non-Communist China . . .

This House must now assume the responsibility of preventing the onrushing tide of Communism from engulfing all of Asia.

Document C

Source: Speech by President Harry Truman, July 29, 1951

This malicious propaganda has gone so far that on the Fourth of July . . . people were afraid to say they believed in the Declaration of Independence. A hundred and twelve people were asked to sign a petition that contained nothing except quotations from the Declaration of Independence and the Bill of Rights. One hundred and eleven of these people refused to sign that paper—many of them because they were afraid that it was some kind of subversive document and that they would lose their jobs or be called Communists.

Document D

Source: Advertisement, *Civil Defender* magazine, 1955

TO: CIVIL DEFENSE AUTHORITIES, EDUCATORS, AND PARENT-TEACHER ASSOCIATIONS

STUDENT IDENTIFICATION DURING AN "ATOMIC" ALERT

NEED: Is Civil Defense needed? If the answer to this question is yes, then we must entertain the thought of evacuation. Since the advent of the Hydrogen Bomb the only safety lies in not being "there."

EVACUATION: Should it be necessary to evacuate the children during school hours, it is also necessary to identify them. Many educators feel that this identification is more necessary for the grades from sixth down through kindergarten.

IDENTIFICATION: Identification must be positive, practical, and nontransferable. Identification must be kept in the school, to be used only during the time of the actual alert or drill. Identification must be inexpensive, since neither the schools nor the Civil Defense people have a lot of money to spend.

How do we of NATIONAL SCHOOL STUDIOS fit in to this picture?

We offer the solution of the Identification problem . . .

We will furnish the Identification Card, chain, and pin (pictured in this ad) for the small sum of 60 cents per student. . . . We will furnish the Identification Card . . . free of charge if we are permitted to submit our envelopes of pictures to the parents for possible purchase of these envelopes by the parents. Incidentally, this entails absolutely NO OBLIGATION on the part of the parent to purchase the envelope of pictures. We submit the envelope of pictures 100% on speculation…

Here's How to Crack It

Document A is a good example of a document that starts out confusing but ends up being pretty straightforward. At first glance, this document makes very little sense; it is just a jumble of words and names. Do not panic; look for familiar elements. First, look at the source information. It is a telegram from a KGB agent. Therefore, it must have something to do with Soviet espionage. Now, look at the notes, and notice that they mention Julius Rosenberg, the Atomic Energy Project, and Los Alamos. Those references are probably all you need to know to understand why this document is included in the DBQ. It presents evidence that the Soviets were spying on the United States while it was developing the atomic bomb.

When you write your essay, do not fall into the trap of explaining every detail of this telegram. Your job is to analyze the importance of the document, not to describe exactly what it contains. This is true of every document in a DBQ, but it is particularly tempting here. You will be so proud that you have figured out what this document is all about that you might be tempted to spend a paragraph describing your achievement. Forget it. You have bigger fish to fry.

You probably asked yourself why this DBQ starts with a document from 1944 since the question is about the period from 1945 through 1960. The document is here to demonstrate that there was some foundation for America's anti-Communist fears after World War II. You can use this document as a springboard to discuss other reasons for that fear such as the relative popularity of the American Communist Party (CPUSA) in the 1930s and the party's disproportionate representation in some labor unions. Mentioning unions then allows you to discuss labor problems in the postwar era. (Labor held more than 5,000 strikes in 1946 and 1947, which spurred the anti-union Taft-Hartley Act).

This document can also be incorporated easily into an "America was too paranoid" essay because it raises the issue of the Rosenberg trial and the controversy over their sentence. Many people believe their execution resulted from anti-Communist paranoia, not from reasoned consideration of their alleged crimes. (Albert Einstein testified that the Rosenbergs gave the Soviets nothing that they wouldn't have figured out on their own.) Of course, the Rosenberg trial generated a national debate which illustrates the nation's preoccupation with communism during this period.

You may have thought of other issues that this document raises. That is good, and it highlights an important point: Most DBQ documents will be adaptable to a discussion of many different events and ideas. Consequently, you have a lot of leeway in your essay. (Remember, there is no single "correct" answer to the DBQ.) It also means you cannot possibly discuss every event that relates to this question. There is simply too much to discuss. Believe it or not, that is good, too. DBQ topics are so large that no one *expects* you to write the definitive essay on the subject. Hence, you will not be penalized for forgetting one or another event that illustrates your point as long as you back your points with other evidence.

Document B is taken from a speech in Congress by John F. Kennedy, and it raises several important issues. Primarily, it brings up the Chinese Revolution, which gives you an opportunity to discuss the expansion of Communist power in other parts of the world. Using Document B as a starting point, you could discuss the Korean War, the crises in Eastern Europe in the 1950s (e.g., Hungary), and the fall of Cuba and other Latin American nations to Communist insurgents. All of these events support the position that America's fear of communism was valid, especially if you choose to attribute these events to Communist expansionism.

On the other hand, you might argue that this speech shows Kennedy demonstrating the same Cold War paranoia that later inspired the Bay of Pigs fiasco. You might attribute this speech to his political skills and argue that Kennedy is exploiting a sensitive issue for his own political gain. (Remember, many early "Cold Warriors" gained political support by accusing the government of "giving away" China to the Communists.) Interestingly, Kennedy felt it so important to keep China from communist control that he was willing to overlook the flagrant corruption of Chiang Kai-shek's government. If you think he was right, this document justifies American fears; if you argue that he was wrong, you can use it to illustrate how anticommunism distorted America's judgment.

Document C clearly supports the argument that Americans were paranoid about communism and that this paranoia was the result of propaganda. President Truman's reference to people "losing their jobs" opens the door for you to talk about blacklisting during the 1950s and, by extension, McCarthyism and other excesses of this anticommunist era. His description of those citizens who thought that the Declaration of Independence was a "subversive document" illustrates the conservatism of the era.

However, Document C also gives you a chance to discuss Truman's anticommunism. Remember, he established loyalty boards with tremendous power to fire government employees merely on the suspicion of Communist tendencies. Plus, his foreign policy initiatives, from containment to the Marshall Plan and the Truman Doctrine, might all be considered the ideas of an overzealous anti-Communist. You certainly could argue that those policies antagonized Communist countries and therefore exacerbated tensions. You could even say that the growing American-Communist tension *resulted* from Truman's policies. Americans, you could conclude, had plenty to fear from the Soviets, but only after Truman finished scaring them. As usual, nothing is cut-and-dried in the DBQ, which means that you have many options available to you.

Document D addresses two important issues, the Hydrogen bomb and its chilling effect on America. The document is an advertisement that very clearly tries to exploit parents' fears as a means of selling them pictures of their children. While it is exploitative, it also indicates just how far fear of the H-bomb had infiltrated the American psyche. You can use this document as a starting point to discuss air-raid shelters, atomic bomb drills in school, the "Duck and Cover" propaganda campaign, and civil defense organizations. All of these events stem from American fear of the Communists. Most Americans were afraid of the U.S.S.R. primarily because the U.S.S.R. had the H-bomb. For many Americans, it was conceivable and even likely that the Soviets would use that bomb against the United States.

That's it for the documents. Now, formulate a thesis, figure out how and where to fit all your information into your argument, and write an essay. Relax. It is easier than it sounds.

DEVELOPING A THESIS

As you finish reading the documents and prepare to formulate your thesis, remember that you do NOT have to answer this question by falling squarely on one side or the other of the issue. In fact, you should not. A safe, effective route to take on your DBQ essay is to indicate that the truth lies in that gray area between extremes.

There are any number of positions you can argue on our sample question. The best route, as we just said, would be to attribute America's fear of the Communists to a combination of justifiable and exaggerated reasons. Furthermore, there are a number of ways you can choose to construct an essay that demonstrates this thesis. You might want to argue chronologically, indicating which events caused justifiable alarm and which were blown out of proportion by anti-Communist propagandists. You might wish to divide the body of your essay into two large paragraphs, one dealing with the Communist threat posed from abroad and the other dealing with the threat posed by American Communists.

Before you decide on your thesis, GO BACK AND READ THE QUESTION ONE MORE TIME! Make sure that your thesis addresses all the pertinent aspects of the question.

BEFORE THE WRITING PERIOD BEGINS . . . CREATE AN OUTLINE

At this point, you should still have time left in the mandatory 15-minute reading period. Create an outline with one roman numeral for each paragraph. Decide on the subject of each paragraph and on what information you will include in each paragraph. Do not rely on your grid/columns if you do not have to. The grid/columns are good for organizing your information but are less efficient for structuring an essay.

If you *still* have time after writing an outline, write a rough draft of your first paragraph in your green booklet, then transcribe it to your essay form once the writing period starts.

WRITE YOUR ESSAY

Go back and read the first chapter in the "Cracking the Essay Questions" to review good essay-writing techniques. And, follow this advice from Jean Bennett:

> "Don't write flowery introductions or conclusions: just say what you are going to say. The readers want to get right to the point and see how much you know. Also remember to back up your thesis statement with lots of facts, even if you are stretching it because they want to hear solid evidence and not a lot of fluff. Lastly, make sure to remember what is being asked in the question, and refer to the question several times during the essay writing as it is easy to wander off from the question."

And, stay confident. Everyone else taking the test, all across the country, is at least as nervous about it as you are.

SUMMARY

- The DBQ consists of an essay question and approximately nine historical documents. Most likely, you will have not seen most of the documents before, but they will all relate to major historical events and ideas. The DBQ begins with a 15-minute reading period, followed by a 45-minute writing period.

- There is no single "correct" answer to the DBQ. DBQs are framed so that they can be successfully argued from many different viewpoints.

- Read the essay question carefully. Circle and/or underline important words and phrases. Once you understand the question, create a grid or columns in which to organize your notes on the essay.

- Before you start reading the documents, brainstorm about the question. This way you will gather the all-important "outside information" before you submerge yourself in the documents.

- Read the documents. Read them in order, as there is usually a logic to the order in which they are presented. Pay attention to contradictions within and among the documents, and also to who is speaking and what socio-political tradition s/he represents. If you have decided on a thesis, keep an eye out for information that might refute your thesis, and be prepared to address it in your essay.

- Decide on a thesis, then write an outline for your essay.

- Try to include as many of the documents as you can in your essay.

- Stay positive. Do not panic. Everyone else is at least as nervous as you are.

6

CRACKING THE FREE-RESPONSE QUESTIONS

WHAT IS THE FREE-RESPONSE QUESTION?

The free-response question is a two-part essay section consisting of two groups of questions. The first group asks questions about the period before the Civil War; the second group asks questions about the period after the Civil War. Each group contains two questions; you must choose one question from each group. The essay questions on the tests your AP teacher gives are probably very similar to the free-response questions on the AP test.

The free-response question is the final section of the AP U.S. History exam. It is administered immediately following the DBQ. (You do not get a break between sections.) You are given 70 minutes to plan and write both essays.

The free-response questions, like the DBQ, have no single "correct" answer. Unlike the DBQ, though, the free-response questions are not accompanied by any documents; *everything* you include in your free-response answer will be outside information. Also, because you have less time to plan and write the free-response essays, these essays can be shorter and less comprehensive than your DBQ essay. A simple, defensible thesis, accompanied by an organized essay filled with as much relevant information as you can remember, should earn a top grade. Most free-response questions ask you to *analyze*, *assess*, or *evaluate* the causes and effects of a historical subject, allowing you to write an essay that is primarily descriptive. Here are two examples:

1. Assess the impact of any THREE of the following on the United States' decision to declare war on England in 1812:

   the Napoleonic wars
   the Embargo Act of 1807
   America's desire for Western land
   America's military preparedness

2. Analyze the reasons for Congress' decision to end Reconstruction in 1877.

As you can see, free-response questions are designed to allow you to recite what you have learned in class. The subjects should be familiar; the questions are straightforward.

The free-response essay is graded according to the same standards as the DBQ, except that each essay is graded on a scale of 1 to 9 instead of 1 to 15. Hence, the free-response section is worth a total of 18 points, slightly more than the 15 points that the DBQ is worth.

WHICH QUESTIONS TO CHOOSE

Choose the questions about which you know the most, NOT the ones that look easiest at first glance. The more you know about the subject, the better your final grade will be.

HOW TO WRITE THE ESSAYS

Since we have covered this information already in the previous two chapters, here are brief directions to structure your essay. First, read the question and analyze it. Second, create a grid or columns and take notes. Third, assess your information and devise a thesis. Fourth, write a quick outline. Lastly, write your essay. If any of these instructions are unclear, reread the previous two chapters.

As best you can, *split your time evenly between the two essays*. Too many students spend most of their time on the first essay, then do not have enough time to write a decent second essay. Both essays are worth the same amount of points. Treat them equally. Pace yourself, watch the clock, and make sure you are finishing (or, better yet, have finished) your first essay when 35 minutes have passed. Then move directly on to the next essay.

A FINAL NOTE

This chapter is short because we have already discussed in previous chapters what you need to know to write successful AP essays, not because the free-response question is unimportant. The free-response question is worth more than one-quarter of your grade; it is VERY important. Many students are tempted to ease up when they finish the DBQ because it is so challenging. Do not make that mistake. Reach down for that last bit of energy, like a long-distance runner coming into the home stretch. When you reach the free-response question, you only have a little more than an hour to go. *Then* you can take it easy.

SUMMARY

- The free-response question consists of two pairs of questions. You must answer one question from each of the pairs. The first pair covers the pre-Civil War period; the second group covers the post-1865 era.

- Choose the questions about which you know the most, not the ones that look easiest.

- Analyze the question. Circle and/or underline important words and phrases. Once you understand the question, create a grid or columns in which to organize your notes on the essay.

- Decide on a thesis, and then write an outline for your essay.

- Follow your outline. Stick to one important idea per paragraph. Support your ideas with historical evidence.

- Write clearly and neatly. Do not write in overly complex sentences. Toss in a couple of "big" words that you know you will not misuse. When in doubt, stick to simple syntax and vocabulary.

- Use transition words to indicate continuity of thought and changes in the direction of your argument.

- Stay positive. Do not panic. Everyone else is at least as nervous as you are.

part 2

INTRODUCTION TO THE HISTORY REVIEW

The history review on the following pages is meant to serve as a supplement to the textbook you use in class. It is not a substitute for your textbook. However, it does cover all major subjects and terms that are likely to appear on the AP U.S. History exam. If you are familiar with everything in this review, you should do very well on the AP exam.

This review covers some subjects more perfunctorily than they would be covered in a serious treatment of American history. We have weighted this review not toward what we think is most important or most interesting about history, but rather toward what we know the AP is likely to cover. Please do not be offended if your favorite subject receives short shrift in this review. Civil War buffs, beware. The AP never asks about military history, and as a result, this review contains very little about its battles. To repeat, it is not that those battles were not important, it is just that they are not important *in the context of preparing for the AP*.

This review summarizes those events and actions that the writers of the AP consider important. Because historical events often exemplify social, political, and economic trends, and because that's what makes those events important to historians (and to test writers), this review focuses on those connections. We have tried to make this section as interesting and as brief as possible while remaining thorough.

7

THE 17TH AND EARLY 18TH CENTURIES

THE EARLY COLONIAL ERA: SPAIN COLONIZES THE NEW WORLD

Christopher Columbus arrived in the New World in 1492. He was not the first European to reach North America. The Norse had arrived in modern Canada around 1000. Unlike Leif Eriksson, Bjarni Herjolfsson, and other Norse explorers, the better-remembered Columbus arrived at a time when Europe had the resources and technology to establish **colonies** far from home. (A *colony* is a territory settled and controlled by a foreign power.) When Columbus returned to Spain and reported the existence of a rich New World with easy-to-subjugate natives (whom he mistakenly called "**Indians**" because he believed he had reached the Indies), he opened the door to a long period of European expansion and colonialism.

During the next century, Spain was *the* colonial power in the Americas. Advanced weaponry and the truly incredible ruthlessness with which the **conquistadors** treated Native Americans allowed them to dominate the New World, while the strength of the **Spanish Armada** (the navy) made it difficult for other countries to send their own expeditions. The Spanish settled a number of coastal towns in Central and South America and the West Indies, where the conquistadors collected and exported as much of the area's wealth as they could. Wherever they went, the conquistadors enslaved the natives and attempted to erase their culture and supplant it with Catholicism. They slaughtered many of the locals, sometimes for sport, but even more Native Americans died from exposure to **smallpox**. (The Europeans were "carriers" of the disease.) In 1588 the English navy defeated the Armada, and consequently, French and English colonization of North America became much easier.

THE ENGLISH ARRIVE

England's first attempt to settle North America came a year prior to its victory over Spain, in 1587, when **Sir Walter Raleigh** sponsored a settlement on Roanoke Island (now part of North Carolina). By 1590 the colony had disappeared, which is why it came to be known as the **Lost Colony**. The English did not try again until 1606 when they settled **Jamestown**. Jamestown was funded by a **joint-stock company**, a group of investors who bought the right to establish New World plantations from the king. (How the monarchy came to sell the rights to land it clearly did not own is just the kind of interesting question that this review will not be covering. Sorry, but it is not on the AP!) The company was called the **Virginia Company**, from which the area around Jamestown took its name. The Jamestown colony nearly went the way of the Lost Colony. The settlers, many of them English gentlemen, were ill-suited to the many adjustments life in the New World required of them. The colony survived only because captain **John Smith** imposed harsh martial law. His motto was, "He who will not work shall not eat." Things got so bad for the colonists that during the **starving time** of 1609 and 1610, some resorted to cannibalism, while others abandoned the settlement to join Indian tribes.

The colony would have perished without the help of the Algonkian leader **Powhatan**, who led a group of tribes called the **Powhatan Confederacy.** The Algonkians taught the English what crops to plant and how to plant them. They also traded with the colonists. Powhatan hoped that alliance with the English settlers would give him an advantage over enemy tribes. Powhatan guessed wrong. The English forgot their debt to Powhatan as soon as they needed more land (to grow tobacco; see the next paragraph). After numerous conflicts, the Powhatan Confederacy was destroyed by English "Indian fighters" in 1644. **Pocahontas** was an Algonkian, and it was her intervention on behalf of John Smith (ca. 1608) that prevented his execution by the Algonkians. The settlers later kidnapped Pocahontas and forced her to marry an Englishman named John Rolfe.

Jamestown's prospects brightened considerably once the colonists started planting and exporting **tobacco**. Tobacco was a huge success in England, and its success largely determined the fate of the Virginia region. Because the crop requires vast acreage and depletes the soil (and so requires farmers to constantly seek new fields), the prominent role of tobacco in Virginia's economy resulted in rapid expansionism. As new settlements sprang up around Jamestown, the entire area came to be known as the **Chesapeake** (named after the bay). That area today is comprised mostly of Virginia and Maryland.

Many who migrated to the Chesapeake did so for financial reasons. Overpopulation in England had led to widespread famine, disease, and poverty. Chances for improving one's lot were minimal. Thus, many were attracted to the New World by the opportunity provided by **indentured servitude**. In return for free passage, indentured servants promised seven years' labor, after which they received their freedom. Throughout much of the seventeenth century, indentured servants also received a small piece of property with their freedom, thus enabling them (1) to survive, and (2) to vote. Indenture was extremely difficult, and nearly half of all indentured servants—most of whom were young, reasonably healthy men—did not survive their period of servitude. Still, indenture was popular. More than 75 percent of the 130,000 Englishmen who migrated to the Chesapeake during the seventeenth century were indentured servants.

American democracy got an early start in the Chesapeake. In 1619 Virginia established the **House of Burgesses**, in which any property-holding, white male could vote. That year also marks the beginning of **slavery** in the colonies. (See "The Establishment of Slavery," below.)

THE PILGRIMS AND THE MASSACHUSETTS BAY COMPANY

During the sixteenth century, a Protestant movement called **Puritanism** arose in England. Its name was derived from its adherents' desire to purify the corrupt Anglican church. English monarchs of the early seventeenth century persecuted the Puritans, and so the Puritans began to look for a new place to practice their faith.

One Puritan group called **Separatists** (because they were so appalled at the corruption of the English church that they had abandoned it) left England around this time. First they went to Holland, but ultimately decided to start fresh in the New World. In 1620 they set sail for Virginia, but their ship, the **Mayflower**, went off course and they landed in modern-day Massachusetts. Because winter was approaching, they decided to settle where they had landed. This settlement was called **Plymouth**.

While on board, the travellers (called **Pilgrims**) signed an agreement establishing a "body politic" and a basic legal system for the colony. That agreement, **the Mayflower Compact**, is important not only because it created a legal authority and an assembly, but also because it asserted that the government's power derives from the consent of the governed and not, as some **monarchists** known as **Absolutists** believed, from God.

Like the settlers in Jamestown, the Pilgrims received life-saving assistance from local Native Americans. To the Pilgrims' great fortune, one of the Pokanokets (**Squanto**) spoke English, having earlier been captured by English traders and imprisoned in England for several years. Squanto served as the Pilgrims' interpreter and taught them how best to plant in their new home. Interaction between Native Americans and settlers was rarer in Massachusetts than in Virginia because the Native Americans of Massachusetts had previously suffered a plague that had decimated much of the population.

In 1629 a larger and more powerful colony called **Massachusetts Bay** was established by **Congregationalists** (Puritans who wanted to reform the Anglican church from within). Led by Governor **John Winthrop**, Massachusetts Bay developed along Puritan ideals. All Puritans believed they had a **covenant** with God, and the concept of covenants was central to their entire philosophy. Government was to be a covenant among the people; work was to serve a communal ideal, and, of course, the true church (that is, the Puritan church) was always to be served. This is why both the Separatists and the Congregationalists did not tolerate religious freedom in their colonies, even though both had experienced and fled religious persecution.

Two major incidents during the first half of the seventeenth century demonstrated Puritan religious intolerance. **Roger Williams**, a teacher in the Salem Bay settlement, taught a number of controversial principles, among them that church and state should be separate. The Puritans banished Williams, who subsequently moved to modern-day Rhode Island and founded a new colony. Rhode Island's charter allowed for the free exercise of religion, and it did not require voters to be church members. **Anne Hutchinson** preached a mystical brand of Christianity that relied on direct communication with God. Her teachings challenged Puritan beliefs and the authority of the Puritan clergy. The fact that she was an intelligent, well-educated, and powerful woman in a resolutely patriarchal society also turned many against her. She was tried of heresy, convicted, and banished.

Puritan emigration to New England came to a near-halt between 1649 and 1660, the years during which **Oliver Cromwell** ruled as Lord Protector of England. Cromwell's reign represented the culmination of the **English Civil Wars**, which the Puritans won. For slightly over a decade, Cromwell ruled England as a republic, complete with a constitution. The death of Cromwell (1658) robbed the Puritans of their best-known and most respected leader, and by 1660 the Stuarts were restored to the throne. During the **Interregnum** (literally "between kings"), Puritans had little motive to move to the New World. Everything they wanted—freedom to practice their religion, as well as representation in the government—was available to them in England. With the restoration of the Stuarts, many English Puritans again emigrated to the New World. Not coincidentally, these emigrants brought with them the republican ideals of the revolution.

The lives of English settlers in New England and the Chesapeake differed considerably. Entire families tended to emigrate to New England; in the Chesapeake, immigrants were often single males. The climate in New England was more hospitable, and so New Englanders tended to live longer and have larger families than Chesapeake residents. A stronger sense of community, and the absence of tobacco as a cash crop, led New Englanders to settle in larger towns that were closer to one another; those in the Chesapeake lived in smaller, more spread-out farming communities. And while both groups were religious, the New Englanders were definitely *more* religious. (Note that the differences between settlers in New England and in the Chesapeake was the subject of the Document-Based Question on the 1993 AP exam.)

OTHER EARLY COLONIES

As the population of Massachusetts grew, settlers began looking for new places to live. One obvious choice was the Connecticut Valley, a fertile region with lots of access to the sea (for trade). The area was already inhabited by the **Pequots**, however, who resisted the English incursions. When the Pequots attacked a settlement in Wakefield and killed nine colonists, members of the Massachusetts Bay Colony retaliated by burning the main Pequot village, killing 400, many of them women and children. The result was the near-destruction of the Pequots in what came to be known as the **Pequot War**.

Several colonies were proprietorships; that is, they were owned by one person, who usually received the land as a gift from the king. **Connecticut** was one such colony, receiving its charter in 1635. **Maryland** was another, granted to Cecilius Calvert, Lord Baltimore. Calvert declared Maryland a haven of religious tolerance for all Christians, and it became the first major Catholic enclave in the New World.

New York was also a royal gift, this time to James, the king's brother. At the time, some of the area was a Dutch settlement called New Netherland. The Dutch considered the area relatively unimportant, except as a trading post. Thus when the English invaded, the leader of the Dutch colony, Peter Stuyvesant, gave up without a fight. Allowed to remain, the Dutch made up a large segment of New York's population for many years. The king also gave **New Jersey** to a couple of friends, who in turn sold it off to investors, many of whom were Quakers.

Ultimately, the Quakers received their own colony. William Penn, a Quaker, was a close friend of King Charles II, and Charles granted Penn what became **Pennsylvania** (hence "The Quaker State"). Charles, like most Anglicans, perceived the egalitarian Quakers as dangerous radicals, but the two men's friendship (and Charles' desire to export the Quakers to someplace far from England) prevailed. Penn established liberal policies toward religious freedom and civil liberties in his colony. That, and the area's natural bounty, made Pennsylvania one of the fastest growing of the early colonies. He also attempted to treat Native Americans more fairly than did other colonies and had mixed results. His attitude attracted many tribes to the area but also attracted many European settlers who bullied tribes off of their land. An illustrative story: Penn made a treaty with the

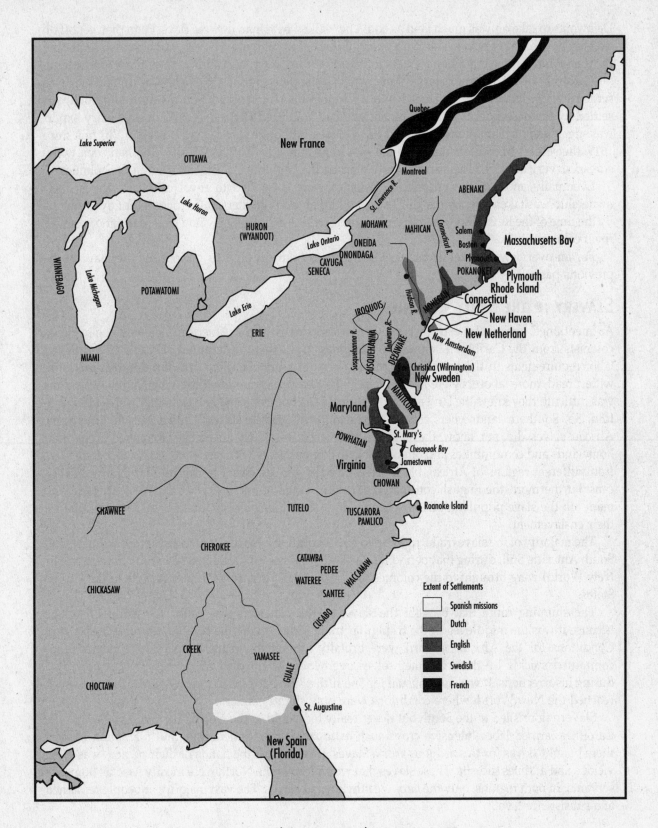

Lake Superior

OTTAWA

New France

Quebec

Lake Huron

Montreal

ABENAKI

St. Lawrence R.

HURON
(WYANDOT)

MOHAWK

MAHICAN

Salem
Boston
Plymouth

Massachusetts Bay

Lake Ontario

WINNEBAGO

Lake Michigan

ONEIDA
ONONDAGA

CAYUGA
SENECA

Connecticut R.

POKANOKET

Plymouth
Rhode Island
Connecticut

Hudson R.

MOHEGAN

New Haven
New Netherland

New Amsterdam

POTAWATOMI

Lake Erie

IROQUOIS

ERIE

Susquehanna R.

SUSQUEHANNA

DELAWARE

Delaware R.

Christina (Wilmington)
New Sweden

MIAMI

NANTICOKE

Maryland

POWHATAN

St. Mary's

Chesapeak Bay

Virginia

Jamestown

CHOWAN

SHAWNEE

TUTELO

TUSCARORA
PAMLICO

Roanoke Island

CHEROKEE

CATAWBA
PEDEE
WATEREE
SANTEE

WACCAMAW

CHICKASAW

CUSABO

Extent of Settlements

CREEK

YAMASEE

GUALE

Spanish missions

Dutch

English

Swedish

French

CHOCTAW

St. Augustine

New Spain
(Florida)

European Settlements in North America, 1650

Delawares to take only as much land as could be walked by a man in three days. Penn then set off on a leisurely stroll, surveyed his land, and kept his end of the bargain. His son, however, renegotiating the treaty, hired three marathon runners for the same task, thereby claiming considerably more land.

Carolina was also a proprietary colony, which ultimately split in two: **North Carolina**, which was settled by Virginians and developed into a Virginia-like colony, and **South Carolina**, which was settled by the descendants of Englishmen who had colonized Barbados. Barbados' primary export was sugar, and its plantations were worked by slaves. Although slavery had existed in Virginia since 1619, the settlers from Barbados were the first Englishmen in the New World who had seen wide-spread slavery at work. Their arrival truly marked the beginning of the slave era in the colonies.

Eventually, most of the **proprietary** colonies were converted to **royal** colonies; that is, their ownership was taken over by the king, who could then exert greater control over their governments. By the time of the Revolution, only Connecticut, Rhode Island, Pennsylvania, and Maryland were *not* royal colonies.

For an overview of what areas were settled by whom during this period, see the map on the previous page.

SLAVERY IN THE EARLY COLONIES

As mentioned above, the extensive use of African slaves in the American colonies began when colonists from the Caribbean settled the Carolinas. Until then, **indentured servants** had satisfied labor requirements in the colonies. As tobacco and, in South Carolina, rice farming became more widespread, more laborers were needed than indenture could provide. Enslaving Native Americans was difficult; they knew the land and so they could easily escape and subsequently were difficult to find. So, Southern landowners turned increasingly to African slaves. Unlike Native Americans, African slaves did not know the land, and so were less likely to escape. Removed from their homelands and communities and often unable to communicate with one another (because they were from different regions of Africa), black slaves initially proved easier to control than Native Americans. Furthermore, the English considered dark skin a sign of inferiority. As the West Africans who made up the slave population had extremely dark skin, the colonists found it easier to rationalize their enslavement.

The majority of the slave trade, right up to the Revolution, was directed toward the Caribbean and South America. Still, during that period nearly 500,000 slaves (of the almost 10 million brought to the New World) were brought to the colonies. By 1790, 700,000 blacks were in servitude in the United States.

The shipping route that brought the slaves to the Americas was called the **Middle Passage** because it was the middle leg of the **triangular trade** route among the colonies, Europe, and Africa. Conditions for the Africans aboard were brutally inhumane, so intolerable that some Africans committed suicide by throwing themselves overboard. Many died of sickness, and others died during insurrections. It was not unusual for one-fifth of the Africans to die on board. Most, however, reached the New World, where conditions were only slightly better.

Slavery flourished in the South but never really took hold in the North. The Chesapeake and the Carolinas farmed labor-intensive crops such as **tobacco**, **rice**, and **indigo**, and plantation owners there bought slaves for this arduous work. Slaves' treatment at the hands of their owners was often vicious and at times sadistic. Those slaves that wound up in the North were mostly used as domestic servants. In both regions, only the very wealthy owned slaves. The vast majority of people remained at a subsistence level.

THE AGE OF SALUTARY NEGLECT (1650 TO 1750)

British treatment of the colonies during the period preceding the **French and Indian Wars** (also called **the Seven Years' War**) is often described as **salutary neglect** (or **benign neglect**). Although England regulated trade and government in its colonies, it interfered in colonial affairs as little as possible. England even occasionally turned its back to the colonies' violations of trade restrictions. Thus, the colonies developed a large degree of autonomy, which helped fuel revolutionary sentiments when the monarchy later attempted to gain greater control of the New World.

During this century, the colonies "grew up," developing fledgling economies. The beginnings of an American culture—as opposed to a transplanted English culture—took root. (This period was recently the subject of a free-response essay question.)

ENGLISH REGULATION OF COLONIAL TRADE

Throughout the colonial period, most Europeans who thought about economics at all subscribed to a theory called **mercantilism**. Mercantilists believed that economic power was rooted in a favorable balance of trade (that is, exporting more than you import) and the control of **specie** (hard currency such as coins). Colonies, they felt, were important mostly for economic reasons, which explains why the British considered their colonies in the West Indies that produced sugar and other valuable commodities to be more important than their American colonies. The American colonies were seen primarily as markets for British and West Indian goods, although they also were valued as sources of raw materials that would otherwise have to be bought from a foreign country.

In order to guarantee a favorable balance of trade, the British government encouraged manufacturing in England and placed **protective tariffs** on imports that might compete with English goods. A number of such tariffs, included in the **Navigation Acts**, were passed between 1651 and 1673. The Navigation Acts required the colonists to buy goods only from England, to sell certain of its products only to England, and to import any non-English goods via English ports and pay a duty on those imports. The Navigation Acts also prohibited the colonies from manufacturing a number of goods that England already produced. In short, the Navigation Acts sought to establish wide-ranging English control over colonial commerce.

The Navigation Acts were only somewhat successful in achieving their goal, as it was easy to smuggle goods into and out of the colonies. Not surprisingly, many merchants did just that. In the 1690s the British took steps to strengthen the Navigation Acts. First, they set up **vice-admiralty courts**—military-style courts, in which defendants were not entitled to a jury—to try violations of the Navigation Acts. The British considered this change necessary because most colonial juries sided with the colonists accused of smuggling, not with the Crown. Second, the British set up **Boards of Trade** to better regulate colonial commerce. The Boards of Trade also reviewed colonial legislation and revoked laws that conflicted with British law, and administered government appointments. Because the colonists understood and accepted the concept of mercantilism, their protests to the Navigation Acts and Boards of Trade were less strenuous than their protests would later be to the Stamp Act and Townshend Acts. (See the next chapter for details on these acts.) The colonists also did not protest aggressively against the Navigation Acts at the time because they were entirely dependent on England for trade and for military protection.

COLONIAL GOVERNMENTS

Despite trade regulations, the colonists maintained a large degree of autonomy. Every colony had a **governor** who was appointed by either the king or the proprietor. Although the governor had powers similar to the king's in England, he was also dependent on colonial **legislatures** for money. Also, the governor, whatever his nominal powers, was essentially stranded in the New World. His power relied on the cooperation of the colonists, and most governors ruled accordingly, only infrequently overruling the legislatures.

Except for Pennsylvania (which had a unicameral legislature), all the colonies had **bicameral** legislatures modeled after the British Parliament. The lower house functioned in much the same way as does today's House of Representatives; its members were directly elected (by white, male property holders), and its powers included the "power of the purse" (control over government salaries and tax legislation). The upper house was made up of appointees, who served as advisors to the governor and had some legislative and judicial powers. Most of these men were chosen from the local population. Most were concerned primarily with protecting the interests of colonial land owners.

The British never tried to establish a powerful central government in the colonies. The autonomy that England allowed the colonies helped ease their transition to independence in the following century.

The colonists did make some small efforts toward centralized government. **The New England Confederation** is the most prominent of these attempts. Although it had no real power, it did offer advice to northeastern colonies when disputes arose among them. It also provided colonists from different settlements the opportunity to meet and to discover and discuss their mutual problems.

Major Events of the Period

Here is a laundry list of events with which you should be familiar:

Bacon's Rebellion took place on Virginia's western frontier during the 1670s. As the farmable land to the east filled up, settlers looked to the western portion of the colony. Many were willing to chance the dangers of frontier life in return for an opportunity to "strike it rich." As they were encroaching on land already inhabited by Native Americans, however, those dangers were considerable. The pioneers soon believed that the colonial government was not making a good-faith effort to protect them, and that, furthermore, the government was using them as a "human shield" to protect the wealthier colonists to the east. Rallying behind **Nathaniel Bacon**, these settlers first attacked both the Doegs and the Susquehannocks, and then turned their attentions toward the colonial governor. The rebels marched on Jamestown and burned it to the ground. When Bacon later died of dysentery, the rebellion dissolved. The war Bacon almost instigated between the colonists and Native American tribes was averted with a new treaty. Bacon's Rebellion is often cited as an early example of a populist uprising in America.

In New England, colonial expansion led to the bloodiest English-Native American conflict of the time. By the 1670s, the Pokanokets (also known as the Wampanoags) living in Narragansett Bay, Massachusetts, were surrounded by white settlements, and colonists were attempting to usurp Indian life with English culture and religion. Their leader, Metacomet (known to the English as King Philip; hence, **King Philip's War**), led attacks on several settlements in retaliation for this intrusion on Pokanoket territory. Soon after, he formed an alliance with two other local tribes. The alliance destroyed a number of English settlements but eventually ran out of food and ammunition. When Metacomet died, the alliance fell apart and the colonists devastated the tribes, selling many into slavery in the West Indies. King Philip's War marks the end of a formidable Native American presence among the New England colonists.

Insurrections led by slaves did not begin until nearly seventy years later with the **Stono Uprising,** the first and one of the most successful slave rebellions. In September 1739, approximately twenty slaves met near the Stono River outside Charleston, South Carolina. They stole guns and ammunition, killed storekeepers and planters, and liberated a number of slaves. The rebels, now numbering about 100, fled to Florida, where they hoped the Spanish colonists would grant them their freedom.

The colonial militia caught up with them and attacked, killing some and capturing most others. Those who were captured and returned were later executed. As a result of the Stono Uprising (sometimes called the **Stono Rebellion**), many colonies passed more restrictive laws to govern the behavior of slaves. Fear of slave rebellions increased, and New York experienced a "witch hunt" period during which 31 blacks and four whites were executed for conspiracy to liberate slaves.

Speaking of witch hunts, the **Salem Witch Trials** took place in 1692. These were not the first witch trials in New England. During the first 70 years of English settlement in the region, 103 people (almost all women) had been tried on charges of witchcraft. Never before had so many been accused at once, however; during the summer of 1692, more than 130 "witches" were jailed or executed in Salem.

Historians have a number of explanations for why the mass hysteria started and ended so quickly. The region had recently endured the autocratic control of **The Dominion of New England**, an English government attempt to clamp down on illegal trade. Massachusetts' charter had been revoked, its assemblies dissolved, and the governor who ruled for two years was granted powers usually exercised only by an absolute monarch. The Dominion of New England came to an end when the **Glorious Revolution** in England overthrew James II and replaced him with William and Mary. In 1691, Massachusetts became a royal colony under the new monarchs, and suffrage was extended to all Protestants (previously only Puritans could vote), thus weakening Puritan primacy. War against French and Native Americans on the Canadian border (called **King William's War** in the colonies and **The War of the League of Augsburg** in England) soon followed and further heightened regional anxieties.

To top it all off, the Puritans feared that their religion—which they fervently believed was the *only* true religion—was on its way out. Many second- and third-generation Puritans lacked the fervor of the original Pilgrim and Congregationalist settlers, a situation that led to the **Halfway Covenant,** which changed the rules governing Puritan baptisms. (Prior to the passage of the Halfway Covenant in 1662, a Puritan had to experience the gift of God's grace in order for his or her children to be baptized by the church. With so many, particularly men, losing interest in the church, the Puritan clergy decided to baptize all children whose parents were baptized. However—here is the "halfway" part—those who had not experienced God's grace were not allowed to vote.) All of these factors, historians argued, combined to create **mass hysteria in Salem in 1692**. The hysteria ended when the accusers, most of them teenage girls, accused some of the colony's most prominent citizens of consorting with the Devil, thus turning town leaders against them. Some historians also feel that the hysteria had simply run its course.

As noted above, the generations that followed the original settlers were generally less religious than those that preceded them. By 1700 women constituted the majority of active church members. However, between the 1730s and 1760 the colonies experienced a wave of religious revivalism known as the **First Great Awakening**. Two men, Congregationalist minister **Jonathan Edwards** and the Methodist preacher **George Whitefield**, came to exemplify the period. Edwards preached the severe, predeterministic doctrines of Calvinism and became famous for his graphic depictions of Hell; Whitefield preached a Christianity based on emotionalism and spirituality, which today is most clearly manifested in Southern **evangelism**. The First Great Awakening is often described as the response of devout people to the **Enlightenment**, a European intellectual movement that borrowed heavily from ancient philosophy and emphasized rationalism over emotionalism or spirituality.

Whitefield was a native of England, where the Enlightenment was in full swing; its effects were also being felt in the colonies, especially in the cities. The colonist who came to typify Enlightenment ideals in America was the self-made and self-educated man, **Ben Franklin**. Franklin was a printer's apprentice who, through his own ingenuity and hard work, became a wealthy printer and a successful and respected intellectual. His *Poor Richard's Almanack* was extremely popular and remains influential to this day. (It is the source of such pithy aphorisms as "A stitch in time saves nine" and "A penny saved is a penny earned.") He did pioneering work in the field of electricity. He invented bifocals, the lightening rod, and the Franklin stove, and he founded the colonies' first fire department and first public library. Franklin espoused Enlightenment ideals about education, government, and religion and was, until Washington came along, the colonists' "favorite son." Toward the end of his life, he served as an ambassador in Europe, where he negotiated a crucial alliance with the French and, later, the peace treaty that ended the Revolutionary War.

LIFE IN THE COLONIES

Perhaps the most important development in the colonies during this period is how quickly they grew. The population in 1700 was 250,000; by 1750, that number was 1,250,000. Throughout these years the colonies began to develop substantial non-English European populations. Scotch-Irish, Scots, and Germans all started arriving in large numbers during the eighteenth century. English settlers, of course, continued to come to the New World as well. The black population in 1750 was more than 200,000.

The vast majority of colonists—over 90 percent—lived in **rural areas**. Life for whites in the countryside was rugged but tolerable. Only in the cities did substantial numbers of people live in destitution. In the country, labor was divided along gender lines, with men doing the outdoor work such as farming, and women doing the "indoor" work of housekeeping and childrearing. Opportunities for social interaction outside the family were limited to shopping days and rare special community events. Both children and women were completely subordinate to men, particularly to the head of the household. Children's education had to be fit in around their work schedules. Married women were not allowed to vote, own property, draft a will, or testify in court. Unmarried women and widows were also not allowed to vote but otherwise had the same legal rights as men. There were very few such women, however, as the social pressure to marry was great.

Blacks, most of whom were slaves, lived predominantly in the countryside and in the South. Their lives varied from region to region, with conditions being most difficult in the South, where the labor was difficult and the climate less hospitable to hard work. Those slaves who worked on large plantations and developed specialized skills such as carpentry or cooking fared better than did field hands. In all cases, though, the condition of servitude was demeaning. Slaves often developed extended-kinship ties and strong communal bonds to cope with the misery of servitude and the possibility that their nuclear families might be separated by sale. In the North, where black populations were relatively small, blacks often had trouble maintaining a sense of community and history.

Conditions in the **cities** were often much worse than those in the country. Because work could usually be found there, most immigrants usually settled in the cities. The work they found usually paid too little, and poverty was widespread. Sanitary conditions were primitive, and epidemics were common. On the positive side, cities offered residents much wider contact with other people and with the outside world. Cities served as centers for progress and education.

Citizens with anything above a rudimentary level of education were rare. In fact, the majority of colonists could neither read nor write. Education was as much a sign of wealth as intelligence. Nearly all **colleges** established during this period served primarily to train ministers.

The lives of colonists in the various regions differed considerably. **New England** society centered on trade. Boston was the colonies' major port city. The population farmed for subsistence, not for trade, and mostly subscribed to rigid Puritanism. The **middle colonies**—New York, Pennsylvania, New Jersey—had more fertile land and so focused primarily on farming. Philadelphia and New York

City like Boston, were major trade centers. The population of the region was more heterogeneous than was that of New England. The **lower South** (the Carolinas) concentrated on such cash crops as tobacco and rice. Slavery played a major role on plantations, although the majority of Southerners were subsistence farmers who had no slaves. Blacks constituted up to half the population of some Southern colonies. The colonies on the **Chesapeake** combined features of the middle colonies and the lower South. Slavery and tobacco played a larger role in the Chesapeake than in the middle colonies, but like the middle colonies, the Chesapeake residents also farmed grain and thus diversified their economies. The development of major cities in the Chesapeake region also distinguished it from the lower South which was almost entirely rural.

Thus, the colonies were hardly a unified whole as they approached the events that led them to rebel. How then did they join together and defeat the most powerful nation in the world? The answer to this and other exciting questions awaits you in the next chapter.

8

THE LATE 18TH AND 19TH CENTURIES

EVENTS LEADING TO THE REVOLUTIONARY WAR (1750–1776)

In 1754 the colonists considered themselves English subjects. Very few could have imagined circumstances under which they would leave the British empire. The events that led from almost universal loyalty to rebellion are frequently tested on the AP U.S. History exam. Here is what you need to know:

THE SEVEN YEARS' WAR (1754–1763)

Yes, the Seven Years' War lasted for ten years. It is also called the **French and Indian War**, which is almost equally confusing because the French and Indians fought on the same side, not against each other. The Seven Years' War was the British name for the war. The colonists called it the French and Indian War because that's who they were fighting.

The war was the inevitable result of colonial expansion. (It was also caused by a number of inter-European power struggles, which is how Spain, Austria, Sweden, Prussia, and others got involved, but that is on the European history test, so you can worry about it some other time.) As English settlers moved into the Ohio Valley, the French tried to stop them by building fortified outposts at strategic entry spots. The French were trying to protect their profitable fur trade and their control of the region. A colonial contingent led by **George Washington** attacked a French outpost and lost badly. Washington surrendered and was allowed to return to Virginia, where he was welcomed as a hero! Other skirmishes and battles ensued, and in 1756 England officially declared war on France. Native Americans, choosing the lesser of two evils, allied themselves with the French (whom, based on Washington's performance, they expected to win the war). The war dragged on for years before the English finally gained the upper hand. When the war was over, England was the undisputed colonial power of the continent. The treaty gave England control of Canada and almost everything east of the Mississippi Valley.

During the Seven Years' War, many Americans served in the English army and, for the first time, came into prolonged contact with English soldiers. The English did not make a good impression, both in how they treated their "regulars" and in how the regulars behaved themselves. These contacts sowed the first seeds of anti-British sentiment in the colonies, particularly in New England, where much of the fighting took place.

The English victory spelled trouble for Native Americans, who had previously been able to use French and English disputes to their own advantage. They negotiated their allegiances in return for land, goods, and the right to be left alone. The Indians particularly disliked the English, though, because English expansionism was more disruptive to their way of life. In the aftermath of the war, the English raised the price of goods sold to the Indians (they now had a monopoly, after all) and ceased paying rent on their western forts. In response, Ottawa war chief **Pontiac** rallied a group of tribes in the Ohio Valley and attacked colonial outposts. The attacks and resultant wars are known as **Pontiac's Uprising**. In response to the initial attacks, the British government issued the **Proclamation of 1763** forbidding settlement west of the rivers running through the Appalachians. The proclamation came too late. Settlers had already moved west of the line. The proclamation did have one effect, however. It agitated colonial settlers, who regarded it as unwarranted British interference in colonial affairs. The wars ended in 1766.

THE SUGAR ACT, THE CURRENCY ACT, AND THE STAMP ACT

One result of the Seven Years' War was that in financing the war the British government had run up a huge debt. The new king, **George III**, and his prime minister, **George Grenville**, felt that the colonists should help pay that debt. After all, they reasoned, the colonies had been beneficiaries of the war; furthermore, their tax burden was relatively light compared to that of taxpayers in England.

Accordingly, Parliament imposed new taxes on the colonists. The first was the **Sugar Act** of 1764, which established a number of new duties and which also contained provisions aimed at deterring molasses smugglers. The Sugar Act differed from previous tariffs such as the **Navigation Acts** in one important way: It was explicitly designed to generate revenue for the British government. (The Navigation Acts were designed to regulate trade, in keeping with **mercantilist** economics.) It was the first piece of legislation ever to do so. Another Parliamentary act, the **Currency Act**, forbade the colonies to issue paper money. Collectively, the Sugar Act, Currency Act, and Proclamation of 1763 caused a great deal of discontent in the colonies, whose residents bristled at what they correctly viewed as British attempts to exert greater control. That these actions came during a post-war economic depression further aggravated the situation. Colonial protest to these acts, however, was uncoordinated and ineffective.

That all changed when Parliament passed the **Stamp Act** the following year. The Stamp Act included a number of provocative elements. First, it was another tax specifically aimed at raising revenue, thus awakening the colonists to the likelihood that even more taxes could follow. The Stamp Act demonstrated that the colonies' tradition of self-taxation was surely being usurped, much to the dismay of many colonists. Second, it was a broad-based tax, covering all legal documents and licenses. Not only did it affect almost everyone, but it particularly affected a group that was literate, persuasive, and argumentative—namely, lawyers. Third, the law established **vice-admiralty courts** to try violators, thereby removing jurisdiction over such cases from the colonists.

Reaction to the Stamp Act built on previous grievances, and consequently was more forceful than any protest preceding it. A pamphlet by James Otis, called *The Rights of the British Colonies Asserted and Proved*, laid out the colonists' argument against the taxes and became a bestseller of its day. Otis put forward the "No taxation without representation" argument that later became a rallying cry of the Revolution. Since the colonists did not elect members to Parliament, he argued, they were not obliged to pay taxes (following the accepted precept that no Englishman could be compelled to pay taxes without his consent). Otis did *not* advocate secession; rather, he argued for either representation in Parliament or a greater degree of self-government for the colonies. Neither the British nor the colonists had much interest in creating a colonial delegation to Parliament. The British scoffed at the notion, arguing that the colonists were already represented in Parliament. Their argument was rooted in the theory of **virtual representation**, which stated that members of Parliament represented all British subjects regardless of who elected them. The colonists, for their part, knew that their representation would be too small to protect their interests and so never pushed the issue. What they wanted, and what the British were refusing to give them, was the right to determine their own taxes.

Opponents to the Stamp Act united in the various colonies. In Virginia, Patrick Henry drafted the Virginia Stamp Act Resolves, protesting the tax and asserting the colonists' right to a large measure of self-government. (The Virginia legislature removed Henry's most radical propositions before passing the resolves.) In Boston, mobs burned the customs officers in effigy, tore down a customs house, and nearly destroyed the governor's mansion. Protest groups formed throughout the colonies, calling themselves "**Sons of Liberty**." The opposition was so effective that, by the time the law was supposed to take effect, not one of the Crown's appointed duty collectors was willing to perform his job. In 1766 Parliament repealed the Stamp Act. Just as important, George III replaced Prime Minister Grenville, whom the colonists now loathed, with Lord Rockingham, who had opposed the Stamp Act. Rockingham oversaw the repeal but also linked it to the passage of the **Declaratory Act**, which asserted the British government's right to tax and legislate in all cases anywhere in the colonies. Thus, although the colonists had won the battle over the stamp tax, they had not yet gained any ground in the war of principles over Parliament's powers in the colonies.

THE TOWNSHEND ACTS

Rockingham remained Prime Minister for only two years. His replacement was William Pitt. Pitt, however, was ill, and the dominant figure in colonial affairs came to be the exchequer, Charles Townshend. Townshend drafted the eponymous **Townshend Acts**. The Townshend Acts, like the Stamp Act, contained several antagonistic measures. First, they taxed goods imported directly from Britain—the first such tax in the colonies. Mercantilism approved of duties on imports from other European nations but not on British imports. Second, some of the tax collected was set aside for the payment of tax collectors, meaning that colonial assemblies could no longer withhold government officials' wages in order to get their way. The Townshend Acts also created even more vice-admiralty courts and several new government offices to enforce the Crown's will in the colonies. Finally, they suspended the New York legislature because it had refused to comply with a law requiring the colonists to supply British troops.

The colonists got better at protesting with each new tax, and their reaction to the Townshend Acts was their strongest yet. The Massachusetts Assembly sent a letter to all other assemblies asking that they protest the new measures in unison. The British fanned the flames of protest by ordering the assemblies *not* to discuss the Massachusetts letter, virtually guaranteeing it to be all anyone *would* talk about. Governors of colonies where legislatures discussed the letter dissolved those legislatures, which, of course, further infuriated colonists. The colonists held numerous rallies and organized boycotts, and for the first time sought the support of "commoners" (previously such protests were confined largely to the aristocratic classes), making their rallies larger and much more intimidating. The boycotts were most successful because they affected British merchants, who then joined the protest. After two years, Parliament repealed the Townshend duties (except the duty on tea), although not the other statutes of the Townshend Acts.

As part of the Townshend Acts, the British stationed a large number of troops in Boston, and even after the duties were repealed, the soldiers remained. Officially sent to keep the peace, these soldiers in fact heightened tensions. For one thing, the detachment was huge—4,000 men in a city of only 16,000. To make matters worse, the soldiers sought off-hour employment and so competed with colonists for jobs. Numerous confrontations resulted, with the most famous on March 5, 1770, when a mob pelted a group of soldiers with rock-filled snowballs. The soldiers fired on the crowd, killing five hence, the **Boston Massacre**. The propaganda campaign that followed suggested that the soldiers had shot into a crowd of innocent bystanders.

The Calm, and then the Storm

And then, oddly, for the next two years, nothing major happened. An uneasy status quo fell into place during the period. Colonial newspapers discussed ways in which the relationship between the mother country and the colonies might be altered so as to satisfy both sides, but still, nobody except a very few radicals suggested independence.

Things picked up in 1772 when the British implemented that part of the Townshend Acts providing for colonial administrators to be paid from customs revenues (and not by the colonial legislatures). The colonists responded cautiously, setting up groups called **Committees of Correspondence** throughout the colonies to trade ideas and apprise each other of the political mood. The committees also worked to convince more citizens to take an active interest in the conflict.

Not long after, the British granted the foundering East India Tea Company a monopoly on the tea trade in the colonies as well as a portion of new duties to be collected on tea sales. The result was cheaper tea for the colonists, but the colonists saw a more important issue: Parliament was once again imposing new taxes on them. In Boston, the colonists refused to allow the ships to unload their cargo, and the governor refused to allow them to leave the harbor. On December 16, 1773, a group of Sons of Liberty, poorly disguised as Mohawks, boarded a ship and dumped its cargo into Boston Harbor. It took them three hours to jettison the approximately £10,000 worth of tea. The incident is known as the **Boston Tea Party**.

The English responded with a number of punitive measures, known collectively as the **Coercive Acts** (also called the **Intolerable Acts**). One measure closed Boston Harbor to all but essential trade (food and firewood) and declared it would remain closed until the tea was paid for. Several measures tightened English control over the Massachusetts government and its courts, and yet another required civilians to house British soldiers. The Coercive Acts convinced many colonists that their days of semi-autonomy were over and that the future held even further encroachments on their liberties by the Crown. To make matters worse, at the same time Parliament passed the Coercive Acts, it also passed the **Quebec Act** which, to the colonists' chagrin, (1) granted greater liberties to Catholics whom the Protestant colonial majority distrusted and (2) extended the boundaries of the Quebec Territory, thus impeding westward expansion.

The colonists soon met to discuss their grievances. All colonies except Georgia sent delegates to the **First Continental Congress**, which convened in late 1774. All perspectives were represented—Pennsylvania's delegation included conservatives such as Joseph Galloway, while Virginia sent two radicals, Richard Henry Lee and **Patrick Henry**. The goals of the meeting were to enumerate American grievances, to develop a strategy for addressing those grievances, and to formulate a colonial position on the proper relationship between the royal government and the colonial governments. The Congress came up with a list of those laws the colonists wanted repealed and agreed to impose a boycott on British goods until their grievances were redressed. The delegates also agreed that towns should set up **committees of observation** to enforce the boycott; in time, these committees became their towns' *de facto* governments. Perhaps most important, the Congress formulated a limited set of parameters within which it considered Parliamentary interference in colonial affairs justified; all other spheres, the delegates agreed, should be left to the colonists themselves. This position represented a major break with British tradition and, accordingly, a major step toward independence.

Throughout the winter of 1774 and the spring of 1775, the committees of observation expanded their powers. In many colonies they supplanted the British-sanctioned assemblies. They led acts of insubordination by collecting taxes, disrupting court sessions, and, most ominously, by organizing militias and stockpiling weapons. As John Adams would later comment about the period: "The revolution was complete, in the minds of the people, and the Union of the colonies, before the war commenced."

THE SHOT HEARD 'ROUND THE WORLD

The British underestimated the strength of the growing pro-revolutionary movement. Government officials mistakenly believed that if they arrested the ring leaders and confiscated their arsenals, violence could be averted. To that end, the English dispatched troops to confiscate weapons in Concord, Massachusetts in April 1775. The troops had to first pass through Lexington, where they confronted a small colonial militia, called **minutemen** because they reputedly could be ready to fight on a minute's notice. Someone, probably one of the minutemen, fired a shot, which drew British return fire. When the **Battle of Lexington** was over, the minutemen had suffered eighteen casualties, including eight dead. The British proceeded to **Concord**, where a much larger contingent of minutemen awaited them. The Massachusetts militia inflicted numerous casualties on the British **Redcoats** and forced them to retreat. That a contingent of colonial farmers could repel the army of the world's largest empire was monumental, which is why the **Battle of Concord** is sometimes referred to as "the shot heard 'round the world." The two opponents dug in around Boston, but during the next year only one major battle was fought. The two sides regrouped and planned their next moves.

For the colonists, the period provided time to rally citizens to the cause of independence. Not all were convinced. Among those remaining loyal to the Crown—such people were called **Loyalists**—were government officials, devout Anglicans, merchants dependent on trade with England, and many religious and ethnic minorities who feared persecution at the hands of the rebels. Many slaves believed their chances for liberty were better with the British than with the colonists, a belief strengthened when the royal governor of Virginia offered to free those slaves who escaped and joined the British army. The pre-Revolutionary War era saw an increase in the number of slave insurrections, dampening some Southerners' enthusiasm for revolution. The **patriots** were mostly white Protestant property holders and gentry, as well as urban artisans. Much of the rest of the population just hoped the whole thing would blow over. The Quakers of Pennsylvania, for example, were pacifists and so wanted to avoid war.

The **Second Continental Congress** convened during this period, just weeks after the battles of Lexington and Concord. Throughout the summer, the Congress prepared for war by establishing a **Continental Army**, printing money, and creating government offices to supervise policy. The Congress chose **George Washington** to lead the army because he was both well-liked and a Southerner (thus bolstering support in a weak area for the rebels). There is lots of interesting military history about Washington's command, but since the AP ignores military history, so does this review. Let's move on.

THE DECLARATION OF INDEPENDENCE

The rebels were still looking for the masterpiece of propaganda that would rally colonists to their cause. They got it in *Common Sense*, a pamphlet by an English printer named **Thomas Paine**. Paine not only advocated colonial independence, he also argued for the merits of republicanism over monarchy. The pamphlet was an even bigger success than that previous colonial rabble-rouser, James Otis' *The Rights of the British Colonies Asserted and Proved*. In a nation of two million, most of whom couldn't read, it sold more than 100,000 copies in its first three months (proportionally, about the same as selling 13 million compact discs today).

In June, the Congress was looking for a rousing statement of its ideals, and it commissioned **Thomas Jefferson** to write the **Declaration of Independence**. He did not let them down. The Declaration not only enumerates the colonies' grievances against the Crown, but it also articulates the principle of individual liberty and the government's fundamental responsibility to serve the people. Despite its obvious flaws—most especially that it pertained only to white, propertied men—it remains a work of enormous power. With the document's signing on July 4, 1776, the Revolutionary War officially began.

Chronology of Events Leading to Revolutionary War			
1763	French-Indian War ends Pontiac's Uprising Proclamation of 1763	1772	Parts of Townshend Acts implemented Committees of Correspondence formed
1764	Sugar Act Currency Act	1773	British give Dutch East India Company monopoly on tea in colonies Boston Tea Party
1765	Stamp Act Sons of Liberty form	1774	Coercive Acts (aka Intolerable Acts) Quebec Act First Continental Congress meets Committees of Observation form
1766	Grenville replaced by Rockingham as Prime Minister Stamp Act repealed Declaratory Act	1775	Battles of Lexington and Concord Second Continental Congress meets
1767	Townshend Acts	1776	Declaration of Independence
1770	Townshend duties repealed (except tea tax) Boston Massacre		

The Revolutionary War was fought from 1776 until 1782, when the two countries negotiated peace. You should remember a few other facts about the war. The Continental Army (as opposed to local militias) had trouble recruiting good soldiers. Eventually, the Congress recruited blacks, and up to 5,000 fought on the side of the rebels (in return, most of those who had been slaves were granted their freedom). The **Franco-American Alliance**, negotiated by **Ben Franklin** in 1778, brought the French into the war on the side of the colonists. This alliance helped the colonists considerably. Ultimately, the colonists won a war of attrition; like the U.S. in Vietnam almost two centuries later, the British were outlasted and ultimately forced to abandon an unpopular war on foreign soil. The **Treaty of Paris**, signed at the end of 1782, granted the United States independence and generous territorial rights.

CREATING A FUNCTIONING GOVERNMENT (1776–1800)

THE ARTICLES OF CONFEDERATION

The colonies did not wait to win their independence from England before setting up their own governments. As soon as the Declaration of Independence was signed, states began writing their own constitutions. In 1777 the Continental Congress sent the **Articles of Confederation**, the first national constitution, to the colonies for ratification. The articles contained several major flaws, as the country would soon learn. For one, it did not give the national government the power to tax or to regulate trade. Furthermore, amendments to the articles required the unanimous consent of all the states. The Articles of Confederation were clearly more concerned with prohibiting the government from gaining too much power than with empowering it enough to function effectively.

With the end of the war, the colonies had other issues to confront as well. The decrease in England's power in the region opened a new era of relations with Native Americans. This new era was even more contentious than the previous one because a number of tribes had allied themselves with the Crown. Second-class citizens and noncitizens—namely, women and blacks—had made sacrifices in the fight for liberation, and some expected at least a degree of compensation. **Abigail Adams** wrote a famous letter to her husband pleading the case for women's rights in the new government, which John Adams answered in a derisive tone that few men would chance today. The number of free blacks in the colonies grew during and after the war, but their increased presence among free whites was also accompanied by a growth of racist publications and legislation. Such conditions led to the early "ghettoization" of blacks and, for similar reasons, other minorities.

The problems with the Articles of Confederation became apparent early on. The wartime government, unable to levy taxes, tried to finance the war by printing more money which led, naturally, to wild inflation. After the war, the British pursued punitive trade policies against the colonies, denying them access to West Indian markets and dumping goods on American markets. The government, unable to impose tariffs, was helpless. Furthermore, when state governments dragged their heels in compensating loyalists for lost property, the British refused to abandon military posts in the States, claiming that they were remaining to protect the loyalists' rights. The government, again, was powerless to expel them. Perhaps the rudest awakening came in the form of **Shays' Rebellion**. In 1787 an army of 1,500 farmers marched on Boston to protest a number of unfair policies, both economic and political. They were armed and very angry, and they gave the elite class the wake-up call that the revolution might not be over yet. Shays' Rebellion helped convince some that a stronger central government was necessary.

The government under the articles was not totally without its successes, though. Its greatest achievements were the adoption of ordinances governing the sale of government land to settlers. Best known is the **Northwest Ordinance of 1787** because it also contained a bill of rights guaranteeing trial by jury, freedom of religion, and freedom from excessive punishment. It abolished slavery in the Northwest territories (northwest of the Ohio River and east of the Mississippi River, up to the Canadian border), and also set specific regulations concerning the conditions under which territories could apply for statehood. Thus, the ordinance is seen as a forerunner to the Bill of Rights and other progressive government policies. It was not so enlightened about Native Americans, however; in fact, it essentially claimed their land without their consent. War ensued, and peace did not come until 1795 when the U.S. gained a military advantage over the Miami Confederacy, their chief Native American opponent in the area. The Northwest Ordinance remained important long after the northwest territories were settled, because of its pertinence to the statehood process and to the issue of slavery.

(The effectiveness of the Articles of Confederation was recently the subject of the document-based essay question [DBQ]).

A NEW CONSTITUTION

By 1787 it was clear that the Articles of Confederation needed fixing, so the state assemblies agreed to a Constitutional Convention. Again, delegates came from many different ideological backgrounds, from those who felt the Articles needed only slight adjustments to those who wanted to tear them down and start from scratch.

The **New Jersey Plan** called for modifications. **The Virginia Plan**, largely the brainchild of **James Madison**, called for an entirely new government based on the principle of **checks and balances**. The convention lasted for four months, over the course of which the delegates hammered out a compromise, the **Constitution**, which more closely resembled the Virginia Plan. The Constitution called for a bicameral legislature, with the lower house (the House of Representatives) elected by the people and the upper house (the Senate) appointed by state governors. (Direct election of senators, believe it or not, is a twentieth-century innovation.) The Constitution also laid out a method for counting slaves among the populations of Southern states, even though those slaves would not be citizens. It also established three branches of government, the **executive**, **legislative**, and **judicial**, with the power of checks and balances on each other. Only three of the 42 delegates refused to sign the finished document (two because it did not include a bill of rights).

Ratification of the Constitution was by no means guaranteed. Opposition forces portrayed the federal government under the Constitution as an all-powerful beast. These opponents, known as **Anti-Federalists**, were particularly appalled by the absence of a bill of rights. Their position rang true in many of the state legislatures where the Constitution's fate lay, and some held out for the promise of the immediate addition of the **Bill of Rights** upon ratification. The **Federalist** position was forcefully and persuasively argued in **the Federalist Papers**, anonymously authored by **James Madison**, **Alexander Hamilton**, and **John Jay**. The Federalist Papers were published in a New York newspaper and were later widely circulated. They were critical in swaying opinion in New York, a large and therefore politically important state. (Virginia and Massachusetts were the other "powerhouses" of the era.) The **Constitution** went into effect in 1789; the **Bill of Rights** was added in 1791.

THE WASHINGTON PRESIDENCY

The electoral college unanimously chose **George Washington** to be the first president. Washington had not sought the presidency, but as the most popular figure in the colonies, he was the clear choice, and he accepted the role out of a sense of obligation.

Knowing that his actions would set precedents for those who followed him in office, Washington exercised his authority with care and restraint. He determined early on to use his veto only if he was convinced that a bill was unconstitutional. He was comfortable delegating responsibility and so created a government made up of the best minds of his time. Prominent among his cabinet selections were **Thomas Jefferson** as Secretary of State and **Alexander Hamilton** as Secretary of the Treasury. These two men strongly disagreed about the proper relationship between the federal government and state governments. Hamilton favored a strong central government and weak state governments, a position that came to be known as **federalism**. Jefferson, fearing the country would backslide into monarchy, favored a small federal government empowered mainly to defend the country and regulate international commerce. All other powers, he thought, should be reserved to the states.

Their argument was not a mere intellectual exercise. The new government was still defining itself, and each man strove to influence that development. The debate came to the forefront when Hamilton proposed a **National Bank** to help regulate and strengthen the economy. Both houses of Congress approved Hamilton's plan, but Washington, uncertain of the bank's constitutionality, considered a veto. In the debate that followed, the two main schools of thought on constitutional law were established. On one side were the **strict constructionists**, led by Jefferson and **James Madison**. They argued that the Constitution allowed Congress only those powers specifically granted to it or those "necessary and proper" to the execution of its **enumerated powers**. While a bank might be convenient and perhaps beneficial, they argued, it was not necessary, and thus its creation was beyond the powers of the national government. Hamilton took the opposing viewpoint, framing the **broad constructionist** position. He argued that the creation of a bank was an **implied power** of the government because the government already had explicit power to coin money, borrow money, and collect taxes. Hamilton put forward that the government could do anything in the execution of those enumerated powers—including creating a bank—that was not explicitly forbidden it by the Constitution. Washington agreed with Hamilton and signed the bill.

Hamilton's tenure at treasury was a busy and successful one. Among his achievements was his successful handling of the **national debt** accrued during the war. Hamilton's plan called for the federal government to assume the states' debts (further increasing the federal government's power over them) and to repay those debts by giving the debt holders land on the western frontier. The plan clearly favored Northern banks, many of which had bought up debt certificates at a small portion of their worth. Northern states also had more remaining debt than Southern states, another reason why the plan drew accusations that Hamilton was helping the monied elite at the expense of the working classes. (Some issues are perennials of American politics: this is one of them. Opposition to tax increases is another.) Hamilton was able to strike a political deal to get most of his plan implemented. His concession was a Southern location for the nation's capital. In 1800 the capital was moved to **Washington, D.C.**

The **French Revolution** took place during the Washington administration, and it too caused considerable debate. Jefferson wanted to support the revolution and its republican ideals. Hamilton had aristocratic leanings and so disliked the revolutionaries, ordinary people who had overthrown the French aristocracy. The issue came to the forefront when France and England resumed hostilities. The British continued to be America's primary trading partner after the war, a situation that argued for neutrality in the French-English conflict. Even Jefferson agreed that neutrality was the correct course to follow. When French government representative **Citizen Edmond Genêt** visited America to seek its assistance, Washington declared the U.S. intention to remain "friendly and impartial toward belligerent powers." Genêt's visit sparked large, enthusiastic rallies held by American supporters of the revolution. The rallies were organized by **Democratic-Republican societies**, which evolved into the Democratic-Republican **political party** (no relation to the contemporary **Republican** party). The development of political parties troubled the framers of the Constitution, most of whom regarded parties as fractious and dangerous instruments of rabble-rousing.

Washington even accused the Democratic-Republican societies of instigating the **Whiskey Rebellion**, which started when western Pennsylvania farmers resisted a new duty on whiskey. For months, armed rebels across Pennsylvania, Maryland, and Virginia defied government efforts to collect the new tax. Washington, resolute that his government would not tolerate armed disobedience, sent a large troop detachment to disperse the rebels, who, lacking strong leadership, simply went home. The decisive federal action, though probably necessary, alienated many and began the long demise of the **Federalists** as a political force.

During his second term, Washington sent John Jay to England to negotiate a treaty concerning free trade and the continued British presence in the New World. Not everyone was happy with the resultant **Jay Treaty**, although the Senate ratified it. The next year, however, Congress attempted to withhold funding to enforce the treaty. The House of Representatives asked Washington to submit all documents pertinent to the treaty for consideration. Washington refused, establishing the precedent of **executive privilege** (the right of the president to withhold information when doing so would protect national security, e.g., in the case of diplomatic files and military secrets).

The end of Washington's presidency was as monumental as its beginning. Wishing to set a final precedent, Washington declined to run for a third term. In his famous **farewell address**, which was principally authored by Alexander Hamilton, he warned future presidents to avoid foreign entanglement.

THE ADAMS PRESIDENCY

The electoral college selected **John Adams**, a Federalist, as Washington's successor. Under the then-current rules, the second-place candidate became vice-president, and so Adams' vice-president was the Democratic-Republican Thomas Jefferson. After the election of 1800, the Constitution was amended to allow a presidential and vice-presidential candidate to run together, as a **ticket**.

Following the Washington era, Adams' presidency was bound to be an anticlimax. Adams, argumentative and elitist, was a difficult man to like. He was also a hands-off administrator, often allowing his political rival **Alexander Hamilton** to take charge. The animosity between the two men and the growing belligerence between the nascent political parties (the Federalists and the Democratic-Republicans) set the ugly, divisive tone for Adams' term.

Perhaps Adams' greatest achievement was avoiding war with France. After the U.S. signed the Jay Treaty with Britain, France began seizing American ships on the open seas. Adams sent three diplomats to Paris where French officials demanded a huge bribe before they would allow negotiations even to begin. The diplomats returned home, and Adams published their written report in the newspapers. Because he deleted the French officials' names and replaced them with the letters X, Y, and Z, the incident became known as the **XYZ Affair**. As a result, popular sentiment did a complete turnaround; formerly pro-French, the public became vehemently anti-French to the point that a declaration of war seemed possible. Adams avoided the war (a war Hamilton wanted) and negotiated a settlement with a contrite France.

The low point of Adams' tenure was the passage and enforcement of the **Alien and Sedition Acts**, which allowed the government to forcibly expel foreigners and to jail newspaper editors for "scandalous and malicious writing." The acts were purely political, aimed at destroying the Democratic-Republicans, whom the Federalists held in deep contempt. In a scenario almost unimaginable today, Vice President Jefferson led the opposition to the Alien and Sedition Acts. Together with Madison, he drafted the **Virginia and Kentucky Resolutions**, which argued that the states had the right to judge the constitutionality of federal laws. The resolutions went on to exercise this authority they claimed, later referred to as **nullification**, by declaring the Alien and Sedition Acts void. Virginia and Kentucky, however, never prevented enforcement of the laws. Rather, Jefferson used the laws and the resolutions as key issues in his 1800 campaign for the presidency. (The Alien and Sedition Acts have been the subject of the DBQ.)

THE ELECTION OF 1800

By 1800 the Federalist party was split, clearing the way to the presidency for the Democratic-Republicans. Two men ran for the party nomination: **Thomas Jefferson** and **Aaron Burr**. Each received an equal number of votes in the Electoral College, which meant that the Federalist-dominated House of Representatives was required to choose a president from between the two. It took 35 ballots, but Jefferson finally won. Alexander Hamilton swallowed hard and campaigned for Jefferson, with whom he disagreed on most issues and whom he personally disliked, because he believed Burr to be "a most unfit and dangerous man." Burr later proved Hamilton right by killing him (in an old-fashioned duel).

The election was noteworthy for two reasons. For the second time in as many elections, a president was saddled with a vice-president he did not want. That problem was remedied in 1804 with the **Twelfth Amendment** to the Constitution, which allowed electors to vote for a party ticket. The other, more important reason the election was important is that in America's first transfer of power—from the Federalists to the Democratic-Republicans—no violence occurred, a feat practically unprecedented for the time. Jefferson referred to his victory and the subsequent change-over as "the bloodless revolution."

THE JEFFERSONIAN REPUBLIC (1800–1823)

Note: The next two chapters primarily review political history. They are followed by a review of social and economic history between 1800 and 1860 because many of the important socio-economic trends of the era developed over the course of several decades. The economic and social conditions of this period also played a major role in bringing about the Civil War, and the AP often tests them in this context. That's why we'll review them as we get closer, chronologically, to the Civil War.

JEFFERSON'S FIRST TERM

The transition of power from the Federalists to the Democrat-Republicans may have been a bloodless one, but it was not a friendly one. Adams was so upset about the election that he left the capital before Jefferson took office in order to avoid attending the inauguration ceremony. Before he left town, however, he made a number of **"midnight appointments,"** filling as many government positions with Federalists as he could. Jefferson's response was to refuse to recognize those appointments. He then set about replacing as many Federalist appointees as he could. He dismissed some, pressured others to retire, and waited out the rest. By his second term, the majority of public appointees were Democratic-Republicans. Upon taking office, Jefferson also immediately pardoned all those convicted under the Alien and Sedition Acts, then persuaded Congress, now controlled by his party, to repeal the laws.

Next, Jefferson and his treasurer Albert Gallatin set out to reduce the national debt. Under Hamilton's leadership, the government had borrowed to finance national growth. Hamilton had also believed that a national debt was a good thing: If the government borrowed from its rich citizens, those citizens would have a vested interest in the country's growth. Jefferson decided to abandon that policy, trim the federal budget, and cut taxes, all of which he succeeded in doing.

Meanwhile, Jefferson's refusal to accept Adams' midnight appointments resulted in a number of lawsuits against the government. One, the case of *Marbury v. Madison*, reached the Supreme Court in 1803. William Marbury, one of Adams' last-minute appointees, had sued Secretary of State James Madison for refusing to certify his appointment to the federal bench. Chief Justice **John Marshall** was a Federalist, and his sympathies were with Marbury, but Marshall was not certain that the court could force Jefferson to accept Marbury's appointment. Marshall's decision in the case established one of the most important principles of the Supreme Court: **judicial review**. The court ruled that Marbury did indeed have a right to his judgeship, but that the court could not enforce his right. Why? Although the power to do so had been granted to the Supreme Court in the Judiciary Act of 1789, Marshall now declared it unconstitutional. In one fell swoop, Marshall had handed Jefferson the victory he wanted while simultaneously claiming a major role for the Supreme Court: the responsibility for reviewing the constitutionality of Congressional acts. Throughout the rest of his tenure, Marshall worked to strengthen that doctrine and, thus, the court.

The major accomplishment of Jefferson's first term was the **Louisiana Purchase**. When Spain gave New Orleans to the French in 1802, the government realized that a potentially troublesome situation was developing. The French, they knew, were more likely to take advantage of New Orleans' strategic location at the mouth of the Mississippi, almost certainly meaning that American trade along the river would be restricted. In hopes of averting that situation, Jefferson sent James Monroe to France. Monroe's mandate was to buy New Orleans for $2 million. Monroe arrived at just the right time. Napoleon was gearing up for war in Europe, and a violent slave revolt in Haiti against the French further convinced him to abandon French interests in the New World. The French offered to sell Monroe the whole Louisiana territory for $15 million, and the rest, as they say, is history. Ironically, Jefferson the antifederalist had undertaken the largest federal action in the nation's brief history.

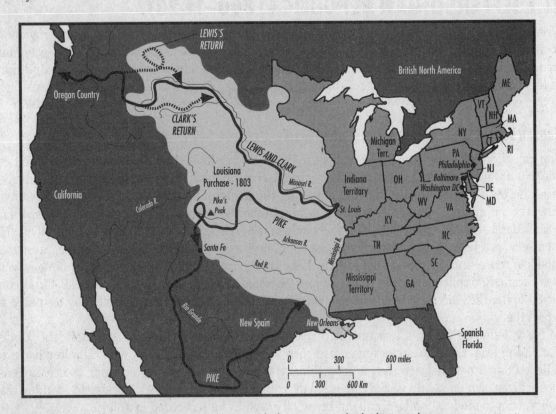

The Louisiana Purchase and The Lewis and Clark Expedition

Jefferson sent explorers, among them **Lewis and Clark**, to investigate the western territories, including much of what was included in the Louisiana territory. All returned with favorable reports, causing many pioneers to turn their attentions westward in search of wealth and freedom.

In 1804 Jefferson won reelection in a landslide victory. During the 1804 elections, Aaron Burr ran for governor of New York. Again, Alexander Hamilton campaigned against Burr and for a Democratic-Republican (a party, you should recall, that he detested). When Burr lost, he accused Hamilton of sabotaging his political career and challenged him to a **duel** in which he killed Hamilton. Afterward, Burr fled to the Southwest where he plotted to start his own nation in parts of the Louisiana Territory. He was later captured and tried for treason but was acquitted because of lack of evidence.

JEFFERSON'S SECOND TERM

Jefferson's second term did not go nearly as smoothly as his first. During these years, the U.S. got caught in the middle of yet another French-English dispute. The resulting situation led to the **War of 1812**.

In 1805 the British and French were at war and at a stalemate. In an effort to gain an advantage, each side began blockading the other's trade routes. The U.S., dependent on both as trade partners, suffered greatly from the blockades. To add insult to injury, the British began stopping American ships and **impressing** those sailors who *might* have deserted the British navy. Unfortunately, the English were not as particular about whom they "reenlisted" as the Americans would have liked them to be. Tensions mounted, then boiled over when a British frigate attacked an American ship in American waters. Jefferson was at a loss. He couldn't go to war against the British because the U.S. Navy was no match for England's forces. So, Jefferson responded with a boycott, biding his time while increasing military and naval appropriations.

Because both the British and the French continued to harass American ships, Jefferson lobbied for and won the **Embargo Act of 1807**. The law basically shut down America's import and export business, with disastrous economic results. New England's economy collapsed, and smuggling became widespread. As had Washington before him, Jefferson decided that two terms as president were enough. He endorsed his Secretary of State, **James Madison**, who defeated the ever-weakening Federalists handily. Jefferson repealed the unsuccessful Embargo Act in the final days of his presidency.

MADISON'S PRESIDENCY AND THE WAR OF 1812

Madison, seeking a solution to America's trade problems, reopened trade with both France and England. However, he promised that if either of the countries would renounce its interference with American trade, he would cut off trade with the other one. Napoleon made that promise, forcing the U.S. to cut off trade with England, but then continued to harass American ships. The British, angry at the new embargo, stepped up their attacks on American ships, making a bad situation even worse. These developments helped build pro-war sentiments in the U.S. Particularly anxious for a confrontation with the British were the Southern **War Hawks**, who saw war as an opportunity to grab new territories to the west and southwest. Their leaders were **Henry Clay** and **John Calhoun**. Madison held out as long as he could, but finally he relented and declared war in 1812.

You should know several important points about the **War of 1812**. Once again, Native Americans aligned themselves with the British. The great chief **Tecumseh** unified area tribes in an effort to stop American expansion into Indiana and Illinois, both before and during the war. Meanwhile, his brother **Prophet** led an extensive revival of traditional Indian culture and religion. Tecumseh's coalition fell apart after he was killed in battle.

American forces were ill-prepared for the war, and much of the fighting went badly. The British captured Washington, D.C., in 1814 and set the White House on fire. However, in most battles America was able to fight to a stalemate. When English-French hostilities ended (with Napoleon's defeat), many of the issues that had caused the war evaporated, and the British soon negotiated peace. The Federalists, opposed to the war and not aware that its end was coming, met in the **Hartford Convention** to consider a massive overhaul of the Constitution or, failing that, secession. When the war ended soon after, most people considered the Federalists to be traitors, and their national party dissolved (although the party continued to exert influence in some states through the next decade).

The war had one clear positive result, which is that it spurred **American manufacturing**. Cut off from trade with Europe, the states became more self-sufficient by necessity. New England became America's manufacturing center during the war, and after the war, the U.S. was less dependent on imports than it had been previously. (For more information on economic developments of the period, see pp. 92–96.)

Throughout the rest of his tenure, Madison worked to promote national growth. At the same time, he remained true to his Democratic-Republican principles, and so extended federal power only cautiously. Madison championed a combination of programs that included protective tariffs on imports, improvements to interstate roads (including expansion of the **National Road** from Maryland to Ohio), and the rechartering of the National Bank (the first National Bank's charter had expired). The programs were known collectively as the **American System**. Speaker of the House **Henry Clay** lobbied for them so aggressively that many history books refer to "Henry Clay's American System."

MONROE'S PRESIDENCY

The demise of the Federalists briefly left the U.S with only one political party. This period of unity is referred to as **"the Era of Good Feelings."** During this period, Chief Justice John Marshall's rulings continued to strengthen the federal government and its primacy. For example, he ruled in *McCulloch v. Maryland* that the states could not tax the National Bank, thus establishing the precedence of national law over state law.

The good feelings nearly came to an abrupt end in 1819 when a financial scare called **the Panic of 1819** threw the American economy into turmoil. The panic followed a period of economic growth, inflation, and land speculation, all of which had destabilized the economy. When the national bank called in its loans, many borrowers couldn't repay them. The consequences included numerous mortgage foreclosures and business failures. Many people were thrown into poverty. Nonetheless, no nationally organized political opposition resulted from the panic, and Monroe easily won reelection in 1820.

The post-war period had also ushered in a new wave of westward expansionism. As Secretary of State under Monroe, **John Quincy Adams** (son of former president John Adams) deftly negotiated a number of treaties that fixed U.S. borders, opened new territories, and acquired Florida from the Spanish. Adams also had to handle international tensions caused by a series of revolutions in Central America and South America (against European imperialism). Ultimately, events compelled Monroe and Adams to recognize the new nations. At the same time, they decided that America should assert its authority over the Western Hemisphere. The result was the **Monroe Doctrine**, a policy of mutual noninterference. You stay out of the West, Monroe told Europe, and we'll stay out of your squabbles. The Monroe Doctrine also claimed America's right to intervene anywhere in its own hemisphere, if it felt its security was threatened. No European country tried to intercede in the Americas following Monroe's declaration, and so the Monroe Doctrine *appeared* to work. No one, however, was afraid of the American military; Spain, France, and others stayed out of the Western Hemisphere because the powerful British Navy made sure they did.

The new period of expansion also resulted in a national debate over slavery, as would every period of expansion to follow. In 1820 the Union consisted of twenty-two states. Eleven allowed slavery, eleven prohibited it. Missouri's application for statehood, however, threatened the balance. The two sides worked out the **Missouri Compromise**, which (1) admitted Missouri as a slave state; (2) carved off a piece of Massachusetts, called it Maine, and admitted Maine as a free state; and (3) established the southern border of Missouri as the northernmost point in which slavery would then be allowed in the United States. The compromise was the first in a series of measures forestalling the Civil War. It also split the powerful Democratic-Republican coalition, ending its twenty-year control of national politics.

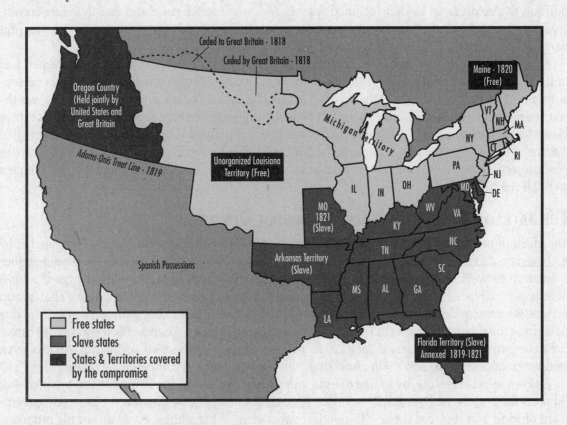

Missouri Compromise, 1820

BEGINNINGS OF MODERN AMERICAN DEMOCRACY (1824–1844)

THE ELECTION OF 1824 AND JOHN QUINCY ADAMS' PRESIDENCY

The **election of 1824** marked a major turning point in presidential elections. Prior to 1824, electors (who selected the president in the electoral college) had been chosen by a variety of methods. State legislatures chose many electors, although with each election the number of states using this method decreased. By 1824 a majority of states allowed voters to choose their presidential electors directly. In earlier elections, **congressional caucuses** had chosen their parties' nominee, and electors (often chosen by those same congressmen or by their friends) had not challenged the choices. With more people voting directly for electors, however, the caucus nominee was no longer guaranteed to represent his party. When the Democratic-Republican caucus chose William H. Crawford in 1824, others—among them John Quincy Adams, Henry Clay, and Andrew Jackson—decided to challenge the nomination. Their opposition, along with their accusations that the caucuses were undemocratic, brought about the **demise of the caucus system**. Of the four, Andrew Jackson received the greatest number of popular votes and electoral votes; however, as none of the four had won a majority, the election was decided in the House of Representatives. There, Clay threw his support to Adams, thereby handing Adams the victory. Adams reciprocated by naming Clay Secretary of State, a position whose previous holders included Adams, Monroe, and Jefferson and was therefore considered the threshold to the presidency. Opponents referred to Clay's appointment as the "**corrupt bargain**."

Adams' presidency was impeded by a contrary Congress. (Remember, more congressmen had initially supported Jackson than Adams.) Adams was also handicapped with an obnoxious personality, a trait that apparently ran in the family. He had also been a Federalist congressman and was the son of a Federalist president, and every effort he made to strengthen the central government was thus viewed with deep suspicion. Jackson's supporters strongly favored **states' rights** and thwarted all of Adams' efforts to initiate improvements through the federal government. His proposals to impose new protective tariffs, build interstate highways, and establish federal schools and research centers were all rejected.

THE JACKSON PRESIDENCY AND JACKSONIAN DEMOCRACY

The **election of 1828** ushered in the beginning of the modern political party system. Furious that he had been denied the presidency in 1824 despite winning a plurality of the vote, Jackson put together a support network to assure wide popular support. A coalition of state political organizations, newspaper publishers, and other community leaders rallied around the campaign. That group became the present-day **Democratic** party. The campaign itself was vicious, with Jackson and Adams devoting little time to the issues of the day. Instead, Jackson accused Adams of being a corrupt career politician, while Adams accused Jackson of being a stupid and violent drunkard. Adams even stooped to attacking Jackson's wife. And thus, the modern political campaign was born.

Jackson won the election by a large margin; in so doing, he became the first president who was not (1) born in Virginia, or (2) named "Adams." Among his first acts, he dismissed numerous government officials and replaced them with political supporters. While almost every one of his predecessors had done exactly the same thing, Jackson was the first to be widely criticized for the practice. Trading jobs for political favors came to be known as the "**spoils system**."

Jackson's popularity ushered in the age of **Jacksonian democracy**, which replaced **Jeffersonian democracy**. Jefferson had conceived of a nation governed by middle- and upper-class educated property holders, in which the government would be only as large as necessary to provide an acceptable level of services. Jacksonian democracy, on the other hand, was based on **universal manhood suffrage**, meaning the extension of voting rights to all white males, even those who did not own property. A strong presidency also characterized Jacksonian democracy. Jackson parlayed his wide popularity into a mandate to challenge both Congress and the Supreme Court in a way that none of his predecessors had. You should note that, unlike Jeffersonian democracy, Jacksonian democracy is *not* a coherent vision of how a government should function. Jackson was not a great thinker, as Jefferson was.

Jackson's strongest support came from the western frontier states, where the demand for expansion was strong. Accordingly, Jackson pursued an aggressive **Indian removal** program. Although the

Supreme Court had protected Native American rights to their land in *Cherokee Nation v. Georgia* and *Worcester v. Georgia*, Jackson forcibly evicted tribes that would not otherwise relocate to the West. The **Removal Act of 1830** set in motion the events that resulted in the **Trail of Tears**, an 1838 forced march of Cherokees that resulted in thousands of deaths by sickness and starvation.

Jackson spent much of his two terms "downsizing" the federal government. He saw to it that the **Second Bank of the United States** failed (by withdrawing federal funds and depositing them in state banks). Jackson also fought the many **reform** movements of the time that were lobbying for increased government activism against social and economic problems. (For more information on the reform movements, see page pp. 100-101.) In addition, he put a halt to programs associated with Clay's American System. At the same time, Jackson strengthened the office of the presidency through his popularity and by making extensive use of the presidential veto.

One of the major issues of Jackson's presidency focused on **nullification**. The doctrine of nullification, first expressed by Jefferson and Madison in the Virginia and Kentucky Resolutions, holds that the individual states have the right to judge the constitutionality of federal laws and to disobey those laws if they find them unconstitutional. The **Tariff of 1828**, also known as the **Tariff of Abominations**, was passed during the Adams administration, but it almost turned into a national crisis during Jackson's administration, when some states started to consider nullifying the tariff in 1830. Jackson, though a strong supporter of **states' rights**, thought nullification endangered the Union and was thus too extreme. The 1830 nullification movement failed, but it laid the groundwork for opposition to the **Tariff of 1832**, which South Carolina nullified. Jackson threatened to call in troops to enforce the tariff, but in the meantime he worked behind the scenes to reach a compromise that would diffuse tensions. Although the crisis subsided with the compromise, no resolution was reached over the question of nullification, and it would continue to be an issue until the Civil War. In fact, nullification remains an issue today, albeit only among a small group on the radical right known as the "militia movement." (Note: As you read the newspaper, which you should do daily, take note of contemporary issues with deep roots in American history, such as nullification. Using current events to illustrate historical principles, when done correctly, will earn you big bonus points on your essays.)

Jackson's economic policies demonstrated his distrust of both big government and Northeastern power brokers. He fought the Second Bank of the United States because he felt it protected Northeastern interests at the expense of the West. He was also suspicious of paper money, preferring "hard currency" such as gold or silver. His **Specie Circular**, which ended the policy of selling government land on credit (buyers now had to pay "hard cash"), caused a money shortage, a sharp decrease in the treasury, and overall economic hardship. Congress overturned the circular in the final days of Jackson's final term.

Slavery grew to be an ever-more controversial issue during Jackson's tenure. As the Northern abolition movement grew stronger (see p. 101 for more about the abolitionists), the South experienced several slave revolts which resulted in the use of more brutal disciplinary measures by slave holders. The most famous of the insurrections was **Nat Turner's Rebellion**. Turner, a well-read preacher, had a vision, and he took this vision as a sign from God that a black liberation movement would succeed. As a result, he rallied a gang that proceeded to kill and then mutilate the corpses of sixty whites. In retaliation, 200 slaves were executed, some with no connection at all to the rebellion. Fearful that other slaves would hear of and emulate Turner's exploits, Southern states passed a series of restrictive laws, known as **black codes**, prohibiting blacks from congregating and learning to read. Other state laws even prevented whites from questioning the legitimacy of slavery.

THE ELECTION OF 1836 AND THE RISE OF THE WHIGS

Jackson's Democratic party could not represent the interests of all its constituencies (Northern abolitionists, Southern plantation owners, Western pioneers), and inevitably, an opposition party, the **Whigs**, was formed. By 1834 almost as many Congressmen supported the Whig Party as the Democratic Party. The Whigs were a loose coalition that shared one thing in common: opposition to one or more of the Democrats' policies. For example, while the Democrats favored limited federal government, many Whigs believed in government **activism** especially in the case of social issues. Many Whigs were also deeply religious and supported the temperance movement and enforcement of the Sabbath. Still, the defining characteristic of the Whigs was their opposition to the Democrats. They differed on many issues which is why their candidates were often famous military heroes whose political beliefs were politically less important than their popularity.

Still, in the election of 1836, Jackson supported his second vice-president, democrat **Martin Van Buren**. Van Buren had the misfortune to take over the presidency just as the country entered a major economic crisis (the **Panic of 1837**). Van Buren made the situation worse by continuing Jackson's policy of favoring hard currency, thereby insuring that money would be hard to come by. The economic downturn lasted through Van Buren's term, practically guaranteeing that he would not be reelected.

In 1841, former military hero **William Henry Harrison** became the first Whig president. He died of pneumonia a month after taking office. His vice-president, **John Tyler**, a former Democrat, assumed the presidency and began championing states' rights, much to his own party's chagrin. Tyler vetoed numerous Whig bills, which alienated Whig leadership; eventually his entire cabinet resigned in protest. Tyler is often referred to as the "president without a party," and his presidency lasted only one term.

ECONOMIC HISTORY, 1800–1860

This chapter discusses economic developments in the United States during the first part of the nineteenth century. These developments played an important role in the political events that led to the Civil War, and they helped to determine the different characteristics of the country's regions. Along with other social developments (discussed in the next chapter), these economic factors laid the foundation for issues that would be important to American society for the following century (such as abolitionism, women's suffrage, and temperance).

BEGINNINGS OF A MARKET ECONOMY

From the time the first settlers arrived until the Revolutionary War era, most settlers in the United States produced almost everything they needed to survive. Nearly all raised crops for subsistence, rather than for sale at market. Surplus crops were bartered with other farmers, so each farmer did not have to produce every crop his family needed. Most people made their own clothing and built their own furniture and homes, and they got by without many other conveniences. Cash transactions were relatively rare.

Developments in manufacturing and transportation changed all that, however. By making it possible to mass produce goods and transport them across country cheaply, a **market economy** began to develop. In a market economy, people trade their labor or goods for cash which they then use to buy other people's labor or goods. Market economies favor those who specialize. For example, farmers who grow a single crop usually do better in a market economy than those who produce many different crops: One-crop farmers can offer buyers more of what they want. These farmers also do not have to look for different buyers for their many products. The trade-off, of course, is that these farmers are no longer self-sufficient. Instead, they become dependent on the market to provide some necessities. Furthermore, such farmers sometimes fall victim to overproduction, resulting in an unexpected, unwelcome drop in the price of their crop.

Market economies grow more quickly and provide more services than subsistence economies, and they also make people more interdependent. However, they are also much more prone to change. Any number of factors can halt a period of prosperity and throw the economy into a skid like the panics of 1819 and 1837 (previously mentioned; see pp. 88 and 92). These changes are referred to as **boom-and-bust cycles**. During the first decades of the nineteenth century, the United States made a rapid transition from a subsistence economy to a market economy.

As stated earlier, the **War of 1812** and the events leading up to it forced the United States to become less dependent on imports, and, consequently, to develop a stronger national economy. Two key advances, both developed by **Eli Whitney**, also played a major part in the process. The **cotton gin**, invented in 1793, revolutionized Southern agriculture by making it much easier to remove the seeds from cotton plants. (The machine was 5,000 percent more efficient than a human being.) The cotton gin made it easier and cheaper to use cotton for textiles, and as a result, the demand for cotton grew very rapidly in the late 1700s and early 1800s. As demand grew, so did cotton production in the South. Because cotton farming is labor intensive, the spread of cotton as the region's chief crop also intensified the South's dependence on slave labor.

Whitney's second innovation was the use of **interchangeable parts** in manufacturing. Whitney originally struck upon the idea while mass-producing rifles for the U.S. Army. Prior to Whitney's breakthrough, manufacturers had built weapons (and other machines) by hand, custom-fitting parts so that each weapon was unique. The process was costly, time consuming, and inconvenient, since replacing broken parts was extremely difficult. Whitney demonstrated the practicality of his invention to Thomas Jefferson and James Madison by disassembling a number of rifles, scrambling the parts, and then reassembling the rifles from whichever parts he picked out of the pile. Whitney's demonstration was a huge success—"number one with a bullet," so to speak—and soon his idea was being applied to all aspects of manufacturing.

Interchangeable parts gave birth to the **machine-tool industry**, which produced specialized machines for such growing industries as textiles and transportation. (Without interchangeable parts, such machines would have been impractical because they would have been too expensive to build and too difficult to fix.) Whitney's advances also helped promote **assembly line production**. On an assembly line, products are constructed more efficiently by dividing the labor into a number of tasks and assigning each worker one task. Prior to assembly lines, each worker would create a product in its entirety. The result was a product that took longer to produce and was less uniform in quality.

THE NORTH AND THE TEXTILE INDUSTRY

The above-mentioned developments first benefited the textile industry. Advances in machine technology, coupled with a U.S. embargo on British goods prior to and during the War of 1812 (England was then America's chief source of textiles), spurred the development of textile mills in New England. During the first decade of the nineteenth century, mills produced thread and hired local women to spin the thread into cloth at home. The mills would then buy the finished cloth and sell it on the open market. The invention of the first **power loom** in 1813 meant that textile manufacturers could produce both thread and finished fabric in their own factories, and do so quickly and efficiently. The resulting product was both of high quality and inexpensive—so much so that women who had previously woven their own fabrics at home started to buy cloth.

The rapid growth of the textile industry resulted in a shortage of labor in New England. Consequently, textile manufacturers had to "sweeten the pot" to entice laborers (almost all of whom were women from nearby farms) to their factories. The most famous worker-enticement program was called the **Lowell system** (also called the **Waltham system**), so named after the Massachusetts town in which many mills were located. The Lowell system guaranteed employees housing in a respectable, chaperoned boardinghouse, cash wages, and participation in cultural and social events organized by the mill. The system, widely copied throughout New England, lasted until great waves of Irish immigration in the 1840s and 1850s made factory labor plentiful. Later, as working conditions started to deteriorate, workers began to organize **labor unions** to protect their interests. These early unions in the mid-1800s met with strong, frequently violent opposition from industry. Still, they succeeded in shortening the typical workday to ten hours. They also got the courts to confirm their right to organize. (We'll discuss labor unions in much more detail later, when we discuss the post-Civil War, Gilded Age, and Progressive eras.)

Other industries inevitably sprung up around the textile industry. **Clothing manufacturers**, also located primarily in the Northeast, transformed the textiles into finished products. **Retailers** sold the clothing and other manufactured products in their stores. **Brokers** acted as middlemen, buying and selling raw and finished products and trafficking them among manufacturers and retailers. **Commercial banks** lent money to everyone so that the wheels of commerce stayed well-greased. Most significant, the **transportation industry** grew as a result of the need to ship these and other products across the country.

TRANSPORTATION: CANALS, RAILROADS, HIGHWAYS, AND STEAMSHIPS

Prior to the 1820s, travel and shipping along east-west routes was difficult, and most trade centered on the north-south routes along the Ohio and Mississippi Rivers. The construction of the **National Road** from Maryland to West Virginia (and ultimately to central Ohio) made east-west travel easier, but the big change came with the completion of the **Erie Canal** in 1825. The canal linked the Great Lakes region to New York and, thus, to European shipping routes. Suddenly, it became lucrative for a Midwestern merchant or farmer to sell his products to Eastern buyers, and as a result the Northeast soon established itself as the United States' center of commerce. The Erie Canal was so successful that, by 1835, its width and depth had to be nearly doubled to handle the traffic. Other regions tried to duplicate the Erie Canal's success, and during the 1830s thousands of miles of canals were constructed throughout the Northeast and Midwest. None performed as well as the Erie Canal, and a number of those canals failed. Meanwhile, the railroads developed into a convenient means of transporting goods; by 1850, the **canal era** had ended.

The end of this era, however, did not mark the end of shipping as an important industry. The invention of the steam engine allowed for **steamships** that traveled faster than sailing vessels. Steamships became important freight carriers and replaced sailing ships for long sea voyages. By 1850 passengers could travel by steamship from New York to England in ten days; by sails the same trip had taken more than a month.

Similarly, railroads redefined land travel. America's first **railroads** were built during the 1830s, the first typically connecting only two cities. As the nation's rail network grew, a major problem arose: Different railroad lines could not be connected to one another because the width, or **gauge**, of their tracks was different. As a result, rail development proceeded slowly. When different railways converted to compatible systems, the government often paid the bill even though the railroads were privately owned. This hastened progress, and by 1853, New York and Chicago were linked by rail, as were Pittsburgh and Philadelphia. (Southern rail development was much slower, and superior rails gave the North a huge advantage during the Civil War.) We'll discuss the railroads further in the post-Civil War period, during which railroad construction really "picked up steam."

The increase in travel and shipping was helped considerably by the invention of the **telegraph**, which allowed immediate long-distance communication for the first time. The telegraph was like a primitive telephone except that people communicated in **Morse code** rather than by speaking to one another. Americans immediately understood the benefits of telegraphic communications, and widespread use followed its invention almost immediately.

In conclusion, developments in transportation and communication during the first half of the nineteenth century literally revolutionized American commerce and culture. Products, people, and ideas traveled much faster in 1850 than they had in 1800.

FARMING

Although American manufacturing grew at a rapid pace, agriculture remained by far the most common profession throughout the first half of the nineteenth century. Mechanization revolutionized farming during the period, as many of the machines came into common use during this time: including the mechanical plow, sower, reaper, thresher, baler, and cotton gin—the growth of the market economy also changed farming. In 1820 about one-third of all the food grown in the U.S. went to market. (The rest was kept for personal consumption.) By 1860 that fraction had doubled.

Farming continued in the Northeast, but not without difficulties. The region's rocky, hilly terrain was unsuitable to many of the machines that were making farming on the plains easier and cheaper. Furthermore, much of the farmland in the region had been overfarmed, and as a result, the quality of the soil had grown poor. Unable to compete with Midwestern grain farmers, some New England farmers quit cultivating grain and started raising livestock and growing fruits and vegetables. Others quit farming entirely and headed to the cities to take manufacturing jobs.

As mentioned above, the Midwest became America's chief source of grains such as wheat and corn. Midwestern farms—much larger than New England farms—were also much more adaptable to the new technology that allowed farmers to nearly double production. **Banks** sprang up to lend farmers the capital necessary to buy modern equipment, and the trade routes created by rail and ship provided access to the markets these farmers needed to sell their crops in order to pay off their loans. The system worked well, except during the various financial crises of the first half of the century. The panics of 1819 and 1837 resulted in bank foreclosures on mortgages and other business loans, not just in the Midwest but all across the country. Not surprising, many people were thrown into poverty.

In the South, plantations focused primarily on cotton, especially in the Deep South; tobacco continued to be a major cash crop in the Upper South. The majority of Southerners were small farmers who did not own slaves. (In 1860 approximately one-quarter of white Southern families owned slaves.)

WESTWARD EXPANSION

The Louisiana Purchase removed one major obstacle to U.S. western settlement, and victory in the War of 1812 removed another by depriving Native Americans of a powerful ally in Great Britain. By 1820 the United States had settled the region east of the Mississippi River and was quickly expanding west. Americans began to believe that they had a God-given right to the Western territories, an idea that came to be known as America's **manifest destiny**. Some took the idea of manifest destiny to its logical conclusion and argued that Canada and Mexico eventually would be annexed by the United States.

Western settlement was dangerous. The terrain and climate could be cold and unforgiving, and these settlers from the East were moving into areas that rightfully belonged to Native Americans and Mexicans, none of whom were about to cede their homes without a fight.

Texas presents a good case in point. When Mexico declared its independence from Spain in 1821, the new country included what is now Texas and much of the Southwest, including California. The Mexican government established liberal land policies to entice settlers, and tens of thousands of Americans (many of them cattle ranchers) flooded the region. In return for land, the settlers were supposed to become Mexican citizens, but they never did. Instead, they ignored Mexican law, including—and especially—the one prohibiting slavery. When Mexico attempted to regain control of the area, the settlers rebelled and declared independence from Mexico. It was during this period that the famous battle at the **Alamo** was fought (1836). For a while Texas was an independent country, called the **Republic of Texas**. The existence of slavery in the area guaranteed a Congressional battle over statehood, and Texas was not admitted to the Union until 1845. We'll discuss this further when we discuss the **Polk** presidency.

Farther west and north, settlers were also pouring into the **Oregon Territory**. During the early 1840s, thousands of settlers traveled to the Willamette Valley, braving a six-month journey on the Oregon Trail. Again, the Americans were not the first ones in; not only was there a large Native American population, but the British were also there, claiming the territory for Canada. The Polk administration eventually settled the territorial dispute by signing a treaty with England.

By the late 1840s, though, those heading along the Oregon Trail had a new destination—**California**. In 1848 the discovery of gold in the California mountains set off the **Gold Rush**, attracting more than 100,000 people to the Golden State in just two years. Most of those who did not strike it rich—that is, all but a small minority of prospectors—settled the area after discovering that it was very hospitable to agriculture. Its access to the Pacific Ocean allowed major cities such as San Francisco to develop as important trade centers.

ECONOMIC REASONS FOR REGIONAL DIFFERENCES

Throughout the first half of the nineteenth century, three different sections of the country—North, South, and West—developed in very different directions. Accordingly, they did not see eye to eye on many issues; thus, historians often refer to **sectional strife** during this period.

The **North**, as mentioned earlier, was becoming industrialized. Technological advances in communications, transportation, industry, and banking were helping it become the nation's commercial center. Farming played less of a role in the Northern economy than it did elsewhere in the country, and slavery was illegal in the region's states.

The **South**, meanwhile, remained almost entirely agrarian. Its chief crops, tobacco and cotton, required vast acreage, and so Southerners were constantly looking west for more land. Anxious to protect slavery, which the large landholders depended on, Southerners also looked for new slave territories to include in the Union in order to strengthen their position in Congress and protect slavery from Northern legislators, who in ever increasing numbers sought to make slavery illegal.

Western economic interests were varied but were largely rooted in commercial farming, fur trapping, and real estate speculation. Westerners generally distrusted the North, which they regarded as the home of powerful banks that could take their land away. They had little more use for the South, whose rigidly hierarchical society was at odds with the egalitarianism of the West. Most Westerners wanted to avoid involvement in the slavery issue— regarded as irrelevant to their lives. Ironically, western expansion was the core of the most important conflicts leading up to the Civil War.

SOCIAL HISTORY, 1800–1860

The growth of the American economy in the early nineteenth century brought about numerous social changes. The invention of the cotton gin altered Southern agriculture, resulting in the region's increased reliance on slave labor. The development of commerce led to a larger middle class, especially in the North but also in the cities of the South and Midwest. Industrialization resulted in bigger cities with large (and often impoverished) migrant and immigrant neighborhoods. Westward migration created a new frontier culture as pioneers dealt with the uniqueness of the West's landscape and climate. Each of these sets of circumstances influenced people's attitudes and ambitions and set the scene for the social and political events of the era.

Remember these generalizations about the different regions of the U.S., because by using them and some common sense, you can often answer a specific AP questions. Take, for example, a question dealing with a specific tariff. Even if you do not remember the details of the tariff—and chances are you will not—you should remember that the North, as a commercial and manufacturing center, would probably support it because a tariff makes imports more expensive and therefore reduces competition with American goods. Southerners would probably oppose it because a tariff reduces competition and therefore raises prices. (Also, tariffs helped the North, and Southerners did not like the North.) Note: The AP test asks about events that illustrate important general trends in American history. If there were a nineteenth-century tariff that the South supported and the North opposed, the *test would not ask about it*!

THE NORTH AND AMERICAN CITIES

As we discussed in the previous chapter, the North became the nation's industrial and commercial center during the first half of the nineteenth century. Accordingly, it became home to many of the nation's major cities. In their early years, American cities faced numerous problems, chiefly the lack of powerful urban governments to oversee their rapid expansion. Modern waste disposal, plumbing, sewers, and incineration were still a long way off, and as a result, cities could be extremely unhealthy environments. The proximity in which people lived and worked, coupled with sanitation problems, made epidemics not only likely but inevitable.

City life was not, however, without its benefits. First, cities meant jobs. Many Northern farmers, unable to compete with cheaper produce carted in from the West and South (by steamship and rail), moved to cities to work in the new factories. Craftsmen—tailors, cobblers, blacksmiths, etc.—also found it easier to make a living in cities. Second, cities offered more opportunities for social advancement. In the 1830s and 1840s, as municipal governments grew, cities began to provide important services, such as public schooling. Labor unions began to form; although it would be many decades until they would come close to matching the power of business management, these unions still brought about some improvements in the lives of working people. Middle- and upper-class Americans in cities formed clubs and associations through which they could exert more influence on government and in society. Finally, cities provided a wide variety of leisure-time options, such as theater and sports.

As in the South, there was a great disparity in the **distribution of wealth** in Northern cities. A very few (the **aristocracy**) controlled most of the personal wealth and led lives of power and comfort. Beneath them were the **middle class**, made up of tradesmen, brokers, and other professionals. They worked to reach the plateau at which the women in their families could devote themselves to homemaking instead of wage earning. (Many middle-class women worked in their teens and early twenties—as sales clerks, teachers, and such—before settling down to marriage.) As wage-earning labor was more often performed away from the home, in factories and offices, the notion developed that men should work while women kept house and raised children. That notion, known as the **cult of domesticity**, was supported by popular magazines and novels that glorified home life. The middle classes also constituted much of the market for luxury goods such as housewares and fine furniture. Members of the middle class often rose from the **working class**. In working-class families, men often worked in factories or at low-paying crafts; women often worked at home, taking in sewing. Others worked as domestic servants, and most worked throughout their lives. Such families lived just above the poverty level, and any calamity—loss of a job, injury, sickness, or a death in the family—could plunge them irretrievably into debt. Those in **poverty** were most often recent immigrants. Their numbers swelled in the 1840s and 1850s when the great **immigration waves** from **Ireland** and then **Germany** reached the U.S. These immigration waves met with hostility, especially from the working classes, who feared competition for low-paying jobs. The Irish, in particular, were subject to widespread bias, directed in part at their Catholicism.

Occasionally tensions would boil over, and American cities were frequently the sites of riots. Particularly in the 1830s and 1840s, religious, ethnic, and/or class strife could escalate to violence and could even result in fatalities. Such disturbances were largely responsible for the formation of municipal police departments, which replaced privately run security companies in enforcing the peace.

THE SOUTH AND RURAL LIFE

There were few major urban centers in the South. The majority of Southerners lived instead in the country in near isolation. In 1860 the population density of Georgia was 18 people per square mile. (In Massachusetts, the most populous state, it was 153 people per square mile.) Family, not surprisingly, played a dominant role in social life. After family came the church, and after the church, little else. There simply were not enough people around to support organized cultural and leisure events.

With almost no major cities, the South also lacked centers of commerce. And while the North developed canals, railroads, and highways, the South did not. The major city of the South, New Orleans, relied almost completely on waterways for its trade routes, and therefore grew much more slowly than did Northern cities such as New York and Boston. Consequently, the South did not develop a strong market economy, as did the North; many more Southerners made and grew most of their necessities for survival.

The wealthiest Southern citizens consisted mainly of plantation owners; as in the North, the wealthy made up a small minority. Plantation owners also owned most of the slaves. In fact, more than three-quarters of white Southerners owned no slaves. Of the rest, half owned five or fewer slaves. Only 10 percent of actual slave holders — fewer than about 2 percent of the white population —held twenty or more slaves.

Plantation owners grew cotton throughout the Deep South and tobacco in the Middle Atlantic, alongside the crops they needed to support their families and slaves. Most convinced themselves that the slave system benefited all of its participants, *including* the slaves. This attitude, called **Southern paternalism**, relied on the perception of blacks as childlike and unable to take care of themselves. Many slaves discovered that life became easier for them when they reinforced such paternalistic instincts and adopted a submissive and grateful demeanor (which will be familiar to you if you've ever seen old Hollywood movies about this period). Slave owners almost always converted their slaves to Christianity, again convinced that they were serving the slaves' best interests. The Africans, in turn, adapted Christianity to their cultures and incorporated their own religions and traditions into their new faith.

Slaves lived in a state of subsistence poverty. They were usually housed in one-room cabins with their families, and often with another family. Conditions were overcrowded and unsanitary. Although work conditions varied from region to region and farm to farm, most worked extremely long hours at difficult and tedious labor. (Any concern that slave holders had for their slaves' welfare could arguably be attributed to the fact that importing African slaves was banned in 1808, making it essential to keep one's slaves alive and reproducing. In addition, the purchase price of a slave was always fairly high.) Moreover, most slaves lived in fear that their families would be broken up by the sale of one or more of them. Many were subjected to the abuses of vicious overseers.

The majority of Southern planters farmed smaller tracts of land. Some owned a few slaves, alongside whom they often worked in their own fields. Generally, such people could afford the basic comforts and little else; they were often very provincial and poorly educated. **Yeomen** were similar but owned no slaves and worked their small tracts of land with only their families. Most were of Scottish and Irish descent and farmed in the hills, which were unsuitable for plantation farming. They grew subsistence crops, raised livestock, and sometimes produced a few cash crops, though limited access to Northern markets hindered profit making. Less fortunate were **landless whites**, who either farmed as tenants or hired themselves out as manual laborers. Elevation from this social stratum to the level of yeoman proved very difficult.

The South was also home to more than 250,000 **free blacks**, the descendants of slaves freed by their owners or freed for having fought in the Revolutionary War. Special laws, called **black codes**, prevented them from owning guns, drinking liquor, and assembling in groups of more than three (except in church). Prejudice was a constant fact of life. Some owned land or worked at a trade, but most worked as tenant farmers or day laborers. Some were mulattos, a number of whom (mostly descendants of wealthy whites) led lives of relative luxury and refinement in the Deep South, particularly in and around New Orleans.

THE WEST AND FRONTIER LIVING

During this period, the frontier's boundaries constantly changed. In 1800 the frontier lay east of the Mississippi River. By 1820 nearly all of this eastern territory had attained statehood, and the frontier region consisted of much of the Louisiana Purchase. Settlers also moved to Texas, then a part of Mexico, in the late 1820s and 1830s. By the early 1840s, the frontier had expanded to include the Pacific Northwest. In 1848 the Gold Rush drew numerous settlers to California.

The United States government actively encouraged settlers to move west. It gave away, or sold at reduced rates, large tracts of land to war veterans. The government also loaned money at reduced rates to civilians so that they too could move west. Some settlers, called **squatters**, ignored the requirement to buy land and simply moved onto and appropriated an unoccupied tract as their own.

Settlers in the Ohio Valley and points west soon found that the area was hospitable to grain production and dairy farming. As previously discussed, much of the area was flat and could easily be farmed by new farm implements such as mechanical plows and reapers. Transportation advances made shipping produce easier and more profitable, and soon the Midwest came to be known as "the nation's breadbasket."

Fur trading was another common commercial enterprise on the frontiers. Fur traders, often the first pioneers in a region, constantly moved west, one step ahead of farming families. When they reached Oregon, they ran out of places to go. Furthermore, they had hunted beaver to near extinction. A group of former trappers formed the first American government in the Oregon Territory and began lobbying for statehood. The western frontier was also home to **cattle ranchers** and **miners**.

Frontier life was rugged, to say the least. To survive, settlers constantly struggled against the climate, elements, and Native Americans who were not anxious for the whites to settle, having heard about the their treatment of Eastern tribes. Still, the frontier offered pioneers opportunities for wealth, freedom, and social advancement, opportunities that were rarer in the heavily populated, competitive East and the aristocratic South. Those women who could handle the difficulties of frontier life found their services in great demand, and many made a good living at domestic work and, later, running boardinghouses and hotels. Because of the possibilities for advancement and for "getting a new start in life," the West came to symbolize freedom and equality to many Americans.

RELIGIOUS AND SOCIAL MOVEMENTS

The nineteenth century saw the beginnings of social reform in the United States, and much of the impulse to improve the lives of others came from citizens' religious convictions. In fact, early social reform movements grew out of the **Second Great Awakening**, which, like the first, was a period of religious resurgence. The Second Great Awakening began in the Northeast in the 1790s and then spread throughout the country, sparking an intense period of evangelism in the South and West. Numerous churches formed in places where previously there had been only occasional religious meetings (called **revivals**). A few reform societies sprang up in the South and West, but in the Northeast, the Second Great Awakening gave birth to numerous societies dedicated to the task of saving humanity from its own worst impulses.

Usually, the most active members of reform groups were women, particularly those of the middle and upper classes. **Temperance societies**, dedicated to the prohibition of liquor, formed and remained powerful until they achieved nationwide prohibition in 1919. (Not coincidentally, prohibition finally succeeded at the same time it became evident to politicians that women would soon gain the right to vote.) These groups battled other vices as well, particularly **gambling**. By 1860 every state in the Union had outlawed **lotteries,** and many had prohibited other forms of gambling. Many Northern states also prohibited the manufacture or purchase of alcoholic beverages during this period. A group called "The Female Moral Reform Society" led the battle against **prostitution** in the cities, focusing not only on eliminating the profession but also on rehabilitating those women involved in it.

Reform societies also helped bring about **penitentiaries**, **asylums**, and **orphanages** by popularizing the notion that society is responsible for the welfare of its least fortunate. Penitentiaries sought to rehabilitate criminals (rather than simply isolate them from society, as prisons do) by teaching them morality and a "work ethic." Asylums, orphanages, and houses of refuge for the poor were built to care for those who would previously have been imprisoned or run out of town. While some of the methods used in these institutions would seem primitive and cruel today, the impulses motivating them were largely compassionate.

Before we discuss the reform movement with the greatest impact—the **abolition** movement—we need to mention a few other important religious groups of the period. The **Shakers,** a utopian group that splintered from the Quakers, believed that they and all other churches had grown too interested in this world and too neglectful of their afterlives. The Shakers isolated themselves in communes where they shared work and its rewards; they also granted near-equal rights to women, even allowing them to attain priesthood. Believing the end of the world was at hand and that sex was an instrument of evil, the Shakers practiced celibacy; their numbers, not surprisingly, diminished. The Shaker revival ended during the 1840s and 1850s.

The **Mormons**, on the other hand, continue to thrive today. In response to divine revelation, Joseph Smith formed the Mormon Church of Jesus Christ of Latter-Day Saints in 1830. Smith's preaching, particularly his acceptance of polygamy, drew strong opposition in the East and Midwest, culminating in his death by a mob while imprisoned in Illinois. The Mormons, realizing that they would never be allowed to practice their faith in the East, made the long, difficult trek to the Salt Lake Valley. There, they settled and transformed the area from desert into farmland through extensive irrigation. The Mormons' success was largely attributable to the settlers' strong sense of community and selflessness. Through their communal efforts, they came to dominate the Utah territory.

The Abolition Movement

Before the 1830s, few whites fought aggressively for the liberation of the slaves. The Quakers, to their credit, believed slavery morally wrong and argued for its end. Most other anti-slavery whites, though, sought gradual abolition, coupled with a movement to return blacks to Africa. The religious and moral fervor that accompanied the Second Great Awakening, however, persuaded more and more whites, particularly Northerners, that slavery was a great evil. As in other reform movements, women played a prominent role.

White abolitionists divided into two groups. Moderates wanted emancipation to take place slowly and with the cooperation of slave owners. **Immediatists**, as their name implies, wanted emancipation at once. Most prominent among white immediatists was **William Lloyd Garrison,** who began publishing a popular abolitionist newspaper called the *Liberator* in 1831. His early subscribers were mostly free blacks, but as time passed, his paper caught on with white abolitionists as well.

Garrison fought against slavery and against moderates as well, decrying their plans for black resettlement in Africa as racist and immoral. Garrison's persistence and powerful writing style helped force the slavery issue to the forefront. His message, as you may imagine, did not go over well everywhere; some Southern states banned the newspaper, and others prohibited *anyone* from discussing emancipation. When Congressional debate over slavery became too heated, Congress adopted a **gag rule** that automatically suppressed discussion of the issue. It also prevented Congress from enacting any new legislation pertaining to slavery. The gag order, which lasted from 1836 to 1844, along with Southern restrictions of free speech, outraged many Northerners and convinced them to join the abolition movement.

The abolition movement existed prior to 1830, but it had been primarily supported by free blacks. Abolition associations formed in every large black community to assist fugitive slaves and publicize the struggle against slavery; these groups met at a national convention every year after 1830 to coordinate strategies. In the 1840s, **Frederick Douglass** began publishing his influential newspaper *The North Star*. Douglass, an escaped slave, gained fame as a gifted writer and eloquent combatant for freedom and equality; his *Narrative of the Life of Frederick Douglass* is one of the great American autobiographies. Other prominent black abolitionists included **Harriet Tubman,** who escaped slavery and then returned south repeatedly to assist more than 300 slaves escape via the **underground railroad** (a network of hiding places and "safe" trails), and **Sojourner Truth**, a charismatic speaker who campaigned for emancipation and women's rights.

Abolitionists' determination and the South's inflexibility pushed the issue of slavery into the political spotlight. Westward expansion, and the question of whether slavery would be allowed in the new territories, forced the issue further. Together, they set in motion the events that led up to the Civil War.

Heading Toward the Civil War (1845–1860)

The election of 1844 pitted **James Polk**, a Democrat expansionist, against Whig leader Henry Clay. One of Polk's slogans—"54º40′ or Fight,"—meant that America's Northwestern border should be extended to the 54º40′ latitude, deep in Canadian territory. Polk's supporters also wanted the immediate annexation of Texas as well as expansion into the Mexican-claimed territories of New Mexico, Arizona, and California. Clay too favored expansion, but at a slower rate. He also hoped to avoid war by negotiating with Mexico and Britain for the land America wanted. The election was close, but Polk won. In the last days of his administration, President Tyler proposed the annexation of Texas, arguing that Polk's victory amounted to a mandate for annexation. Again, the vote was close and divided along sectional lines. The annexation vote passed, the U.S. annexed Texas, and Mexico broke off diplomatic relations. Under these circumstances, war with Mexico seemed likely.

THE POLK PRESIDENCY

Polk realized almost immediately upon taking office that, campaign rhetoric aside, the United States could hardly afford to fight two territorial wars at the same time, particularly if one was against Great Britain. Consequently, he almost immediately conceded on demands for expansion deep into Canada and set about instead to negotiate a more reasonable American-Canadian border. The **Oregon Treaty**, signed with Great Britain in 1846, allowed the United States to acquire peacefully what is now Oregon, Washington, and parts of Idaho, Wyoming, and Montana. It also established the current northern border of the region.

Reasonably certain that war in the Northwest could be avoided, Polk concentrated on efforts to claim the Southwest from Mexico. He tried to buy the territory, and when that failed, he provoked Mexico until it attacked American troops. Polk then used that attack to argue for a declaration of war. Congress granted the declaration, and in 1846 the **Mexican-American War** began.

The Mexican-American War did not have universal support from the American public. Abolitionists, largely in the North but elsewhere as well, feared that new states in the West would become slave states, thus tipping the balance in Congress in favor of proslavery forces. Opponents argued that Polk had provoked Mexico into war at the request of powerful slave holders, and the idea that a few slave owners had control over the government became popular. Those rich Southerners who allegedly were "pulling the strings" were referred to as the **Slave Power** by abolitionists. The **gag rule** in 1836 raised suspicions of a Slave Power, and the defeat of the **Wilmot Proviso**, a Congressional bill mandating the prohibition of slavery in any territory gained from Mexico during the war, reinforced those suspicions. The failure of the proviso, strongly supported in the North, led to the formation of the **Free Soil Party**, a regional, single-issue party devoted to the goals of the Wilmot Proviso. Many Southerners, on the other hand, now felt that it was the choice of the settlers in new territories, and not of the federal government, as to whether to permit slavery. The two sides were growing farther apart and more rigid in their determination not to give in.

While debate raged on, so too did the war, which went very well for American forces. The United States dominated so easily in Texas that Polk ordered troops across the Southwest and into California, hoping to grab the entire region by war's end. When the U.S. successfully invaded Mexico City, the war was over. In the **Treaty of Guadalupe Hidalgo (1848)**, Mexico handed over almost all of the modern Southwest: Arizona, New Mexico, California, Nevada, and Utah.

The addition of this new territory greatly increased the nation's potential wealth. However, it also posed major problems regarding the status of slavery. Although both Democrats and Whigs tried to skirt the issue, the electorate was interested in nothing but the slavery question. The Democrats' strong support in the South guaranteed that the party would never oppose slavery, and when forced to confront the issue, they settled on the policy of **popular sovereignty**. Popular sovereignty meant that the territories themselves would decide, by vote, whether to allow slavery within their borders. When the Whigs also refused to oppose slavery, the party split. Anti-slavery Whigs began to join the Free Soil Party. The Whigs managed to win the election of 1848 by running another nondescript military hero, **Zachary Taylor**, but the party was on its way out. Its two great leaders, Daniel Webster and Henry Clay, died before the next presidential election in 1852, leaving a huge leadership void in the Whig Party. The political upheaval caused by the slavery issue eventually proved too divisive to the Whigs (not to mention the entire country). In 1856 the Whigs did not even field a presidential candidate; they were finished as a national power.

THE COMPROMISE OF 1850

Sectional strife over the new territories started as the ink was drying on the Treaty of Guadalupe Hidalgo. During the gold rush, settlers had flooded into California, and the populous territory wanted statehood. Californians had already drawn up a state constitution. That constitution prohibited slavery, and so, of course, the South opposed California's bid for statehood. At the very least, proslavery forces argued, southern California should be forced to accept slavery, in accordance with the boundary drawn by the Missouri Compromise of 1820. The debate grew so hostile that Southern legislators began to discuss openly the possibility of secession.

Democrat **Stephen Douglas** and Whig Henry Clay hammered out what they thought to be a workable solution, known as the **Compromise of 1850**. When presented as a complete package, the compromise was defeated in Congress. Douglas, however, realized that different groups supported different parts of the compromise, and so he broke the package down into separate bills. He managed to organize majorities to support each of the component bills, and thus ushered the entire compromise through Congress. Together, the bills admitted California as a free state; created the territories of Utah and New Mexico, but left the status of slavery up to each territory to decide only when it came time for each to write its constitution, thus reinforcing the concept of **popular sovereignty**; and enacted a stronger **fugitive slave law**. The last two accomplishments were seriously flawed: Its definition of popular sovereignty was so vague that Northerners and Southerners could interpret the law entirely differently so as to suit their own positions. The compromise left the status of slaves undetermined in each territory joining the Union. The fugitive slave law, meanwhile, made it much easier to retrieve escaped slaves and required free states to cooperate in their retrieval. Abolitionists considered it coercive, immoral, and an affront to their liberty.

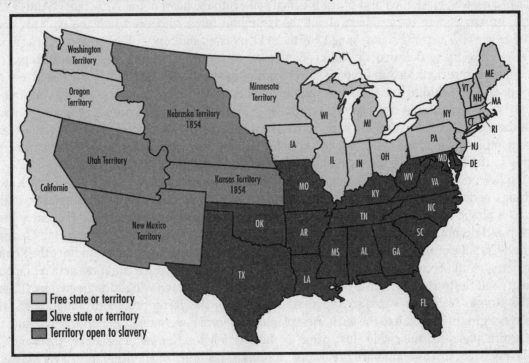

Kansas-Nebraska Act, 1854

Antislavery sentiments in the North grew stronger in 1852 with the publication of **Uncle Tom's Cabin**, a sentimental novel written by a then-obscure writer named Harriet Beecher Stowe. Stowe, a

Northerner, based her damning depictions of plantation life on information provided her by abolitionist friends. She wisely avoided political preaching, instead playing on people's sympathies. The book sold more than a million copies and was turned into a popular play that toured America and Europe. It was an extremely powerful piece of propaganda, awakening antislavery sentiment in millions who had never before given the issue much thought. It was in this atmosphere that **Franklin Pierce**, perceived in both the North and South as a moderate, was elected president.

THE KANSAS-NEBRASKA ACT AND "BLEEDING KANSAS"

After California, no new states would be admitted to the Union until 1858. However, the contentious status of the new territories proved increasingly problematic. Settlers entering the Kansas and Nebraska territories found no established civil authority. Congress also wanted to build railways through the territory, but they needed some form of government to impose order, secure land (a task that included driving out Native Americans), and supervise construction.

Stephen Douglas sought to address these issues with the **Kansas-Nebraska Act of 1854**. Again, Douglas formulated and ushered through Congress a law that left the fate of slavery up to residents without specifying *when* or *how* they were to decide. To make matters worse, by opening the two territories to slavery, the Kansas-Nebraska Act repealed the Missouri Compromise, thus further destabilizing the political situation. Northerners considered the new law a betrayal, regarding it as further evidence of the Slave Power's domination of government. In response, many Northern states passed laws weakening the fugitive slave act. These laws, called **personal liberty laws**, required a trial by jury for all alleged fugitives and guaranteed them the right to a lawyer. Southerners, who thought the fugitive slave law would be the final word on the issue, were furious.

The Kansas-Nebraska Act also drove the final stake into the heart of the Whig party. Antislavery Whigs, growing more impassioned about the issue and more convinced that the national party would never take a strong stand, joined Northern Democrats and former Free Soilers (whose single issue was effectively defeated by Kansas-Nebraska) to form a new party, the **Republicans**. The Republicans were dedicated to keeping slavery out of the territories, but they championed a wider range of issues, including the further development of national roads, more liberal land distribution in the West, and increased protective tariffs. As a result, the Republicans appealed to a wider constituency than the Free Soilers had. Midwestern merchants and farmers, Western settlers, and Eastern importers all found something to like in the Republican platform. The Republican party grew quickly in the North, where it won a majority of Congressional seats in 1854.

Another new party formed during this period. The **American** party, often called the **Know-Nothings** because they met privately and remained secretive about their political agenda, rallied around a single issue: hatred of foreigners, a perennial favorite in U.S. politics. The party grew quickly and dominated several state legislatures. It also spread some ugly anti-Irish, anti-German, and anti-Catholic propaganda. For a while it appeared that the Know-Nothings, and not the Republican party, would become the Democrats' chief competition. Yet, before it could reach that pinnacle, the party self-destructed, primarily because its Northern and Southern wings disagreed over slavery.

The Kansas-Nebraska Act also provoked violence in the territories. Both abolitionists and proslavery groups rushed into the territories, planning to form governments in hopes of winning the two future states for their side. Just prior to the election for Kansas' legislature, thousands of proslavery Missourians temporarily relocated in Kansas, resulting in an illegal, proslavery government. The new legislature, which President Pierce recognized, promptly declared Kansas a slave territory. Abolitionists refused to accept this outcome and set up their own government. Pro-slavery forces took Pierce's recognition as a license to expel the abolitionists, and they demolished the abolitionist city of Lawrence. In retaliation, radical abolitionist **John Brown** led a raid on a proslavery camp, murdering five. After that, the gloves *really* came off, as gangs from both sides roamed the territory and attacked the opposition. More than 200 people died in the conflict, which is how Kansas came to be known as **Bleeding Kansas**, or **Bloody Kansas**, during this period.

The events in Kansas further polarized the nation. The passions raised were even reflected in Congress when proslavery Congressman Andrew Butler pummeled abolitionist Senator Charles Sumner on the head with a cane. The crisis destroyed Pierce's political career, and the Democrats chose **James Buchanan** as their 1856 candidate. Buchanan's greatest political asset was that he had been out of the country for the previous four years and so could avoid blame for the disastrous results of the Kansas-Nebraska Act. In a sectional vote, Buchanan won the election, carrying the South, while Republican John Frémont carried the North. The Know-Nothings ran Millard Fillmore, who won 20 percent of the vote. It was the Know-Nothings' last hurrah.

BUCHANAN, DRED SCOTT, AND THE ELECTION OF 1860

As president, **James Buchanan** tried to maintain the status quo. He worked to enforce the fugitive slave act and opposed abolitionist activism in the South and West. Like many of the nation's leaders at the time, he was at a loss when it came to a permanent solution to the question of slavery. He hoped merely to maintain the Union until a solution presented itself.

Months after Buchanan took office, the crisis over slavery escalated when the Supreme Court ruled in the *Dred Scott Case*. Scott, a former slave whose master had taken him to territories where slavery was illegal, declared himself a free man and sued for his freedom. Scott won the case, then lost the appeal, and the case finally wound up in the Supreme Court, where Scott lost. At a time when many wanted to ignore the big questions surrounding slavery, Chief Justice **Roger Taney** (who wrote the majority decision) chose to attack them head-on. Taney's one-sided, proslavery decision declared that slaves were property, not citizens. Because slaves were not citizens, Taney argued, they could not sue in federal courts, as Scott had done. Moreover, he ruled that Congress could not regulate slavery in the territories, as it had in the Missouri Compromise. This part of the decision not only nullified the now-obsolete Missouri Compromise but also the Kansas-Nebraska Act, the Wilmot Proviso (still championed by abolitionists), and the concept of popular sovereignty. Taney essentially told Republicans that their goal— freedom for slaves in the territories— was illegal.

In the North, the Supreme Court decision was viciously denounced. Even those who lacked strong abolitionist sentiments feared that the decision tilted the balance of power too far in the South's favor. Many, including the press, regarded the decision as further proof of a Slave Power that, if left unchecked, would soon dominate the entire country, perhaps even forcing slavery on those states that did not want it. Meanwhile, the Democratic party was dividing along regional lines, raising the possibility that the Republicans might soon control the national government. As a result, many in the South started to accept the inevitability of secession. Adding fuel to the secessionist fire was **John Brown**'s raid on **Harper's Ferry** in 1859. Brown hoped to spark a slave revolt but failed. After his execution, news spread that Brown had received financial backing from Northern abolitionist organizations. Brown became a martyr for the cause, celebrated throughout the North.

Democrat **Stephen Douglas** did his best to hold his party together. He attempted to cobble together a concept of popular sovereignty that could get around the Taney decision. His solution, called the **Freeport Doctrine**, was doomed to failure because any position that backed away from the Dred Scott decision would be opposed in the South. When it came time for the Democrats to choose their 1860 presidential candidate, their convention split. Northern Democrats backed Douglas, Southerners backed John Breckinridge. A new party centered in the Upper South, the Constitutional Union party, nominated John Bell. The Republicans nominated **Abraham Lincoln**. The vote was neatly divided along sectional lines. Lincoln attracted 40 percent of the vote and won the election in the House of Representatives.

Immediately after the election, Southern leaders who wanted to maintain the Union tried to negotiate a compromise. All hope of resolution died, however, when Lincoln refused to soften the Republican demand that all territories be declared free. Lincoln probably had no other political option, as to do otherwise would have been to abandon the principles of those who had supported his election. Lincoln and other Northern leaders were banking on the hope that the South was bluffing and would not secede.

In December 1860, a month before Lincoln's inauguration, South Carolina seceded from the Union. Within months, seven states had joined South Carolina to form the **Confederate States of America**; the states chose **Jefferson Davis** to lead the Confederacy. Cautiously, Lincoln decided to maintain control of federal forts in the South while waiting for the Confederacy to make a move. On April 12, 1861, it did, attacking and capturing **Fort Sumter**. Inauspiciously, no one died in this first battle of America's bloodiest war, the **Civil War**.

THE CIVIL WAR AND RECONSTRUCTION (1860–1877)

For many people of the era, the Civil War was not solely (or even primarily) about slavery. Except for active abolitionists, most Northerners believed they were fighting to preserve the Union. Most Southerners felt they were fighting for their **states' rights** to govern themselves. Many on both sides thought that slavery was simply the issue that had caused the argument over states' rights to escalate to war. As late as 1862, Lincoln stated: "If I could save the Union without freeing *any* slaves I would do it, and if I could save the Union by freeing *all* the slaves I would do it. . . . What I do about slavery, and the colored race, I do because I believe it helps to save the Union."

The Civil War took place not only on the battlefields but also in political, economic, and social realms. Although you do not need to know about the military battles, you do need to know how political, social, and economic conditions influenced the outcome of the war.

THE CIVIL WAR AND THE CONFEDERACY

Ironically, as the Southern states fought to maintain the right to govern themselves locally, the Confederate government brought them under greater central control than they had ever experienced. Jefferson Davis understood the North's considerable advantages in population, transportation, and economics, and he knew that the weak, poorly organized state governments of the South could not mount an effective defense. Davis took control of the Southern economy, imposing taxes and using the revenues to spur industrial and urban growth; he took control of the railroads and commercial shipping; and, he created a large government bureaucracy to oversee economic developments. Davis, in short, forced the South to compensate quickly for what it had lost when it cut itself off from Northern commerce. When Southerners opposed his moves, he declared martial law and suspended the writ of *habeas corpus* in order to maintain control.

Davis had some success in modernizing the Southern economy, but the Confederacy lagged too far behind in industrialization to catch up to the Union. Rapid economic growth, furthermore, brought with it rapid **inflation**. Prices rose so quickly that paychecks and payments for crops became worthless almost as soon as they were made, plunging many Southerners into poverty. In 1862 the Confederacy imposed **conscription** (a military draft), requiring many small farmers and yeomen to serve in the Confederate Army. This act caused even greater poverty in the country, as many families could not adequately tend their farms without their men.

Confederate conscription also created class conflict. The government allowed the wealthy to hire surrogates to perform military service in their place and exempted anyone who owned more than twenty slaves from military service (on the grounds that the large plantations these men ran fed the Confederacy and its army). In effect, the wealthy did not have to serve, while the poor had no choice. As a result, **class tensions** increased, leading ultimately to widespread desertions from the Confederate Army. Toward the end of the war, it also led many Southerners in small towns to ignore the government and try to carry on as if there was no war. Many resisted when asked to feed, clothe, or house passing troops.

The Civil War and the Union

The Northern economy received a boost from the war as the demand for war-related goods, such as uniforms and weapons, spurred manufacturing. The loss of Southern markets harmed the economy at first, but soon the war economy brought about a boom period. A number of entrepreneurs became extremely wealthy; many succumbed to the temptations of greed, overcharging the government for services and products. Some sold the Union government worthless food and clothing (called **shoddy**) while government bureaucrats looked the other way (for the price of a bribe). Corruption was fairly widespread, eventually prompting a year-long Congressional investigation.

Like the South, the North experienced a period of accelerated inflation, although Northern inflation was nowhere as extreme as its Southern counterpart. (In the North, prices rose between 10 and 20 percent annually; in the South, the inflation rate was well over 300 percent.) Workers, worried about job security (in the face of mechanization) and the decreasing value of their wages, formed **unions**. Businesses, in return, blacklisted union members, forced new employees to sign contracts in which they promised not to join unions, and used violence to break strikes. The Republican Party, then (as now) believing that government should help businesses but regulate them as little as possible, supported business in its opposition to unions.

Lincoln, like Davis, oversaw a tremendous increase in the power of the central government during the war. He implemented economic development programs without waiting for Congressional approval, championed numerous government loans and grants to businesses, and raised tariffs to protect Union trade. He also suspended the writ of *habeas corpus* in the border states, mainly to prevent Maryland from seceding. During the war, Lincoln strengthened the **national bank** and initiated the printing of **national currency**. (Previously, each state had circulated its own bank notes.)

Emancipation of the Slaves

As previously stated, neither the Union nor the Confederacy initially declared the Civil War to be a war about slavery. As a presidential candidate, Lincoln had argued for gradual emancipation, compensation to slave holders for liberated slaves, and the colonization of freed slaves somewhere outside the United States, perhaps in Africa. When the Union dissolved and the South left Congress, Lincoln was faced with a legislature much more progressive in its thoughts on slavery than he was. The **Radical Republican** wing of Congress wanted immediate emancipation. To that end, the radicals introduced the **confiscation acts** in Congress. The first (1861) gave the government the right to seize any slaves used for "insurrectionary purposes." The second (1862) was much wider in scope, allowing the government to liberate any slave owned by someone who supported the rebellion, even if that support was limited to paying taxes to the Confederate government. The second confiscation act, in effect, gave the Union the right to liberate all slaves. This act had little effect, however, because Lincoln refused to enforce it.

Soon after, however, Lincoln took his first cautious steps toward emancipation. In September 1862, Lincoln issued the **Emancipation Proclamation**. Note that the Emancipation Proclamation did not free all the slaves. Instead, it stated that on January 1, 1863, the government would liberate all slaves residing in those states still in rebellion. The proclamation did not liberate the slaves in the border states such as Maryland, nor did it liberate slaves in Southern counties under the control of the Union Army. Abolitionists complained that the proclamation liberated slaves only where the Union had no power to enforce emancipation and maintained slavery precisely where it could liberate the slaves. The proclamation also allowed southern states to rejoin the Union *without* giving up slavery. On the positive side, the emancipation proclamation finally declared that the Civil War was, for the Union, a war against slavery.

The Emancipation Proclamation had an immediate effect on the war. **Escaped slaves** and **free blacks** enlisted in the Union Army in substantial numbers (a total of nearly 200,000), greatly tipping the balance in the Union's favor. Furthermore, the infusion of new, enthusiastic recruits to the Union Army discouraged European nations from recognizing and trading with the Confederate government. This prevented the Confederacy from forging the military alliances it needed, and it weakened the Confederate economy.

Not until two years later, while campaigning for reelection, did Lincoln give his support to complete emancipation. Just before the Republican convention, Lincoln lobbied for a party platform that called for a constitutional amendment prohibiting slavery; the result was the **Thirteenth Amendment**. Yet even then, Lincoln remained equivocal. After his reelection, Lincoln considered allowing defeated Southern states to reenter the Union and to vote on the Thirteenth Amendment. He tried to negotiate a settlement with Southern leaders along those lines at the **Hampton Roads Conference**. Lincoln also offered a five-year delay on implementing the amendment if it passed, as well as $400 million in compensation to slave owners. Jefferson Davis' commitment to complete Southern independence scuttled any chance of compromise.

THE ELECTION OF 1864 AND END OF THE CIVIL WAR

As the 1864 presidential election approached, popular opinion in both the North and South favored an end to the war. Lincoln's opponent, General George McClellan, campaigned on a peace platform. In the South, citizens openly defied the civil authority. And yet, both sides fought on. Just when a stalemate might have forced a negotiated end to the war, everything started going the North's way. Victories throughout the summer of 1864 played a large part in helping Lincoln gain reelection. By the early spring of 1865, a Union victory was virtually assured, and the government established the **Freedman's Bureau** to help newly liberated blacks establish a place in postwar society. The Bureau helped with immediate problems of survival (food, housing) and developed social institutions such as schools. In April 1865 the Confederate leaders surrendered. John Wilkes Booth assassinated Lincoln just weeks before the final surrender took place.

The Civil War was fought at enormous personal and economic cost. More than three million men fought in the war, and of them, more than 500,000 died. At least as many were seriously wounded. Both governments ran up huge debts during the war, and much of the South was decimated by Union soldiers. During **Sherman's March** from Atlanta to the sea in the fall of 1864, the Union Army burned everything in its wake (to destroy Confederate morale and deplete the South's material resources). From a political perspective, the war permanently expanded the role of government. On both sides, government grew rapidly to manage the economy and the war. After the war, the federal government remained large.

RECONSTRUCTION AND JOHNSON'S IMPEACHMENT

At war's end, two major questions faced the reunited nation. First, under what conditions would the Southern states be readmitted to the Union? Second, what would be the status of blacks in the postwar nation? Black leaders hoped that their service in the military would earn blacks equal rights. The newly liberated slaves, called **freedmen**, were primarily interested in the chance to earn wages and own property.

With Lincoln's assassination, vice-president **Andrew Johnson** assumed the presidency. Johnson, a Southern Democrat, had opposed secession and strongly supported Lincoln during his first term. In return, Lincoln rewarded Johnson with the vice-presidency. When the war ended, Congress was in recess and would not reconvene for eight months. That left the early stages of Reconstruction entirely in Johnson's hands.

Johnson had lifted himself from poverty and held no great love for the South's elite planters, and at first he seemed intent on taking power away from the old aristocracy and giving it to the yeomen and small farmers. **Johnson's Reconstruction** plan, which was based on a plan approved by Lincoln, called for the creation of provisional military governments to run the states until they were readmitted to the Union. It also required all Southern citizens to swear a **loyalty oath** before receiving amnesty for the rebellion. However, it barred many of the former Southern elite (including plantation owners, Confederate officers, and government officials) from taking that vow, thus prohibiting their participation in the new governments. According to this plan, the provisional governments would hold state constitutional conventions, at which time the states would have to write new constitutions eliminating slavery and renouncing secession. Johnson did not require the states to enfranchise blacks.

The plan did not work, mostly because Johnson **pardoned** many of the Southern elite who were supposed to have been excluded from the reunification process. After the states drafted new constitutions and elected new governments, former Confederate officials were again in positions of great power. Furthermore, many of their new constitutions were only slight revisions of previous constitutions. Southern legislators also passed a series of laws defining the status of freedmen. These laws, called **black codes**, limited freedmen's rights to assemble and travel, and restricted their access to public institutions. The codes also instituted curfew laws and laws requiring blacks to carry special passes. In the most egregious instances, state legislatures simply took their old slave codes and replaced the word *slaves* with *freedmen*. When Congress reconvened in December 1865, the new Southern senators included the vice-president of the Confederacy and other Confederate officials. Northern Congressmen were not pleased. Invoking its constitutional right to examine the credentials of new members, Congress voted not to seat the new Southern delegations. Then, it set about examining Johnson's Reconstruction plan.

Congress was divided among conservative Republicans, who generally agreed with Johnson's plan; moderates, who were a large enough contingent to swing a vote in one or the other direction; and **Radical Republicans**. The radicals wanted a Reconstruction that punished the South for seceding, confiscated land from the rich and redistributed it among the poor (including, of course, the freedmen), and extended democratic rights in the South. (In many Southern states at the time, all important political positions were held by appointees; very few officials were directly elected.) All Republicans agreed that Johnson's Reconstruction needed some modification, but Johnson refused to compromise. Instead, he declared Reconstruction over and done with, vetoing a compromise package that would have extended the life of the Freedman's Bureau and enforced a uniform civil rights code on the South.

In response, the radicals drew up the plan that came to be known as **Congressional Reconstruction**. Its first component was the **Fourteenth Amendment** to the Constitution. The amendment (1) prohibited states from depriving any citizen of "life, liberty, or property, without due process"; (2) gave states the choice either to give freedmen the right to vote or to stop counting them among their voting population for the purpose of Congressional apportionment; (3) barred prominent Confederates from holding political office; and (4) excused the Confederacy's war debt. The first two points held the most importance. The first meant to override the effect of the black codes, while the second aimed to force states to either extend suffrage to black men or lose power in Congress. Johnson campaigned against the amendment and lost. In the Congressional election of 1866, the North voted for a Congress more heavily weighted toward the radical end of the political spectrum.

The new Congress quickly passed the **Military Reconstruction Act of 1867**. It imposed martial law on the South; it also called for new state constitutional conventions and forced the states to allow blacks to vote for convention delegates. The act also required each state to ratify the Fourteenth Amendment and to send its new constitution to Congress for approval. Aware that Johnson would oppose the new Reconstruction, Congress then passed a number of laws designed to limit the president's power. As expected, Johnson did everything in his power to counteract the Congressional plan. The conflict reached its climax when the House Judiciary Committee initiated **impeachment proceedings** against Johnson, ostensibly for violating the Tenure of Office Act (which stated that the President had to secure the consent of the Senate before removing his appointees once they'd been approved by that body. Johnson had fired Secretary of War, Edwin Stanton.) but really because he was getting in the way of Reconstruction. Although impeachment failed (by one vote), the trial rendered Johnson politically impotent, and he served the last few months of his presidency and retired.

With a new president, **Ulysses S. Grant**, in office, Congress forged ahead in its efforts to remake the South. The **Fifteenth Amendment**, proposed in 1869, finally required states to enfranchise black men. (Women's suffrage would have to wait another half-century.) Ironically, the Fifteenth Amendment passed only because Southern states were required to ratify it as a condition of reentry into the Union; a number of northern states opposed the amendment.

THE FAILURE OF RECONSTRUCTION

Reconstruction had its share of **successes**. New state constitutions allowed all Southern men to vote (previous constitutions had required voters to own property) and replaced many appointed government positions with elected positions. New Southern governments, directed mostly by transplanted Northern Republicans, blacks, and Southern moderates, created public schools and those social institutions such as orphanages popularized in the North during the reform movement of the 1830s. The new governments also stimulated industrial and rail development in the South through loans, grants, and tax exemptions. The fact that blacks were serving in Southern governments represented a huge step forward, given the seemingly insurmountable restrictions placed on blacks only a few years earlier.

However, ultimately, Reconstruction **failed**. Although government industrialization plans helped rebuild the Southern economy, these plans also cost a lot of money. High tax rates turned public opinion, already antagonistic to Reconstruction, even more hostile. Opponents waged a propaganda war against Reconstruction, calling Southerners who cooperated **scalawags** and Northerners who ran the programs **carpetbaggers**. (The name came from the suitcases they carried, implying they had come to the South merely to stuff their bags with ill-gotten wealth.) Many who participated in Reconstruction were indeed **corrupt**, selling their votes for money and favors. Accompanying the propaganda war was a war of intimidation, spearheaded by the **Ku Klux Klan**. The Klan targeted those who supported Reconstruction; it attacked and often murdered scalawags, black and white Republican leaders, community activists, and teachers. The Klan successfully intimidated many of its opponents, preventing a more complete implementation of Reconstruction.

Also, because Reconstruction did nothing to redistribute the South's wealth or guarantee that the freedmen would own property, it did very little to alter the basic power structure of the region. Southerners knew that when the Northerners left, as they inevitably would, things would return to a condition much closer to the way they were before Reconstruction. As early as 1869, the federal government began sending signals that it would soon ease up restrictions. President Grant enforced the law loosely, hoping to lessen tensions and thereby hasten an amicable reunion. Worse, throughout the 1860s and 1870s, the Supreme Court consistently restricted the scope of the Fourteenth and Fifteenth Amendments. In the *Slaughter-House* case, the court ruled that the Fourteenth Amendment applied only to the federal government, not to state governments, an opinion the court strengthened in *United States v. Cruikshank*. In *United States v. Reese*, the court cleared the way for "grandfather clauses," poll taxes, property requirements, and other restrictions on voting privileges. Soon nearly all Southern states had restrictive laws that effectively prevented blacks from voting. Finally, because Grant's administration was so thoroughly corrupt, it tainted everything with which it was associated, including Reconstruction.

During the 1872 election, moderates calling themselves **Liberal Republicans** abandoned the coalition that supported Reconstruction. Angered by widespread corruption, this group hoped to end federal control of the South. Although their candidate, **Horace Greeley**, did not defeat Grant, they made gains in Congressional and state elections. As a result, Grant moved further away from the radical position and closer to conciliation. Several Congressional acts, among them the **Amnesty Act of 1872**, pardoned many of the rebels, thus allowing them to reenter public life. Other crises such as the financial **Panic of 1873** drew the nation's attention away from Reconstruction. By 1876 Southern Democrats had regained control of most of the region's state legislatures. The election of 1876 was extremely close, with the vote in several states contested on charges of fraud. Although Republican **Rutherford B. Hayes** was ultimately declared the victor, the election demonstrated that the nation was now evenly split on Reconstruction. The final withdrawal of federal troops from the South began with Hayes' inauguration.

SOUTHERN BLACKS DURING AND AFTER RECONSTRUCTION

At the end of the Civil War, the former slaves were thrust into an ambiguous state of freedom. Most reacted cautiously, remaining on plantations where they had been relatively well-treated and fleeing those with cruel overseers. Many set out in search of family members from whom they had been separated. The **Freedman's Bureau** helped them find new jobs and housing, as well as provided money and food to those in need. The Freedman's Bureau also helped establish schools at all levels for blacks, among them Fisk University and Howard University.

When it became evident that the government would not redistribute land, blacks looked for other ways to work their own farms. The Freedman's Bureau attempted to establish a system in which blacks contracted their labor to whites, but the system failed. Instead, blacks preferred **sharecropping**, in which they traded a portion of their crop in return for the right to work someone else's land. The system worked at first, but unscrupulous landowners eventually used the system as a means of keeping poor farmers in a state of near slavery and debt. Abuses of the sharecropping system grew more widespread at the end of Reconstruction, at which point no court would fairly try the case of a sharecropper against a landowner.

Disenchantment with white society led many freedmen to found communities as far removed from the sphere of whites as possible. Black churches sprang up as another means by which the black community could bond and gain further autonomy. When Reconstruction ended, many blacks anticipated the fate that awaited them in the South and left. These people, called **exodusters**, picked up and moved to the Midwest (especially Kansas) where they attempted to start fresh in new black communities.

THE MACHINE AGE (1877–1900)

In 1876 **Thomas A. Edison** built his workshop in Menlo Park, New Jersey, and proceeded to produce some of the most important inventions of the century. Edison's greatest invention was the **light bulb**. Edison's pioneering work in the development of **power plants** also proved immensely important. His advances allowed for (among other things) the extension of the work day (which previously ended at sundown) and the wider availability of electricity. With that wider availability, Edison and other inventors began to create new uses for electricity, both for industry and the home. The last quarter of the nineteenth century is often called the **age of invention** because so many technological advances like Edison's were made. These advances, in turn, generated greater opportunities for **mass production**, which then caused the economy to grow at a tremendous rate. Not surprisingly, the "captains of industry" who owned and controlled the new manufacturing enterprises became extremely rich and powerful during this period.

INDUSTRIALIZATION, CORPORATE CONSOLIDATION, AND THE GOSPEL OF WEALTH

As more and faster machines became available to manufacturers, businessmen discovered that their cost per unit decreased as the number of units they produced increased. The more raw product they bought, the cheaper the suppliers' asking price. The closer to capacity they kept their new, faster machines running, the less the cost of labor and electricity per product. The lower their costs, the cheaper they could sell their products. The cheaper the product, the more they sold. That, simply put, is the concept of **economies of scale**.

The downside of this new business practice was that it required employees to work as efficiently, and repetitively, as machines. **Assembly line production** required workers to perform a single task over and over, often (before labor reform) for 12 to 14 hours a day. Factories were dangerous; machine malfunctions and human error typically resulted in more than 500,000 injuries to workers per year.

The overriding concern for businessmen, however, was that profits continued to increase by huge margins. Although government made some efforts to regulate this rapid growth, these were tentative. Furthermore, the government remained uncertain as to how to enforce regulations, and widespread corruption existed among those bureaucrats charged with enforcing the regulations. Finally, the courts of the era (especially the Supreme Court) were extremely pro-business. With almost no restraint, businesses followed the path that led to greater economies of scale, which meant larger and larger businesses. They aimed for control of all facets of production, an idea known as **vertical integration**. Ideal vertical integration, from the standpoint of business, would include a central organization called a **holding company** that owned the controlling interest in the production of raw material, the means of transporting that material to a factory, the factory itself, and the distribution network for selling the product. The logical conclusion is a **monopoly**, or complete control of an entire industry.

Numerous problems arose because of this consolidation of power. First, rapid growth required lots of money. Businessmen borrowed huge sums, and when their businesses occasionally failed, bank failures could result. During the last quarter of the nineteenth century, the United States endured one major financial panic per decade. Although irresponsible investors caused the panics, the lower classes suffered the most, as jobs and money became scarce. Second, monopolies created a class of extremely powerful men whose interests did not agree with those of the rest of society. As these businessmen grew more powerful, public resentment increased, and the government responded with laws to restrict monopolies (which the courts, in turn, weakened). The back-and-forth battle among the public, the government, and the courts is best exemplified by the **Sherman Anti-Trust Act of 1890**. Public pressure led to the passage of this law forbidding any "combination . . . or conspiracy in the restraint of trade." The Supreme Court then ruled (1) that a company that controlled 98 percent of the nation's sugar refining business did *not* violate the law, but that (2) trade unions did.

Another response to public pressure for reform came from industrialists themselves. Steel mogul **Andrew Carnegie** developed a philosophy based on the work of Charles Darwin. Using Darwin's theory of evolution as an analogy, Carnegie argued that in business, as in nature, unrestricted competition allowed only the "fittest" to survive, to the benefit of everyone. This theory was called **social Darwinism**. Aside from the fact that Carnegie's analogy to Darwin's theory was at best dubious, it also lacked consistency; while Carnegie argued against government regulation, he supported all types of government assistance to business (in the form of tax abatements, grants, tariffs, etc.). Carnegie further argued that the concentration of wealth among a few was the natural and most efficient result of capitalism—a belief held so dearly that he dubbed it the **Gospel of Wealth**. Carnegie also asserted that great wealth brought with it social responsibility, and consequently, he gave generously to charities. Some of his peers were as generous; others were not.

FACTORIES AND CITY LIFE

Manufacturers cut costs and maximized profits in every way they could imagine. They reduced labor costs by hiring **women** and **children**. In cities, where most factories were located, manufacturers hired the many newly arrived **immigrants** who were anxious for work. Because manufacturers paid as little as possible, the cities in which their employees lived suffered many of the problems associated with poverty, such as crime, disease, and the lack of livable housing for a rapidly expanding population. As mentioned before, factories were dangerous, and many families had at least one member who had been disabled at work. Insurance and workmen's compensation certainly did not exist then, and the cost of caring for an ailing family member fell on the family.

The poverty level in cities also rose because those who could afford it moved away from the city center. As factories sprung up, cities became dirtier and generally less healthy environments. Advances in **mass transportation** allowed the middle class to live in nicer neighborhoods and commute to work. (The middle class was growing, it was made up of managers, secretaries, bureaucrats, merchants, and the like.) As a result, immigrants and migrants made up the majority of city populations. Starting around 1880, the majority of immigrants arrived from southern and eastern Europe. (Prior to 1880, most immigrants to America came from northern and western Europe.) Prejudice against the new arrivals was widespread, and many immigrants settled in **ethnic neighborhoods** to insulate themselves. Worse off still were **black** and **Latino** migrants. Many employers refused them any but the worst jobs, and by necessity they fell into low-end service work such as sanitation.

Municipal governments of the era were not like those of today. In fact, such governments were practically nonexistent. Most Americans expected churches, private charities, and ethnic communities to provide services for the poor. However, many of those services were provided instead by a group of corrupt men called **political bosses**. Bosses helped the poor find homes and jobs; they also helped them apply for citizenship and voting rights. They built parks, funded auxiliary police and fire departments, and constructed roads and sewage lines. In return, they expected community members to vote as they were instructed. Occasionally they also required "donations" to help fund community projects. Political bosses—whose organizations were called **political machines**—rendered services that communities would not otherwise have received. However, because the bosses resorted to criminal means to accomplish their goals, the cost of their services was high.

Widespread misery in cities led many to seek changes. **Labor unions** formed to try to counter the poor treatment of workers. Unions were considered radical organizations by many, and the government was wary of them; businesses and the courts were openly hostile to them. Hired goons often broke strikes, and in some cases, federal troops broke them. Propagandists claimed that unions were subversive forces—a position reinforced in public opinion by the **Haymarket Square Riot**. (During an 1886 labor demonstration in Chicago's Haymarket Square, a bomb went off, killing police.) Many blamed the incident on the influence of radicals within the union movement, although no one knew who set off the bomb. Many early unions did indeed subscribe to utopian and/or socialist philosophies. The **American Federation of Labor** avoided those larger political questions, concentrating instead on such basic issues as higher wages and shorter work days—an approach that proved successful. The history of early unions is marred by the fact that many refused to accept immigrants or blacks among their memberships.

Charitable middle-class organizations, usually run by women, also made efforts at urban reform. These groups lobbied local governments for building-safety codes, better sanitation, and public schools. Frustrated by government's slow pace, their members also founded and lived in **settlement houses** in poor neighborhoods. These houses became community centers, providing schooling, child care, and cultural activities. Settlement houses laid the foundation for the progressive movement (discussed in the next chapter).

While the poor suffered, life improved for both the wealthy and the middle class. Increased production and wealth meant greater access to luxuries and more leisure time. America's entertainment industry grew at this time, as sports, high theater, vaudeville, and, later, movies became popular diversions. It was also during this period that large segments of the public began to read **popular novels** and **newspapers**. The growth of the newspaper industry was largely the responsibility of **Joseph Pulitzer** and **William Randolph Hearst**, both of whom understood the commercial value of bold, screaming headlines and lurid tales of scandal. (Prior to Pulitzer and Hearst, papers were stodgy and looked like the *Wall Street Journal*, but with even more boring graphics.) These men's style of sensational reporting became known as **yellow journalism**.

JIM CROW LAWS AND OTHER DEVELOPMENTS IN THE SOUTH

Most of the advances made during the machine age primarily affected Northern cities. In the South, agriculture continued as the main form of labor. The industrialization programs of Reconstruction did produce some results, however. Textile mills sprang up around the South, reducing cotton farmers' reliance on the North. Tobacco processing plants also employed some workers. Still, the vast majority of Southerners remained farmers.

Postwar economics forced many farmers to sell their land, which wealthy landowners bought and consolidated into larger farms. Landless farmers were forced into **sharecropping**. The method by which they rented land was called the **crop lien system**; it was designed to keep the poor in constant debt. Because these farmers had no cash, they borrowed what they needed to buy seed and tools, promising a portion of their crop as collateral. Huge interest rates on their loans and unscrupulous landlords pretty much guaranteed that these farmers would never overcome their debt, forcing them to borrow further and promise their *next* crop as collateral. In this way landlords kept the poor, both black and white, in a state of virtual slavery.

The advent of **Jim Crow laws** made matters worse for blacks. As the federal government exerted less influence over Southern states, towns and cities passed numerous discriminatory laws. The Supreme Court assisted the states by ruling that the Fourteenth Amendment did not protect blacks from discrimination by privately owned businesses and that blacks would have to seek equal protection from the states, not from the federal government. In 1883 the Court also reversed the Civil Rights Act of 1875, thus opening the door to legal segregation. In 1896 the Supreme Court ruled in *Plessy v. Ferguson* that "separate but equal" facilities for the different races was legal. In so doing, the Court set back the civil rights gains made during Reconstruction.

THE RAILROADS AND DEVELOPMENTS IN THE WEST

On the western frontier, **ranching** and **mining** were growing industries. Ranchers drove their herds across the western plains and deserts, ignoring property rights and Native American prerogatives to the land. Individual miners lacked the resources to mine and cart big loads, so mostly they prospected; when they found a rich mine, they staked a claim and sold their rights to a mining company.

The arrival of the **railroad** changed the West in many ways. The railroads, although owned privately, were built largely at the public's expense. Both federal and local governments were anxious for rails to be completed and so provided substantial assistance. Although the public had paid for the rail system, rail proprietors strenuously objected to any government control of their industry, and it took years for railroad rates to come under regulation. Until they were regulated, the railroads would typically overcharge wherever they owned a monopoly and undercharge in competitive and heavily trafficked markets. This practice was particularly harmful to farmers in remote areas.

As railroad construction crawled across the nation, rail companies organized massive hunts for buffalo (considered a nuisance). Railroad bounty hunters hunted the herds to near extinction, destroying a resource upon which local Native Americans had depended. Some tribes, such as the Sioux, fought back, giving the government an excuse to send troops into the region. While Native Americans won some battles (notably at **Little Big Horn**, where George Custer met his defeat), the federal army ultimately overpowered them.

The railroads brought other changes as well. Rails quickly transformed depot towns into vital cities by connecting them to civilization. Easier, faster travel meant more contact with ideas and technological advances from the East. Developments in railroad technology had applications in other industries and so accelerated the industrial revolution. In addition, "railroad time," by which rail schedules were determined, gave the nation its first standardized method of timetelling.

As the rails pushed the country westward, settlers started filling in the territory. By 1889 North Dakota, South Dakota, Washington, and Montana were populous enough to achieve statehood; Wyoming and Idaho followed in 1890. In 1893 historian Frederick Jackson Turner made his famous pronouncement that the American frontier was gone, and with it the first period of American history.

In the Great Plains, **farming** and **ranching** constituted the main forms of employment. New farm machinery and access to mail (and mail-order retail) made life on the plains easier, but it was still lonely and difficult. The government, realizing the potential of the region as the nation's chief agricultural center, passed the **Morrill Land Grant Act** to provide money for agricultural colleges. Eventually, agricultural science became a huge industry in the United States.

The big losers in this expansionist era, of course, were Native Americans. At first, pioneers approached the tribes as sovereign nations. They made treaties with them, which they or their immediate successors broke. The result was warfare, leading the government to try another approach. The new tack was to force Native Americans onto **reservations**, which typically were made up of the least desirable land in a tribe's traditional home region. The reservation system failed for a number of reasons, including the inferiority of the land, the grouping of incompatible tribes on the same reservation, and the lack of autonomy granted the tribes in managing their own affairs. Moreover, some Westerners simply ignored the arrangement and poached on reservation lands. Reformers pushed for change, which came in the form of the **Dawes Severalty Act**. This law gave tracts of land to those who left the reservations. Its goal was to accelerate the **assimilation** of Native Americans into western society by integrating them more closely with whites; Native Americans, naturally, resisted. Furthermore, poverty drove many to sell their land to speculators, leaving them literally homeless. By the time the policy set by Dawes was reversed (in 1934), the Native American nations were decimated.

NATIONAL POLITICS

Mark Twain dubbed the era between Reconstruction and 1900 the **Gilded Age** of politics. Gilded metals have a shiny, gold-like surface, but beneath lies a cheap base. Twain's point was that politics looked good, but just beneath the surface lay crass corruption and patronage. Political machines, not municipal governments, ran the cities. Big business bought votes in Congress, then turned around and fleeced consumers. Workers had little protection from the greed of their employers because the courts turned a deaf ear to worker complaints. In other words, Twain was right on the money.

The presidents of this era were generally not corrupt. They were, however, relatively weak. (The president is only as powerful as his support allows him to be; thus popular presidents, such as Andrew Jackson and Franklin Roosevelt, were able to accomplish so much.) As a result, we barely remember **Rutherford B. Hayes**, **James A. Garfield**, **Chester A. Arthur**, **Grover Cleveland (both times)**, **Benjamin Harrison**, and **William McKinley**. (Okay, we remember McKinley, but only because he was in business' hip pocket and because his assassination made a president of **Theodore Roosevelt,** whom everyone remembers.)

In response to the outcry over widespread corruption, the government made its first stabs at regulating itself and business. Many states imposed **railroad regulations** because railroads were engaging in price gouging. **The Interstate Commerce Act** went further, creating a federal Interstate Commerce Commission to regulate unfair railroad practices. Although these acts demonstrated the government's good intentions, they were ineffective; the railroads challenged them and usually won in the business-friendly courts. **Civil service reform** came with the **Pendleton Act**, which was passed in response to charges of patronage in the awarding of government jobs. The Pendleton Act created the **Civil Service Commission** to oversee examinations for potential government employees.

It was also during this period that **women's suffrage** became an important political issue. **Susan B. Anthony** led the fight, convincing Congress to introduce a suffrage amendment to the Constitution. The bill was introduced every year and rarely got out of committee, but the fight had begun in earnest. Meanwhile, organizations such as the **American Suffrage Association** fought for women's suffrage amendments to state constitutions. By 1890 they had achieved some partial successes, gaining the vote on school issues.

THE SILVER ISSUE AND THE POPULIST MOVEMENT

In the period after the Civil War, production on all fronts, industrial and agricultural, increased. Greater supply accordingly led to a drop in prices. For many farmers, lower prices meant trouble, as they were locked into long-term debts with fixed payments. Looking for a solution to their problem, farmers came to support **a more generous money supply**. An increase in available money, they correctly figured, would make payments easier. It would also cause inflation, which would make the farmers' debts (held by Northern banks) worth less. Not surprisingly, the banks opposed the plan, preferring for the country to use only gold to back its money supply.

The farmers' plan called for the liberal use of **silver** coins, and because silver was mined in the West, this plan had the added support of Western miners along with that of Midwestern and Southern farmers. Thus, the issue had a regional component. Because it pitted poor farmers against wealthy bankers, it also had elements of class strife. Although a complicated issue, the money issue was also a potentially explosive political issue.

The "silver vs. gold" debate provided an issue around which farmers could organize. They did just that. First came the **Grange Movement**, which by 1875 had more than one million members. The Granges started out as cooperatives, with the purpose of allowing farmers to buy machinery and sell crops as a group and, therefore, reap the benefits of economies of scale. Soon, the Granges endorsed political candidates and lobbied for legislation. The Granges ultimately died out due to lack of money, but they were replaced by **Farmers' Alliances**. The Farmers' Alliances were even more successful than the Grange movement, and they soon grew into a political party called the **People's Party**, the political arm of the **Populist** movement.

The People's Party held a convention in 1892. (The platform it drew up presented many of the ideas that would later be championed by the Progressives.) Aside from supporting the generous coinage of silver, the Populists called for government ownership of railroads and telegraphs, a graduated income tax, direct election of U.S. senators, and shorter work days. Although their 1892 presidential candidate came in third, he won more than one million votes, awakening Washington to the growing Populist movement.

As Cleveland took office in 1893, the country entered a four-year financial crisis. Hard economic times made Populist goals more popular, particularly the call for easy money. (Most people at the time, after all, had no money at all.) Times got so bad that even more progressive (some would say radical) movements gained popularity; in 1894 the **Socialists**, led by **Eugene V. Debs**, gained support. By 1896 the Populists were poised for power. They backed Democratic candidate **William Jennings Bryan** against Republican nominee **William McKinley**, and Bryan ran on a strictly Populist platform; he based his campaign on the call for "**free silver**." He argued that an easy money supply, though inflationary, would loosen the control that Northern banking interests held over the country. He lost the campaign; this, coupled with an improved economy, ended the Populist movement.

AMERICAN IMPERIALISM: FOREIGN POLICY

Throughout the machine age, American production capacities grew rapidly. As we have already discussed, not every American had enough money to buy the products he or she made at work. America began looking overseas to **find new markets**. Increased **nationalism** also led American business to look for new markets. America's centennial celebration in 1876 heightened national pride, as did awareness that the country was becoming a world economic power. As Americans became more certain that their way of life was best, they hoped to spread that around the globe. This philosophy led American influence to expand into a number of new arenas.

First, **William H. Seward**, secretary of state under Lincoln and Johnson, set the precedent for increased American participation in any and all doings in the western hemisphere. In particular, Seward engineered the purchase of Alaska and invoked the Monroe Doctrine to force France out of Mexico. In the following decade, American businesses began developing markets and production facilities in Latin America, and gradually they gained political power in the region.

As long as America moved into regions to do business, it was practicing **expansionism**, which most Americans supported. When the United States took control of another country, however, it was exercising **imperialism**, a more controversial practice. A book by naval Captain Alfred T. Mahan, called *The Influence of Sea Power Upon History* (1890), piqued the government's interest in imperialism. Mahan argued that successful foreign trade relied on access to foreign ports, which in turn required overseas colonies, and colonies in turn required a strong navy. The book popularized the idea of the **New Navy**, and after the United States invested in upgrading its ships, it turned its attention to foreign acquisitions.

The search for a port along the trade route to Asia attracted the U.S. to **Hawaii**. The United States had been involved in Hawaii since the 1870s when American sugar producers started trading with the island. Due in large part to American interference, the Hawaiian economy collapsed in the 1890s. (The U.S. allowed Hawaii tariff-free access to American markets. Then, when Hawaii became dependent on trade with the U.S., the government imposed high tariffs, thereby greatly diminishing Hawaiian exports.) The white minority overthrew the native government, and, eventually, the U.S. annexed Hawaii. Japan was outraged; more than 40 percent of Hawaii's residents were of Japanese descent. That anger would resurface during World War II.

Another opportunity for American expansion arose when Cuban natives revolted against Spanish control. The revolution in **Cuba**, like the Hawaiian revolution, was instigated by U.S. tampering with the Cuban economy (by imposing high import tariffs). A violent Cuban civil war followed, reported in all its gory detail in the sensational Hearst newspaper (see "yellow journalism," page 108). McKinley waited for an opportune moment, which came when an American warship, the *Maine*, exploded in the Havana harbor. To this day no one is sure what destroyed the *Maine*, but the U.S. assumed Spain was responsible and declared war. In the ensuing war, the U.S. not only drove Spain out of Cuba, but also sent a fleet to the Spanish-controlled **Philippines** and drove the Spanish out of there too. In the **Treaty of Paris**, Spain granted Cuba independence and ceded the Philippines, Puerto Rico, and Guam to the United States.

Finally, America hoped to gain entry into Asian markets. To that end, McKinley sought an **open door policy** for all western nations hoping to trade with Asia. The European nations that had colonized China were not so keen on the idea; to their way of thinking, they fought for those markets and planned to keep them. When the Chinese rebelled against European imperialism, the United States sent troops to help suppress the rebels. In return, Germany, France, and England grew more receptive to America's foreign policy objectives.

American imperialism would continue through Theodore Roosevelt's administration. We'll discuss that period in the next chapter.

THE 20TH CENTURY

THE PROGRESSIVE ERA AND WORLD WAR I
(1900–1920)

The Populist movement dissipated, but not before raising the possibility of reform through government. The Populists' successes in both local and national elections encouraged others to seek change through political action. Building on Populism's achievements and adopting some of its goals (e.g., direct election of senators, opposition to monopolies) the **Progressives** came to dominate the first two decades of twentieth-century American politics.

THE PROGRESSIVE MOVEMENT

One of the reasons Populism failed is that its constituents were mostly poor farmers whose daily struggle for survival made political activity difficult. The **Progressives** achieved greater success in part because theirs was an urban, middle-class movement. Its proponents started with more economic and political clout than the Populists. Furthermore, Progressives could devote more time to the causes they championed. Also, because many Progressives were Northern and middle class, the Progressive movement did not intensify regional and class differences, as the Populist movement had.

The roots of Progressivism lay in the growing number of associations and organizations at the turn of the century. The National Woman Suffrage Association, the American Bar Association, and the National Municipal League are some of the many groups that rallied citizens around a cause or profession. Most of these groups' members were educated and middle class; the blatant corruption they saw in business and politics offended their senses of decency, as did the terrible plight of the urban poor.

Progressivism got a further boost from a group of journalists who wrote exposés of corporate greed and misconduct. These writers, dubbed "**muckrakers**" by Theodore Roosevelt, revealed widespread corruption in urban management (**Lincoln Steffens**' *The Shame of the Cities*), oil companies (**Ida Tarbell**'s *History of Standard Oil*), and the meat-packing industry (**Upton Sinclair**'s *The Jungle*). Their books and news articles raised the moral stakes for Progressives.

Over the course of two decades, Progressives achieved great successes on both the local and national levels. They campaigned to change public attitudes toward education and government regulation in much the same way reformers of the 1830s had campaigned for public enlightenment on the plight of the orphans, prostitutes, and the mentally infirm. New groups arose to lead the fight against discrimination but met with mixed success. **W.E.B. Du Bois** headed the **National Association for the Advancement of Colored People** (**NAACP**) in the quest for racial justice, an uphill battle so strenuous that, after a lifelong struggle, Du Bois abandoned the United States and moved to Africa. Meanwhile, women's groups continued to campaign for suffrage. The adamant, conservative opposition they faced gave birth to the **feminist** movement. One early advocate, **Margaret Sanger**, faced wide opposition for promoting the use of contraceptives (illegal in most places). The movement's greatest success was in winning women the right to vote, granted by the **Nineteenth Amendment** in 1920.

Wisconsin governor **Robert LaFollette** led the way for many Progressive state leaders. Under his leadership, Wisconsin implemented plans for direct primary elections, progressive taxation, and rail regulation. Many states extended greater power to voters by adopting the **ballot initiative**, through which the voters could propose new laws; the **referendum**, which allowed the public to vote on new laws; and the **recall election**, which gave voters the power to remove officials from office before their terms expired. Working-class progressives also won a number of victories on the state level, including limitations on the length of the work day, minimum-wage requirements, child labor laws, and urban housing codes. Many states adopted progressive income taxes which served partially to redistribute the nation's wealth.

The most prominent Progressive leader was probably president **Theodore Roosevelt**. People expected Roosevelt, a war hero, to be conservative because he was McKinley's vice-president, but his politics surprised almost everyone. He was the first to successfully use the **Sherman Anti-Trust Act** against monopolies, and he did so repeatedly during his term, earning the nickname "the Trustbuster." Among Roosevelt's other progressive achievements were tightening food and drug regulations, creating national parks, and broadening the government's power to protect land from overdevelopment. (Roosevelt, an avid outdoorsman, was a particularly impassioned conservationist.) Presidents Taft and Wilson continued to promote Progressive ideals. **William Howard Taft** spearheaded the drive for two constitutional amendments, one that instituted a national income tax and another that allowed for the direct election of senators. He pursued monopolies even more aggressively than Roosevelt. **Woodrow Wilson** created the Federal Trade Commission, lobbied for and enforced the Clayton Anti-Trust Act of 1914, and helped create the Federal Reserve, which gave the government greater control over the nation's finances. It was also during his term that the Nineteenth Amendment gave women the right to vote.

Progressivism lasted until the end of World War I, at which point the nation, weary from war, stepped back from its moral crusade. The war had torn apart the Progressive coalition; pacifist Progressives opposed the war while others supported it. A Red Scare, heightened by the Russian

Revolution (see p. 123), further split the Progressive coalition by dividing the leftists from the moderates. Moreover, the Progressive movement had achieved many of its goals, and as it did, it lost the support of those interest groups whose ends had been met. It is possible to argue that the Progressive movement was brought to an end, at least in part, by its own success.

FOREIGN POLICY AND U.S. ENTRY INTO WORLD WAR I

Roosevelt differed from his predecessors on domestic policy, but he concurred with their foreign policy. Roosevelt was, if anything, an even more devout imperialist than McKinley had been. In 1903, the Roosevelt administration strong-armed Cuba into accepting the **Platt Amendment**, which essentially committed Cuba to American semicontrol. Under Platt's stipulations, Cuba could not make a treaty with another nation without U.S. approval, and the United States had the right to intervene in Cuba's affairs if domestic order dissolved. A number of invasions and occupations by the Marines resulted. For ten of the years between 1906 and 1922, the American military occupied Cuba, arousing anti-American sentiments on the island.

Roosevelt's actions were equally interventionist throughout Central America. During his administration, the country set its sights on building a canal through the Central American isthmus, since a canal would greatly shorten the sea trip from the East Coast to California. Congress approved a plan for a canal through **Panama**, at the time a province of Colombia. Because Colombia asked for more than the government was willing to spend, the United States encouraged Panamanian rebels to revolt, then supported the revolution. Not surprisingly, the new Panamanian government gave the United States a *much* better deal. Because American commercial interests were so closely tied to the canal's successful operation, the United States military became a fixed presence throughout the region. During the next twenty years, troops intervened repeatedly, claiming that Latin American domestic instability constituted a threat to American security. This assertion came to be known as the **Roosevelt Corollary to the Monroe Doctrine**.

American foreign policy continued to adhere to the Monroe Doctrine, which asserted America's right to intervene anywhere in the western hemisphere where it felt its national security was at stake. It also stated that the United States wanted no part of Europe's internal disputes. American commitment to that aspect of the Monroe Doctrine would soon be tested, as Europe started down the path leading to **World War I**. Complicating matters was the fact that the United States and England were quickly forming a close alliance. To America's benefit, England had not opposed its many forays into Central American politics, although it could have. The British were not merely being friendly; they were trying to line up the United States as a potential ally in their ongoing rivalry with Germany, the other great European power of the era.

Fortunately, you do not need to know the tangled series of events that led Europe into war in 1914. You do, however, have to know about the United States' initial efforts to stay out of the war and the events that ultimately drew it into the conflict. **Woodrow Wilson** won the election of 1912, a three-way race in which the third party candidate, Theodore Roosevelt, outpolled Taft, the Republican incumbent. Wilson entered office with less than a commanding mandate—only 40 percent of the electorate voted for him. However, with regard to the simmering European conflict, he and the electorate were of the same mind: The United States should stay out of it.

When war broke out in Europe in August 1914, Wilson immediately declared the U.S. policy of **neutrality**. Neutrality called for America to treat all the belligerents fairly and without favoritism. It was Wilson's hope that the United States would help settle the conflict and emerge as the world's arbiter. However, the neutrality policy posed several immediate problems, owing to America's close relationship with England and relatively distant relationship with Germany and Austria-Hungary. A number of Wilson's advisors openly favored the Allies (led by the British).

The situation quickly grew more complicated. England's strategic location and superior navy allowed it to impose an effective **blockade** on shipments headed for Germany, particularly those coming from the east (namely, American shipments). Protests proved futile; the British government impounded and confiscated American ships. They then paid for the cargo, reducing the pressure that American merchants would otherwise have put on the U.S. government to take action against the blockade.

Germany attempted to counter the blockade with **submarines**, or **U-boats**. According to contemporaneous international law, an attacker had to warn civilian ships before attacking. Submarines could not do this, since doing so would eliminate their main advantage (e.g., the enemy doesn't know where they are). Furthermore, when the Germans attacked civilian ships, it was usually because those ships were carrying military supplies. The Germans announced that they would attack any such ship, but that did not satisfy Wilson, who believed that the Germans should adhere to the strict letter of international law. Thus, when the German submarines sank the passenger ship *Lusitania* in 1915 (killing 1,200 passengers), the action provoked the condemnation of both the government and much of the public. That the *Lusitania* was carrying tons of ammunition to the British, was a fact that received much less public attention than did the loss of 1,200 innocent lives.

The sinking of the *Lusitania*, and the bad publicity it generated, led the Germans to cease submarine warfare for a while. Britain made steady gains, however, and as the U-boats were Germany's most effective weapon, the Germans resumed their use. In 1916, while Wilson was campaigning for reelection on the slogan "He kept us out of war," Germany sank another passenger liner, the *Arabic*. In response, Wilson, while still maintaining neutrality, asked Congress to put the military into a state of "**preparedness**" for war, just in case. While most Americans wanted to stay out of the war, popular support for entry was beginning to grow.

Then, in early 1917 the British intercepted a telegram from German Foreign Minister Zimmerman. The telegram, imaginatively called the **Zimmerman Telegram**, outlined a German plan to keep the United States out of the European war. The telegram stated that *if* Mexico were to declare war on the U.S., Germany would help them. The telegram also suggested that Germany would help Japan if it too wanted to go to war against America. Published in newspapers around the country, the telegram convinced many Americans that Germany was trying to take over the world. Although the public was by no means universally behind the idea of war, the balance had shifted enough so that within a month, America would declare war on Germany.

WORLD WAR I AND ITS AFTERMATH

As is often the case during wartime, the government's power expanded greatly during the three years America was involved in World War I. The government took control of the telephone, telegraph, and rail industries, and a massive bureaucracy arose to handle these new responsibilities. The **War Industry Board**, created to coordinate all facets of industrial and agricultural production, sought to guarantee that not only the United States but also the rest of the Allies would be well-supplied. (European production had been drastically cut by the war.) The WIB had mixed success; like most large bureaucracies, it was slow and inefficient.

The government also curtailed individual civil liberties during the war. In response to the still-sizable opposition to U.S. involvement, Congress passed the **Espionage Act** in 1917 and the **Sedition Act** in 1918. The Espionage Act essentially made it illegal to try to convince someone to dodge the military draft. (The draft had been instituted upon America's entry into the war.) The Sedition Act made it illegal to try to prevent the sale of war bonds or to speak disparagingly of the government, the flag, the military, or the Constitution. Both laws were worded vaguely, giving the courts great leeway in their interpretation.

These laws soon became useful tools for the suppression of anyone who voiced unpopular ideas. A mood of increased paranoia pervaded the era, heightened by the **Russian Revolution** in 1917, which placed Russia under Communist control. Suddenly, Americans began to fear a Communist takeover. Radical labor unions, such as the International Workers of the World, were branded enemies of the state, and their leaders were incarcerated. Eugene Debs, the Socialist leader, was also imprisoned for criticizing the war. A new government agency, the **Federal Bureau of Investigation**, was created to prevent radicals from taking over; **J. Edgar Hoover**, headed the nascent agency (and continued to run it until the 1970s). Business assumed greater power, while unions lost power. Under the pretext of stamping out radicalism, businesses increased their use of strike breakers and other forceful tactics against unions. The government helped: In the **Palmer Raids** in early 1920, the government abandoned all pretext of respecting civil liberties as its agents raided union halls, pool halls, social clubs, and residences to arrest 4,000 suspected radicals. Six hundred were eventually deported, some for no other crime than their expression of sympathy for the Communist movement.

The government helped create this frenzied atmosphere through its wartime propaganda arm, the **Committee on Public Information**. As the war progressed, the CPI's messages grew more sensational. At lectures and movie theaters, in newspapers and magazines, the CPI created the image of the Germans as cold-blooded, baby-killing, power-hungry Huns. During this period, Americans rejected all things German; for example, they changed the name of sauerkraut to "liberty cabbage." More serious were the many acts of violence against German immigrants and Americans of German descent.

Wartime also presented new opportunities for **women**. Although the number of women in the work force did not increase greatly during the war, their means of employment did change. Many women quit domestic work and started working in factories; at one point, 20 percent of factory floor manufacturing jobs were held by women. These workplace advances ended with the war, as veterans returned home and replaced the women workers. Southern **blacks**, realizing that wartime manufacturing was creating jobs in the North, migrated to the big cities. During the war, more than 500,000 blacks left the South in search of work. Many blacks joined the army; W.E.B. Du Bois encouraged blacks to enlist, hoping that military service would provide an inroad to social equality. Sadly, the army segregated blacks and assigned them mostly to menial labor. Fearful of the effects of integration, the army assigned black combat units to French command.

American participation in the war tipped the balance in the Allies' favor, and two years after America's entry, the Germans were ready to negotiate a peace treaty. Wilson wanted the war treaty to be guided by his **Fourteen Points** plan. The Fourteen Points called for free trade through lower tariffs and freedom of the seas; a reduction of arms supplies on all sides; and the promotion of self-determination, both in Europe and overseas (in other words, the end of colonialism). The plan also sought to create the **League of Nations**, a mechanism for international cooperation much like today's **United Nations**. Wilson's Fourteen Points served as a basis for initial negotiations, but the negotiations soon took a different direction. The European Allies wanted a peace settlement that punished Germany, and ultimately they got it. Under the **Treaty of Versailles**, Germany was forced to cede German and colonial territories to the Allies, to disarm, to pay huge reparations, and to admit that the war was Germany's fault. Although much of Wilson's plan was discarded, the Treaty of Versailles did create the League of Nations. Wilson hoped that the League would ultimately remedy the peace settlement's many flaws, but when he returned home, a rude surprise awaited him. The Senate rejected the treaty and American participation in the League of Nations. Weary of war, America was receding into a period of **isolationism**. The public wanted less interaction with Europe, not more, as the League would have required. Wilson tried to muster popular support for the treaty. However, while campaigning, Wilson suffered a major stroke, thereby ending whatever chance he might have had for encouraging the treaty's ratification.

THE JAZZ AGE AND THE GREAT DEPRESSION (1920–1933)

After World War I the American economy (after a brief slump) started to grow rapidly. By 1922 America was hitting new peaks of prosperity every day. The invention of a practical electric motor was largely responsible for the economic boom; like computers in the 1990s, electric motors became essential to work and home environments, driving industrial machines and household appliances. With the new prosperity, other industries arose to serve the growing middle class in its search for the trappings of affluence.

PRO-BUSINESS REPUBLICAN ADMINISTRATIONS

As the age of progressive reform ended, many Americans became more comfortable with the idea of large, successful businesses. Some of these businesses, such as department stores, offered both convenience and reasonable prices. Others, like the automobile industry, offered (again at reasonable prices) products that made life more convenient and conferred status on their owners.

The government, which had worked closely with business leaders as part of the war effort, also grew to be more **pro-business** during the era. Government regulatory agencies (such as the FTC) more often assisted business than regulated it. Labor unions fell further out of public favor, particularly when they struck against industries necessary to keep industrial America running smoothly. Unions striking for higher wages and safer work conditions in the steel, coal, and railroad industries were suppressed by federal troops. The Supreme Court overturned a minimum wage law for women and nullified child labor restrictions.

All three of the era's presidents—**Warren Harding**, **Calvin Coolidge**, and **Herbert Hoover**—pursued pro-business policies and surrounded themselves with like-minded advisors. Harding, an honest man, had the misfortune of surrounding himself with corrupt advisors; several of his cabinet members wound up in prison. The most infamous incident of his administration was the **Teapot Dome scandal**, in which oil companies bribed the Secretary of the Interior in order to drill on public lands. Conservative on economic issues, Harding proved more liberal than his predecessor Wilson on issues of civil liberty. He supported antilynching laws and tried to help farmers (who were benefiting less from the new economy than were middle-class city dwellers) by providing more money for farm loans. Harding died in office, and Coolidge, his vice-president, assumed the presidency. When Coolidge ran for the presidency in 1924, he turned the election into a debate on the economy by running on the slogan "Coolidge prosperity." Coolidge won easily and, following his mandate, continued Harding's conservative economic policies. He also pushed for lower income-tax rates. We will discuss Hoover's presidency later, when we discuss the causes of the Great Depression.

The pro-business atmosphere of the era led to a temporary decline in the popularity of labor unions; membership levels dropped throughout the decade. Also contributing to this drop were the efforts of businesses to woo workers with pension plans, opportunities for profit sharing, and company parties and other events designed to foster a communal spirit at work. Businessmen hoped that, if they offered some such benefits, they could dissuade workers from organizing and demanding even more. Such practices were often referred to as **corporate welfare**.

MODERN CULTURE

No consumer product better typified the new spirit of the nation than the **automobile**. At first, automobiles were expensive conveniences, only affordable to the extremely wealthy; then, Henry Ford perfected the assembly line and mass production, which lowered the cost of automobiles. By the end of the decade, most middle-class families could afford a car. The automobile allowed those who worked in the cities to move further away from city centers, thus giving birth to the **suburbs**, which, in turn, transformed the automobile from a convenience to a necessity. The impact of the automobile on the 1920s was tremendous, forcing areas to quickly develop roadways and the means of policing traffic. In 1929, when the population stood at 100 million, more than 23 million automobiles were registered in the United States.

The **radio** followed automobiles in its impact on the nation, quickly becoming a very popular form of entertainment. Ten million families owned them, and in cities it was not unusual for several families to gather at the home of a radio owner and settle in for the evening. As more houses gained access to electric power, household appliance sales boomed as well. The **advertising industry** grew up during the decade to hype all these new products. Although advertisements from that era look pretty goofy to us today, they were quite effective at convincing people to buy stuff they did not really need (as are today's advertisements!).

All this consumerism required money, and as single-earner households often couldn't afford to "keep up with the Joneses," more women entered the working world. Many worked in offices, while others worked in schools. While the vast majority of married women continued to stay at home, more than ever—about 15 percent—entered the work force. Women continued, as they had in the past, to work in predominantly female-dominated professions and earn much less than men. The inequity of the system helped fuel the feminist movement.

The rapid modernization of American society was reflected in the way it entertained itself. **Movies** grew tremendously popular during the decade, reflecting back at the nation its idealized self-image; on movie screens, young, independent-minded, gorgeous heroes and heroines defied all odds to succeed in romance and—at the same time—strike it rich. **Sports** grew more popular as well, especially baseball, whose greatest player of the era, Babe Ruth, was idolized by millions. In **literature**, America gained international prominence through such world-class authors such as **F. Scott Fitzgerald**, **Ernest Hemingway**, and playwright **Eugene O'Neill**. Ironically, many of these writers moved to Europe, where they chronicled their alienation from the modern era, which explains why they came to be known as the **Lost Generation**.

In the largest black neighborhood of New York City, theaters, cultural clubs, and newspapers sprang up—a development called the **Harlem Renaissance**. **W.E.B. Du Bois** opened writers' centers, and his prominence helped draw attention to Harlem's cultural movement. Among the great figures of the Harlem Renaissance were the poets **Langston Hughes** and **Countee Cullen**. Another major black cultural development was the popularization of **jazz music**. Because jazz featured improvisation and free-spiritedness, it came to be seen as emblematic of the era (which is how the decade came to be known as the **Jazz Age**). Probably the most popular and most gifted of the era's jazz musicians was trumpeter **Louis Armstrong**.

Backlash Against Modern Culture

Not all Americans were excited about the rapid transition into the modern age, and the 1920s were also a time of considerable reactionary backlash. Often this backlash took the form of groups opposing and attacking those different from themselves. Most prominently, the **Ku Klux Klan** grew to more than 5 million members and widened its targets, attacking blacks, Jews, urbanites, and anyone whose behavior deviated from the Klan's narrowly defined code of acceptable Christian behavior. Anti-immigration groups grew in strength as well, targeting the growing number of southern and eastern European immigrants. Accusations that America's newcomers were dangerous subversives intensified when two Italian immigrant anarchists, **Sacco and Vanzetti**, were arrested on charges of murder. (Their trial immediately became a cause célèbre for the political left, as the evidence against them was inconclusive. Nonetheless, they were convicted and executed.) Throughout the 1920s, the federal government tightened restrictions and imposed quotas specifically aimed at preventing Italian and Russian immigration to the United States.

Another famous trial also illustrated the societal tensions of the decade. In 1925 Tennessee passed a law forbidding teachers to teach the theory of evolution. **John Thomas Scopes** broke that law, and his trial (dubbed the **Scopes monkey trial**) drew national attention, due in part to the two prominent attorneys arguing the case, **Clarence Darrow** and **William Jennings Bryan**. The case also captivated the nation because, for many, it encapsulated the debate over whether to stick with tradition or abandon it for progress' sake.

Nineteenth-century morals played a part in the institution of **Prohibition**, which banned the manufacture, sale, or transport of alcoholic beverages. The Prohibition movement had its roots in the reform campaigns of the 1830s and remained a mainstay of women's political agendas until, on the eve of women's enfranchisement (1917), the **Eighteenth Amendment** outlawed drinking. Many people soon came to resent the government's intrusion in what they considered a private matter. Prohibition was further weakened by the effectiveness of organized crime in producing and selling liquor, especially in the cities. Open warfare between competing gangs and between criminals and law enforcement earned this period the title of the "**gangster era**," which inspired many movies and television series such as *The Untouchables*. Prohibition was repealed in 1933.

HERBERT HOOVER AND THE BEGINNING OF THE GREAT DEPRESSION

In 1928 the Republicans nominated **Herbert Hoover**. Like Coolidge, Hoover was able to parlay a strong economy into an easy victory. During his campaign, Hoover predicted that the day would soon come when no American would live in poverty. He turned out to be very wrong.

In October 1929, the bottom fell out of the stock market. Prices dropped, and no matter how far they dropped, nobody wanted to buy. Hoover and his advisers underestimated the damage that the stock market crash would eventually cause. Convinced that the economy was sound, Hoover reassured the public that only stock traders would be hurt because of their irresponsible speculation. (Traders had been allowed to buy **on margin**, which allowed them to borrow against future profits that may or may not materialize. Margin buying is a destabilizing practice that was made illegal soon after the crash.) Unfortunately, among those speculators were huge banks and corporations, who suddenly found themselves on the verge of bankruptcy and unable to pay employees or guarantee bank deposits.

Other factors contributed to plunging the nation into a deep depression. Farmers and manufacturers had been overproducing for years, creating large inventories. This led factories to lay off workers and made the farmers' crops worth much less on the market. Furthermore, production of new consumer goods was outstripping the public's ability to buy them. Business failures resulted. Finally, government laxity in regulating large businesses had led to the concentration of wealth and power in the hands of a very few businessmen. When their businesses failed, many people were thrown out of work.

The Depression had a calamitous effect on tens of millions of Americans. People lost their jobs as their employers went bankrupt or, to avoid bankruptcy, laid off the majority of workers. People lost their life savings as thousands of banks failed, and many lost their homes when they could not keep up with mortgage payments. The homeless built shantytowns, sarcastically called "**Hoovervilles**." In rural areas, farmers struggled to survive as produce prices dropped more than 50 percent. Furthermore, a prolonged drought afflicted the Midwest, turning the region into a giant **Dust Bowl**. The situation encouraged **agrarian unrest**; farmers fought evictions and foreclosures by attacking those who tried to enforce them. Farmers also conspired to keep prices at farm auctions low, then returned the auctioned property to its original owner. In addition, they formed the **Farmers' Holiday Association**, which organized demonstrations and threatened a nation wide walk out by farmers in order to raise prices.

Hoover at first opposed any federal relief efforts, but as the Depression worsened, he initiated a few farm assistance programs and campaigned for federal works projects (such as the Hoover Dam and the Grand Coulee Dam) that would create jobs. He hoped that raising tariffs would help American business, but the **Hawley-Smoot Tariff** actually worsened the economy because it resulted in a lower export rate. Hoover's greatest mistake came in 1932 when Congress considered early payment of benefits to World War I veterans. Tens of thousands of impoverished veterans and their families, calling themselves the **Bonus Expeditionary Force**, came to Washington to lobby for the bill. When the bill was narrowly defeated, many refused to leave. They squatted in empty government offices or built shanties and stayed through the summer. In July, Hoover ordered the Army to expel them, which they did with great force. Employing the cavalry and attacking with tear gas, Army forces drove the veterans from D.C., then burned their makeshift homes. One hundred people died during the attack, including two babies who suffocated from exposure to tear gas.

News of the Army attack on the BEF killed any chance Hoover had for reelection, but by the summer of 1932, he had already secured the Republican nomination. He ran a campaign stressing his traditional conservative values. (His main concession was to accept the repeal of Prohibition; Hoover had opposed repeal during his first term.) His opponent, New York governor **Franklin D. Roosevelt**, argued for a more interventionist government. Roosevelt also promised relief payments to the unemployed, which Hoover had opposed throughout his term. Roosevelt won the election easily.

THE NEW DEAL AND WORLD WAR II (1934–1945)

In his inaugural address Roosevelt declared war on the Depression, and he asked the country to grant him the same broad powers that presidents exercise during wars against foreign nations. He also tried to rally the public's confidence. In the most famous line of the speech, Roosevelt declared, "The only thing we have to fear is fear itself—nameless, unreasoning, unjustified fear." A powerful presidency and the people's confidence in Roosevelt both played a large part in the implementation of his sweeping reforms called the **New Deal**.

THE FIRST NEW DEAL

Early in 1933 Roosevelt summoned an emergency session of Congress to work out the details of his recovery plan. The period that followed is often called the **First Hundred Days** because (1) that's how long it lasted, and (2) it was during this time that the government implemented most of the major programs associated with the **First New Deal**. (The **Second New Deal** began two years later.)

Roosevelt first sought to reestablish America's confidence in its banking system. The **Emergency Banking Relief Bill** put poorly managed banks under the control of the Treasury Department and granted government licenses (which functioned as seals of approval) to those that were solvent. In the first of many **fireside chats** broadcast over the radio, Roosevelt reassured the public that the banks were once again secure. More than 60 million Americans listened, and they obviously took Roosevelt at his word. The following week, millions redeposited their savings (which they had withdrawn during the bank failures of the previous years). American banks, once on the verge of ruin, were again healthy and could begin to contribute to the economic recovery. Later during the first hundred days, the government passed the **Banking Act of 1933**, which created the Federal Deposit Insurance Corporation (**FDIC**) to guarantee bank deposits. Roosevelt also instituted a number of intentionally inflationary measures in order to artificially raise prices (to get more money flowing into the economy).

Roosevelt then set out to provide relief for the rural poor. At the time, farmers were overproducing. They hoped that by growing more they could make up for falling produce prices, but their efforts were futile; the more they produced, the farther prices fell. Roosevelt's solution was the **Agricultural**

Adjustment Act, referred to as the **AAA**. (So many of Roosevelt's new agencies were referred to by their acronyms that the entire group became known as the "**alphabet agencies**.") The AAA provided payments to farmers in return for their agreement to cut production by up to one-half; the money to cover this program came from increased taxes on meat packers, millers, and other food processors. A month later, Congress passed the **Farm Credit Act**, which provided loans to those farmers in danger of foreclosure.

Several other New Deal programs established government control over industry. The **National Industrial Recovery Act** (**NIRA**) consolidated businesses and coordinated their activities with the aim of eliminating overproduction and, by so doing, stabilizing prices. The NIRA also established the **Public Works Administration** (**PWA**), which set aside $3 billion to create jobs building roads, sewers, public housing units, and other civic necessities. At the same time, the **Civilian Conservation Corps** (**CCC**) provided grants to the states to manage their own PWA-like projects. In one of the New Deal's most daring moves, the government took over the **Tennessee Valley Authority** (**TVA**). Under government control, the TVA (which provided energy to the Tennessee Valley region) expanded its operations greatly, which led to the economic recovery of the region.

In June 1933 Congress adjourned, ending the first one hundred days. Most of the programs that made up the First New Deal were in place, although others, such as the creation of both the **National Labor Relations Board** (to mediate labor disputes) and the **Securities Exchange Commission** (to regulate the stock market) were not implemented until 1934. The First New Deal was an immediate success, both politically and economically; the unemployment rate lowered and wages rose. In the midterm elections of 1934, the Democrats increased their majorities in both houses.

THE SECOND NEW DEAL

Not everyone, however, was enamored of the New Deal. In fact, both ends of the political spectrum criticized Roosevelt. **Conservatives** opposed the higher tax rates that the New Deal brought; they also disliked the increase in government power over business, and they complained that relief programs removed the incentive for the poor to lift themselves out of poverty. Additionally, the government had to borrow to finance all of its programs, and its **deficit spending** was also anathema to conservatives. **Leftists** complained that the AAA policy of paying farmers *not* to grow was immoral, given that many Americans were still too poor to feed themselves. They also felt that government policy toward businesses was too favorable; they wanted more punitive measures as many on the left blamed corporate greed for the Depression. The despair caused by the Depression provided fodder for a more radical left, and the **Socialists** (and, to a lesser extent, the **Communist Party of America**) were gaining popularity by calling for the nationalization (that is, a takeover by the government) of businesses.

Then, in 1935, the Supreme Court started to dismantle some of the programs of the First New Deal. First, it declared the NIRA illegal; not long after, it invalidated the AAA as well. Roosevelt responded with a package of legislation called the **Second New Deal**. First, he established the Emergency Relief Appropriation Act, which created the **Works Progress Administration** (**WPA**; the name was later changed to the Works Project Administration). The WPA generated more than 8 million jobs, all paid for by the government. Along with public works projects such as construction, the WPA also employed writers, photographers, and other artists to create travel guides and to record local and personal histories. One such project hired writers to track down former slaves and record their recollections, which were later published in the book *Bullwhip Days: The Slaves Remember*.

The summer of 1935 is often called Roosevelt's **Second Hundred Days** because the amount and importance of legislation passed then is comparable to that of the First Hundred Days. During this period, Congress passed legislation that broadened the powers of the **NLRB**, democratized unions, and punished businesses with anti-union policies. During this time, Congress also created the **Social Security Administration** to provide retirement benefits for many workers including the disabled and families whose main bread winner had died. Furthermore, the government increased taxes on wealthy individuals and top-end business profits. The cumulative effect of these programs led to the creation of a **new Democratic coalition**, made up of union members, urbanites, the underclass, and blacks (who had previously voted Republican, out of loyalty to the party of Lincoln). This new democratic coalition swept Roosevelt back into office with a landslide victory in 1936.

ROOSEVELT'S TROUBLED SECOND TERM

Several problems marred Franklin Roosevelt's second term. The first major failure of his presidency came as the term began. Angry that the Supreme Court had overturned much of the First New Deal and worried that the same fate awaited the Second New Deal, Roosevelt drafted a **Judicial Reorganization** bill. The bill proposed that Roosevelt be allowed to name a new federal judge for every sitting judge who had reached the age of 70 and had not retired; if passed, it would have allowed Roosevelt to add six new Supreme Court justices and more than 40 other federal judges. A not-so-subtle effort at **packing the courts** with judges more sympathetic to Roosevelt's policies, the bill was soundly defeated in the Democratic Congress, and Roosevelt came under intense criticism for trying to seize too much power. Ultimately the court situation worked itself out to Roosevelt's benefit. A number of justices retired not long after the incident, and Roosevelt was able to replace them with more liberal judges.

In 1937 the economy went into a **recession** (a period of continually decreasing output). The cause was twofold: Roosevelt, satisfied that the New Deal was doing its job, cut back government programs in an effort to balance the budget. At the same time, the Federal Reserve Board tightened the credit supply in an effort to slow inflation. Both actions took money out of circulation, resulting in a slower economy. The recession lasted for almost three years and caused a substantial increase in the unemployment rate.

To top off Roosevelt's second term, by 1938 it was becoming evident that Europe might soon be at war again. This situation forced Roosevelt to withdraw some money from New Deal programs in order to fund a military buildup. The administration succeeded in passing a second **AAA** that met the standards set by the Supreme Court's rejection of the first AAA; it also secured the Fair Labor Standards Act, which set a minimum wage and established the forty-hour workweek for a number of professions. Not long after, however, the New Deal came to an end.

Did the New Deal work? Historians like to debate this question. Those who argue yes point to the many people who escaped life-threatening poverty because of government assistance, and especially to the immediate relief provided by the First New Deal. They also point to the many reforms of banking, finance, and management/union relations. In these areas the New Deal remade America in ways that are still recognizable today. Finally, proponents of the New Deal argue that Roosevelt should be praised for taking bold chances in a conservative political climate; he risked new initiatives when it was clear that old solutions were failing.

On the other hand, those who assert that the New Deal failed have some compelling statistics to back them. By 1939 the unemployment rate was up near 20 percent, and America did not come close to a decent employment rate again until the war (which invigorated such industries as armaments, airplanes, etc.) revived the economy. Furthermore, today's social welfare system stems from the New Deal; those who feel that the current American system has failed can point to Roosevelt as the man who started it all. Lastly, the New Deal did not benefit all equally. Minorities, in particular, reaped fewer (and sometimes no) benefits. The AAA actually hurt blacks and tenant farmers by putting them out of work; some of the public works projects underhired blacks, and almost all were segregated.

FOREIGN POLICY LEADING UP TO WORLD WAR II

In the decade that followed World War I, American foreign policy objectives aimed primarily at promoting and maintaining peace. The **Washington Conference** (1921-22) gathered eight of the world's great powers; the resulting treaty set limits on stockpiling armaments and reaffirmed the Open Door policy toward China. In 1928 62 nations signed the **Kellogg-Briand Pact**, which condemned warfare. Although it contained no enforcement clauses, the Kellogg-Briand Pact was widely considered a "good first step" toward a postwar age.

In Latin America, the U.S. tried in the 1920s to back away from its previous interventionist policy and replace it with the **Good Neighbor policy**. The name, however, is misleading; the United States continued to actively promote its interests in Latin America, often to the detriment of those who lived there. The main change in policy was that the American government proceeded by less obvious means. The U.S. mainly achieved its foreign policy objectives through economic coercion and support of pro-American leaders (some of whom were corrupt and brutal). The United States also figured out how to maintain a strong but less threatening military presence in the area, both by paying for the privilege of maintaining military bases in the countries and by arranging to train the nations' National Guard units.

In Asia, the United States had less influence. Consequently, when Japan invaded Manchuria in 1931 (and in so doing violated the Kellogg-Briand pact, which Japan had signed), the American government could do little. When Japan went to war against China in 1937, the United States sold arms to the Chinese and called for an embargo on arms sales to Japan. However, fearful of provoking a war with Japan, the government did not order an embargo on commercial shipments to Japan from the United States.

Throughout the Republican administrations of the 1920s, government set tariffs high; this policy is called **protectionism**. Early in Franklin Roosevelt's presidency, the government devised a method of using economic leverage as a foreign policy tool. The **Reciprocal Trade Agreements Act** allowed the president to reduce tariffs if he felt doing so would achieve foreign policy goals. Countries granted **most-favored-nation (MFN) trade status** were eligible for the lowest tariff rate set by the United States, if they played their cards right. MFN trade status remains a foreign policy tool today.

In all other ways, however, the United States receded from active participation in overseas politics, particularly in Europe. This desire to remain apart from the developing conflict in Europe during the 1930s was called **isolationism**. Isolationist thought sprang in part from America's perception that western Europe expected the United States to solve the "Hitler problem." Disenchantment with the results of the First World War also fed isolationism, a stance amplified by the findings of the **Nye Commission**. Led by Senator Gerald Nye, the commission's report in 1936 revealed unwholesome activities by American arms manufacturers; many had lobbied intensely for entry into World War I, others had bribed foreign officials, and still others were currently supplying Fascist governments with weapons. Roosevelt pursued isolationist goals through the **neutrality acts**. The first neutrality act (1935) prohibited the sale of arms to either belligerent in a war. (Roosevelt sidestepped this act in the 1937 sale of arms to China by simply refusing to acknowledge that China and Japan were at war.) The second neutrality act banned loans to belligerents.

All the while, Roosevelt poured money into the military—just in case. As it became more apparent that Europe was headed for war, Roosevelt lobbied for a repeal of the arms embargo stated in the first neutrality act so that America could help arm the Allies (primarily England, France, and, later, Russia). When war broke out, Congress relented with a third neutrality act, which allowed arms sales. However, it required the Allies to (1) pay cash for their weapons, and (2) come to the United States to pick up their purchases and carry them away on their own ships. From the outset of the war until America's entry in 1941, Roosevelt angled the country toward participation, particularly when, after Poland fell to German troops, other countries followed in rapid succession. In 1940, Hitler invaded France, and a German takeover of both France and England appeared a real possibility. The chance that America might soon enter the war convinced Roosevelt to run for an unprecedented third term. Again, he won convincingly.

Within the limits allowed by the neutrality acts, Roosevelt worked to assist the Allies. He found creative ways to supply them with extra weapons and ships; he appointed pro-Ally Republicans to head the Department of War and the navy; and he instituted the nation's first peacetime military draft. In 1941 Roosevelt forced the **Lend-Lease Act** through Congress, which permitted the United States to "lend" armaments to England, which no longer had money to buy the tools of war. Roosevelt sent American ships into the war zone to protect Lend-Lease shipments, an act which could easily have provoked a German attack. Later in the year, Roosevelt and British Prime Minister Winston Churchill met at the **Atlantic Charter Conference**. The Atlantic Charter declared the Allies' war aims, which included disarmament, self-determination, freedom of the seas, and guarantees of each nation's security.

Given all this activity in the European theater, it seems odd that America's entry to the war came not in Europe, but in the Asia. Japan entered into an alliance (called the **Tripartite Pact**) with Italy and Germany in 1940. Immediately, Roosevelt imposed a fuel embargo on Japan, in hopes of weakening its air force; later, when Japan invaded the Philippines, an American ally, Roosevelt froze Japanese assets in the United States. By the autumn of 1941, the United States knew that Japan was planning an attack but did not know the location. Secretary of War Henry Stimson encouraged Roosevelt to wait for the Japanese attack in order to guarantee popular support for the war at home. He did not have to wait long. The Japanese attacked **Pearl Harbor**, Hawaii, on December 7, and U.S. participation in the war had begun.

WORLD WAR II

Complicated military strategy and the outcome of key battles played a big part in World War II. Fortunately, you do not have to know much about them for the AP; nor do you need to know about the many truly unspeakable horrors the Nazis perpetrated on Europe's Jews, gypsies, homosexuals, and dissidents. You do have to know that the Allies fought the Germans primarily in Russia and in the Mediterranean until early 1944 when Allied forces invaded occupied France (on **D-Day**). Russia paid a huge price in human and material loss for this strategy and after the war sought to recoup its losses by occupying Eastern Europe. In the Pacific, both sides incurred huge numbers of casualties. The Allies eventually won a war of attrition against the Germans, and the Americans accelerated victory in the East by dropping two atomic bombs on Japan.

As it had during World War I and during the New Deal, the government acquired more power than it previously had. The War Production Board allowed government to oversee the mobilization of industry toward the war effort; in return, businesses were guaranteed generous profits. **Rationing** of almost all consumer goods was imposed. The government also sponsored scientific research directed at improving weaponry. **Radar** was developed during this period, as was, of course, the atomic bomb. The government also exerted greater control over labor. The **Labor Disputes Act** of 1943 (passed in reaction to a disconcerting number of strikes in essential industries) allowed government takeover of businesses deemed necessary to national security and gave the government authority to settle labor disputes. **Hollywood** was enlisted to create numerous propaganda films, both to encourage support on the home front and to boost morale of the troops overseas. Not surprisingly, the size of the government more than tripled during the war.

Again, as during World War I, the government restricted civil liberties. Probably the most tragic instance was the **internment of Japanese Americans** from 1942 to the end of the war. Fearful that the

Japanese might serve as enemy agents within U.S. borders, the government imprisoned more than 110,000 Japanese Americans, over two-thirds of whom had been born in the United States. None of those interned was ever charged with a crime; imprisonment was based entirely on ethnic background. The government placed these Japanese Americans in desolate prison camps far from the West Coast, where they feared a Japanese invasion would take place. Most lost their homes and possessions as a result of the internment.

THE END OF THE WAR

As the war neared its end in Europe, the apparent victors—the Allies (hooray!)—had to discuss the fate of postwar Europe. In early 1945 the Allied leaders met at **Yalta** to redraw the world map. By this time, the Soviet army occupied parts of Eastern Europe; a result of the campaign to drive the German army out of the U.S.S.R. The Allies agreed on a number of issues concerning borders and postwar alliances. They also agreed that once the war in Europe ended, the U.S.S.R. would soon after declare war on Japan. Finally, the Allies agreed to help create the **United Nations** to mediate future international disputes. The Allies met again later in the year at **Potsdam** to decide how to implement the agreements of Yalta. This time, **Harry S Truman** represented the United States, as Roosevelt had died in the interim. Things did not go as well at Yalta; with the war's end closer and the Nazis no longer a threat, the differences between the United States and the Soviet Union were growing more blatant.

Some argue that American-Soviet animosity prompted Truman's decision to use the **atomic bomb** against the Japanese. (By this argument, America feared Soviet entry into the Asian war where they might then attempt to expand their influence, as they were doing in Eastern Europe. Along the same line of reasoning, one could assert that the United States wanted to put on a massive display of power to intimidate the Soviets.) However, the manner in which the war in the Pacific had been fought to that point also supported Truman's decision. The Japanese had fought tenaciously and remained powerful despite the long war; casualty estimates of an American invasion of Japan ran upward of 500,000. Some military leaders estimated that such an invasion would not subdue Japan for years. In August, the United States dropped two atomic bombs, first on **Hiroshima**, and then, three days later, on **Nagasaki**. The Japanese surrendered soon after.

TRUMAN AND THE BEGINNING OF THE COLD WAR (1945–1952)

The end of the World War II raised two major questions: The first issue concerned the survival of the combatants; with the exception of the United States, the nations involved in World War II had all seen fighting within their borders, and the destruction had been immense. The second issue involved the shape of the new world and what new political alliances would be formed. This question would become the major source of contention between the world's two leading political-economic systems, capitalism and communism.

The stakes in this power struggle, called the **Cold War** (because there was no actual combat as there is in a "hot war") were high. To begin with, the American economy was growing more dependent on exports; American industry also needed to import metals, a process requiring (1) open trade, and (2) friendly relations with those nations that provided those metals. In addition, with many postwar economies in shambles, competition for the few reasonably healthy economies grew more fierce. Finally, those countries that were strongest before the war—Germany, Japan, and Great Britain—had either been defeated or seen their influence abroad greatly reduced. The United States and the Soviet Union now constituted the two new world powers. Although allies during the Second World War, the war's end bared the countries' many ideological differences, and they soon became enemies.

TRUMAN AND FOREIGN POLICY

The differences between Soviet and American goals became apparent immediately after the war, when the Soviets refused to recognize Poland's conservative government-in-exile. (The Polish government had moved to England to escape the Nazis; this government was backed by the U.S.) A Communist government took over Poland. Within two years, pro-Soviet Communist coups had also taken place in Hungary and Czechoslovakia. The propaganda in the U.S. and U.S.S.R. during this period reached a fever pitch. In each country, the other was portrayed as trying to take over the world for its own sinister purposes.

Then, in 1947, Communist insurgents threatened to take over both Greece and Turkey, but Truman was intent on preventing it. In a speech before Congress in which he asked for almost $500 million in aid to the two countries, Truman asserted, "I believe it must be the policy of the United States to support free peoples who are resisting attempted subjugation by armed minorities or outside pressures." This policy, called the **Truman Doctrine**, became the cornerstone of a larger policy toward the U.S.S.R. called **containment**. Containment provided that while the United States would not instigate a war with the Soviet Union, it would come to the defense of countries in danger of Soviet takeover. The policy aimed to check further Soviet expansion and encourage the Soviets to abandon its aggressive strategies.

Meanwhile, the United States used a tried-and-true method to shore up its alliances—it gave away money. The **Marshall Plan** (named for Secretary of State George Marshall) sent more than $12 billion to Europe to help rebuild its cities and economy. In return for that money, of course, countries were expected to become American allies. Although the Marshall Plan was offered to Eastern Europe and the Soviet Union, no countries in the Soviet sphere participated in the program. The United States also formed a mutual defense alliance with Western Europe called the **North Atlantic Treaty Organization (NATO)** in 1949. Truman did not have an easy time convincing Congress that NATO was necessary; remember, from the time of Washington's Farewell Address, American sentiment has strongly favored avoiding all foreign entanglements.

The crisis in **Berlin** the previous year, however, helped convince Congress to support NATO. The crisis represented a culmination of events after World War II. In 1945 Germany had been divided into four sectors, with England, France, the United States, and the U.S.S.R. each controlling one. Berlin, though deep in Soviet territory, had been similarly divided. Upon learning that the three western Allies planned to merge their sectors into one country and to bring that country into the western economy, the Soviets responded by imposing a **blockade** on Berlin. Truman refused to surrender the city, however, and ordered airlifts to keep that portion under western control supplied with food and fuel. The blockade continued for close to a year, by which point the blockade became such a political liability that the Soviets gave it up. Afterward, Germany was split into West Germany and East Germany. (Reunification came in 1990.)

Not long after the U.S. joined NATO, the Soviets detonated their first atomic bomb, further convincing many of NATO's necessity. Fear of Soviet invasion or subterfuge also led to the creation of the **National Security Council** (a group of foreign affairs advisers who work for the president) and the **Central Intelligence Agency** (the United States' spy network).

As if Truman didn't have enough headaches in Europe, he also had to deal with Asia. Two issues dominated U.S. policy in the region: the **reconstruction of Japan** and the **Chinese Revolution**. After the war, the United States occupied Japan, and its colonial possessions were divided up. The U.S.

took control of the Pacific islands and the southern half of Korea, while the U.S.S.R. took control of the northern half of the country. Under the command of General Douglas MacArthur, Japan renounced its emperor, wrote a democratic constitution, demilitarized, and started a remarkable economic revival. The U.S. was not as successful in China, where it chose to side with Chiang Kai-shek's Nationalist government against **Mao Zedong**'s Communist insurgents. Despite massive American military aid, the Communists overthrew the Nationalists, and their government was exiled to Taiwan. For decades the United States refused to recognize the legitimacy of Mao's regime, creating another international "hot spot" for Americans. To further rebuff communism, the U.S. sought alliances with all anti-Communist countries in the region, one of which was Vietnam.

THE RED SCARE

All this conflict with Communists resurrected anti-Communist paranoia (the **Red Scare**) at home. In 1947 Truman ordered investigations of 3 million federal employees in a search for "security risks." Those found to have a potential Achilles' heel—either previous association with "known Communists" or a "moral" weakness such as alcoholism or homosexuality (which, the government reasoned, made them easy targets for blackmail)—were dismissed without a hearing. In 1949 former State Department official **Alger Hiss** was found guilty of consorting with a Communist spy. When a nuclear scientist was arrested for passing information about the atomic bomb to the Soviet Union, Americans realized just what was at stake. They began to passionately fear the "enemy within."

It was this atmosphere that allowed a demagogic senator named **Joseph McCarthy** to rise from near anonymity to national fame. In 1950 McCarthy claimed to have a list of more than 200 known Communists working for the State Department. He subsequently changed that number several times, which should have clued people in to the fact that he was lying. Unchallenged, McCarthy went on to lead a campaign of innuendo that ruined the lives of thousands of innocent people. Without ever uncovering a single Communist, McCarthy held years of hearings with regard to subversion, not just in the government, but in education and the entertainment industry as well. Those subpoenaed were often forced to confess to previous associations with Communists and name others with similar associations. Industries created lists of those tainted by these charges, called **blacklists**, that prevented the accused from working. McCarthy's demise came in 1954, during the Eisenhower administration when he accused the Army of harboring Communists. He had finally chosen too powerful a target. The Army fought back hard, and in the televised **Army-McCarthy hearings**, McCarthy was made to look foolish. The public turned its back on him, and the era of **McCarthyism** ended.

TRUMAN'S DOMESTIC POLICY AND THE ELECTION OF 1948

The end of the war meant the end of wartime production. With fewer Jeeps, airplanes, guns, bombs, and uniforms to manufacture, American businesses started laying off employees. Returning war veterans further crowded the job market, and unemployment levels rose dramatically. At the same time, many people who had hoarded their savings during the war started to spend more liberally, causing prices to rise. In 1946, the inflation rate was nearly 20 percent. The poor and unemployed felt the effects the most. Truman offered some New Deal—style solutions to America's economic woes, but a new conservatism had taken over American politics. Most of his proposals were rejected, and the few that were implemented had little effect.

The new conservatism brought with it a new round of anti-unionism in the country. Americans were particularly upset when workers in essential industries went on strike as when the coal miners' strike (by the **United Mine Workers**, or **UMW**) cut off the energy supply to other industries, shutting down steel foundries, auto plants, and others. Layoffs in the affected industries exacerbated tensions. Americans cared little that the miners were fighting for basic rights. Truman followed the national mood, ordering a government **seizure of the mines** when a settlement could not be reached. During a later railroad strike, Truman threatened to draft into the military those strikers who held out for more than he thought they deserved. Consequently, Truman alienated labor, one of the core constituencies of the new Democratic coalition. Labor and consumers angry at skyrocketing prices formed an alliance that helped the Republicans take control of the **Eightieth Congress** in the 1946 midterm elections.

Truman also alienated many voters (particularly in the South) by pursuing a civil rights agenda that, for its time, was progressive. He convened the **President's Committee on Civil Rights** which in 1948 issued a report calling for an end to segregation and poll taxes, and for more aggressive enforcement of antilynching laws. Truman also issued an executive order forbidding racial discrimination in the hiring of federal employees. Blacks began to make other inroads. The NAACP won some initial, important law suits against segregated schools and buses; **Jackie Robinson** broke the color barrier in baseball, a very important symbolic advance; and black groups started to form coalitions with liberal white organizations, thereby gaining more political clout. These advances provoked an outbreak of flagrant racism in the South, and in 1948 segregationist Democrats abandoned the party to support Strom Thurmond for president.

With so many core Democratic constituencies—labor, consumers, Southerners—angry with the president, his defeat in 1948 seemed certain. Truman's popularity, however, received an unintentional boost from the Republican-dominated Congress. The staunchly conservative legislature passed several antilabor acts too strong even for Truman. The **Taft-Hartley Act**, passed over Truman's veto, prohibited "union only" work environments (called *closed shops*), restricted labor's right to strike, prohibited the use of union funds for political purposes, and gave the government broad power to intervene in strikes. The same Congress then rebuked Truman's efforts to pass health care reform, increase aid to schools, farmers, the elderly, and the disabled, and promote civil rights for blacks. The cumulative effect of all this acrimony made Truman look a lot better to those he had previously offended. Still, as election time neared, Truman trailed his chief opponent, Thomas Dewey. He then made one of the most brilliant political moves in American history: He recalled the Congress, whose majority members had just drafted an extremely conservative Republican platform at the party convention, and Truman challenged them to enact that platform. Congress met for two weeks and did not pass one significant piece of legislation. Truman then went out on a grueling public appearance campaign, everywhere deriding the "do-nothing" Eightieth Congress. To almost everyone's surprise, Truman won reelection, and his coattails carried a Democratic majority into Congress.

THE KOREAN WAR

The Korean War began when Communist North Korea invaded U.S.-backed South Korea. Believing the Soviet Union to have engineered the invasion, the U.S. took swift countermeasures. Originally intending only to repel the invasion, Truman decided to attempt a reunification of Korea after some early military successes. American troops attacked North Korea, provoking China, Korea's northern neighbor. (The Chinese were not too keen on the idea of hostile American troops on their border.) China ultimately entered the war, pushing American and South Korean troops back near the original border dividing North and South Korea. U.S. commander **Douglas MacArthur** recommended an all-out confrontation with China, with the objective of overthrowing the Communists and reinstating Chiang Kai-shek. Truman thought a war with the world's largest country might be imprudent and so decided against MacArthur. When MacArthur started publicly criticizing the president, Truman **fired** him. MacArthur was very popular at home, however, and his firing hurt Truman politically.

Although peace talks began soon after, the war dragged on another two years, into the Eisenhower administration. When the 1952 presidential election arrived, the Republicans took a page from the Whig playbook and chose **Dwight D. Eisenhower**, a war hero. By this point, the presidency had been held by the Democratic party for twenty years. Truman was unpopular; his bluntness is now seen as a sign of his integrity, but during his terms, it offended a lot of potential constituents. In short, America was ready for a change. Eisenhower beat Democratic challenger **Adlai Stevenson** easily.

THE EISENHOWER YEARS (1953–1960)

The Fifties are often depicted as a time of **conformity**. Across much of America, a **consensus of values** reigned. Americans believed that their country was the best in the world, that Communism was evil and had to be stopped, and that a decent job, a home in the suburbs, and access to all the modern conveniences (aka **consumerism**) did indeed constitute "the good life." While this image is based in fact, it is also an oversimplification. The fifties also proved to be an era in which the civil rights movement made its first strides and met some violent resistance; an era plagued by frequent economic recessions; and an era of spiritual unrest which manifested itself in the such emerging art forms as **beat poetry and novels** (*On the Road*, "Howl"), **teen movies** (*Blackboard Jungle*, *The Wild One*, *Rebel Without a Cause*) and **rock and roll** (Elvis Presley, Little Richard, Jerry Lee Lewis, Chuck Berry).

DOMESTIC POLITICS IN THE FIFTIES

Eisenhower arrived at the White House prepared to impose conservative values on the federal government, which had mushroomed in size under Roosevelt and Truman. He sought to balance the budget, cut federal spending, and ease government regulation of business. In these goals he was, at best, only partly successful. The military buildup required by the continuing Cold War prevented Eisenhower from making the cuts to the military budget that he would have liked. He reduced military spending by reducing troops and buying powerful weapons systems (thus shaping the **New Look Army**), but not enough to eliminate deficit spending. The popularity of remaining New Deal programs made it difficult to eliminate them; furthermore, circumstances required Eisenhower to increase the number of Social Security recipients and the size of their benefits. Under Eisenhower, the government also began developing the **Interstate Highway System**. The results of the highway system were ultimately economically beneficial; the new roads not only sped up travel, but they also promoted tourism and the development of the suburbs. The initial cost, however, was extremely high. As a result, Eisenhower managed to balance the federal budget only three times in eight years. (He was shooting for a perfect eight-for-eight.)

Some of the most important domestic issues during the Eisenhower years involved minorities. In 1953 Eisenhower sought to change federal policy toward Native Americans. His new policy, called **termination**, would liquidate reservations, end federal support to Native Americans, and subject them to state law. In devising this policy, Eisenhower did not take Native American priorities into account; in fact, he did not consult any tribes before implementing the plan. He aimed simply to reduce federal responsibilities and bolster the power of the states. Native Americans protested, convinced that termination was simply a means of stealing what little land the tribes had left. The plan failed and was ultimately stopped in the 1960s, but not before causing the depletion and impoverishment of a number of tribes.

The **civil rights movement** experienced a number of its landmark events during Eisenhower's two terms. In 1954 the Supreme Court heard the case of **Brown v. Board of Education of Topeka**, a lawsuit brought on behalf of Linda Brown (a black school-age child) by the NAACP. Future Supreme Court justice Thurgood Marshall argued the case for Brown. In its ruling, the Court overturned the "separate but equal" standard as it applied to education; "separate but equal" had been the law of the land since the Court had approved it in *Plessy v. Ferguson* (1896). In a 9-to-0 decision, the court ruled that "separate educational facilities are inherently unequal." Although a great victory for civil rights, *Brown v. Board of Education* did not immediately solve the school segregation problem. Some Southern states started to pay the tuition of white children who went to private schools in order to maintain segregation. Some states actually closed their public schools rather than integrate them. Although Eisenhower personally disapproved of segregation, he also opposed rapid change, and so did little. This inactivity encouraged further Southern resistance, and in 1957 the governor of Arkansas called in the state **National Guard** to prevent blacks from enrolling in a **Little Rock** high school. Eisenhower did nothing until one month later, when the courts ordered him to enforce the law. Arkansas, in response, closed all public high schools in the city for two years.

Another key civil rights event, the **Montgomery bus boycott**, took place in the fifties. The arrest of **Rosa Parks**, who refused to give up her seat on a bus to a white man as was required by **Jim Crow laws**, sparked the boycott. Outrage over the arrest, coupled with long-term resentment over unfair treatment, spurred blacks to impose a year-long boycott of the bus system. The boycott brought **Martin Luther King, Jr.** to national prominence. Barely twenty-seven years old at the time, King was pastor at Rosa Parks' church. Although clearly groomed for greatness—his grandfather had led the protests resulting in Atlanta's first black high school, his father was a minister and community leader, and King had already amassed impressive academic credentials (Morehead College, Crozier Theological Seminary, University of Pennsylvania and finally a Ph.D. from Boston University)—the year-long bus boycott gave him his first national podium.

King encouraged others to organize peaceful protests, a plan inspired by his studies of Henry David Thoreau and Mohandas Gandhi. In 1960 black college students in **Greensboro** tried just that approach, organizing a **sit-in** at a local Woolworth's lunch counter designated "whites only." News reports of the sit-in, and the resultant harassment the students endured, inspired a sit-in movement that spread across the nation to combat segregation.

AMERICA V. THE COMMUNISTS

There are a number of terms associated with the Cold War policy of Eisenhower and Secretary of State **John Foster Dulles** that you need to know. The administration continued to follow the policy of containment, but called it **liberation** to make it sound more intimidating. It carried the threat that the United States would eventually free Eastern Europe from Soviet control. Dulles coined the phrase **"massive retaliation"** to describe the nuclear attack that the U.S. would launch if the Soviets tried anything too daring. **Deterrence** described how Soviet fear of massive retaliation would prevent their challenging the U.S. Dulles allowed confrontations with the Soviet Union to escalate toward war, an approach called **brinksmanship**. Finally, the Eisenhower administration argued that the spread of Communism had to be checked quickly—once Communists took over one country, the others surrounding it would fall quickly like dominoes; hence, the **domino theory**.

Cold War tensions remained high throughout the decade. Eisenhower had hoped that the death of **Joseph Stalin** in 1953 might improve American-Soviet relations. Initially, the new Russian leader **Nikita Khrushchev** offered hope. Khrushchev denounced Stalin's totalitarianism and called for "peaceful coexistence" among nations with different economic philosophies. Some Soviet client states took Khrushchev's pronouncements as a sign of weakness; rebellions occurred in Poland and Hungary. When the Soviets crushed the uprisings, U.S.-Soviet relations returned to where they were during the Stalin era. Soviet advances in nuclear arms development (the U.S.S.R. exploded its first hydrogen bomb a year after the U.S. blew up its first H-bomb) and space flight (the U.S.S.R. launched the first satellite, motivating the U.S. to quickly create and fund the **National Aeronautic and Space Agency**, or **NASA**) further heightened anxieties.

Meanwhile, the U.S. narrowly averted war with the *other* Communists, the Chinese. American-allied Taiwan occupied two islands close to mainland China, **Quemoy** and **Matsu**. The Taiwanese used the islands as bases for commando raids on the Communists, which eventually irritated the Chinese enough that they bombed the two islands. In a classic example of brinksmanship, Eisenhower declared that the United States would defend the islands and strongly hinted that he was considering a nuclear attack on China. Tensions remained high for years, and Eisenhower's stance forced him to station American troops on the islands. During the 1960 presidential election, Kennedy used the incident as a campaign issue, arguing that the two small islands were not worth the cost of defending them.

THIRD WORLD POLITICS

World War II resulted in the breakup of Europe's huge overseas empires. In the decades that followed the war's end, numerous countries in Africa, Asia, and South America broke free of European domination. These countries allied themselves with neither of the two major powers; for this reason they were deemed the **Third World**. Both America and the Soviets sought to bring Third World countries into their spheres of influence as these nations represented potential markets as well as sources of raw materials. The two superpowers particularly prized strategically located Third World countries if they were willing to host military bases.

Neither superpower, it turned out, was at first able to make major inroads in the Third World. **Nationalism** swept through most Third World nations, recently liberated from a major world power. Enjoying their new found freedom, these countries were reluctant to foster a long-term alliance with a large, powerful nation. Furthermore, most Third World countries regarded both powers with suspicion. America's wealth fostered both distrust and resentment, prompting questions about U.S. motives. America's racist legacy also hurt it in the Third World, where most residents were nonwhite. However, most Third World nations also saw how the Soviets dominated Eastern Europe, and so had little interest in close relations with them. These new nations were not anxious to fall under the control of either superpower.

However, the United States tried to expand its influence in the Third World in other ways. For example, in Egypt the U.S. tried offering foreign aid, hoping to gain an ally by building the much-needed **Aswan Dam**. Egypt's nationalist leader Gamal Nasser suspected the western powers of subterfuge; furthermore, he detested Israel, a western ally. Eventually, he turned to the Soviet Union for that aid. The American government also used **CIA covert operations** to provide a more forceful method of increasing its influence abroad. In various countries, the CIA coerced newspapers to report "disinformation" and slant the news in a way favorable to the United States, bribed local politicians, and tried by other means to influence local business and politics. The CIA even helped overthrow the governments of Iran and Guatemala in order to replace anti-American governments with pro-American governments. It also tried, unsuccessfully, to assassinate Cuban Communist leader **Fidel Castro**.

THE 1960 PRESIDENTIAL ELECTION

In 1960 Eisenhower's vice-president, **Richard Nixon**, received the Republican nomination. The Democrats nominated Massachusetts senator **John F. Kennedy**. Similar in many ways, particularly in foreign policy, both candidates campaigned against the "Communist menace" as well as against each other. Aided by his youthful good looks, Kennedy trounced an awkward Nixon in their first televised debate. Kennedy's choice of Texan **Lyndon Johnson** as a running mate helped shore up the Southern vote for the Northern (and therefore, in the South, suspect) candidate. Nixon, meanwhile was hurt by his vice-presidency, where he had often served the role of Eisenhower's "attack dog." The fact that Eisenhower did not wholeheartedly endorse Nixon also marred his campaign. Still, it turned out to be one of the closest elections in history, and some believe that voter fraud turned a few states Kennedy's way, without which Nixon would have won.

In his final days in office, Eisenhower warned the nation to beware of a new coalition that had grown up around the Cold War which he called the **"military-industrial complex."** The combination of military might and the highly profitable arms industries, he cautioned, created a powerful alliance whose interests did not correspond to those of the general public. In retrospect, many would later argue that in his final statement, Eisenhower had identified those who would later be responsible for the escalation of the **Vietnam War**. (See next chapter.)

THE SIXTIES AND BEYOND (1961–THE NEAR PRESENT)

At the outset, the sixties seemed the start of a new, hope-filled era. Many felt that Kennedy, his family, and his administration were ushering in an age of "Camelot," a revival of the glory days of heraldry and King Arthur's roundtable. As Arthur had had his famous knights, Kennedy too surrounded himself with an entourage of young, ambitious intellectuals who served as his advisers. The press dubbed these men and one woman "the best and the brightest" America had to offer. Kennedy's youth, good looks, and wit earned him the adoration of millions. Even the name of his domestic program, the **New Frontier**, connoted hope. It promised that the fight to conquer poverty, racism, and other contemporary domestic woes would be as rewarding as the efforts of the pioneers who settled the West.

The decade did not end as it had begun. By 1969 America was bitterly divided. Many progressives regarded the government with suspicion and contempt, while many conservatives saw all dissidents as godless anarchists and subversives. Although other issues were important, much of the conflict centered around two issues: the Vietnam war, and blacks' struggle to gain civil rights. As you read through this summary of the decade, pay particular attention to the impact of both issues on domestic harmony.

KENNEDY AND FOREIGN POLICY

Like Truman and Eisenhower, Kennedy perceived the Soviet Union as the major threat to the security of America and its allies. All the major foreign policy issues and events of his administration related primarily to these **Cold War** concerns.

Two major events during Kennedy's first year in office heightened American-Soviet tensions. The first involved **Cuba**, where a U.S.-friendly dictatorship had been overthrown by Communist insurgents led by **Fidel Castro**. When Castro took control of the country in 1959, American businesses owned more than 3 million acres of prime Cuban farmland and also controlled the country's electricity and telephone service. Because so many Cubans lived in poverty, Cuban resentment of American wealth was strong, so little popular resistance occurred when Castro seized and nationalized some American property. The United States, however, was not pleased. When Castro signed a trade treaty with the Soviet Union later that year, Eisenhower took punitive steps, imposing a partial trade embargo on Cuba. In the final days of his presidency, Eisenhower broke diplomatic relations with Cuba, and Cuba turned to the Soviet Union for financial and military aid.

Taking office in 1961, President Kennedy inherited the Cuban issue. Looking to solve the dilemma, the CIA presented the ill-fated plan for the **Bay of Pigs invasion** to the new president. The plan involved sending Cuban exiles, whom the CIA had been training since Castro's takeover, to invade Cuba. According to the strategy, the army of exiles would win a few battles and then the Cuban people would rise up in support, overthrow Castro, and replace his government with one more acceptable to the United States. Kennedy approved the plan, and the U.S. launched the invasion in April 1961. The invasion failed, the Cuban people did not rise up in support, and within two days Kennedy had a full-fledged disaster on his hands. Not only had he failed to achieve his goal, but he had also antagonized the Soviets and their allies in the process. His failure also diminished America's stature with *its* allies.

Later in the year, Kennedy dealt with a second foreign policy issue when the Soviets took aggressive anti-West action by erecting a wall to divide East and West Berlin. The **Berlin Wall**, built to prevent East Germans from leaving the country, had even greater symbolic significance to the democratic West. It came to represent the repressive nature of Communism and was also a physical reminder of the impenetrable divide between the two sides of the Cold War. In a show of solidarity with the West Germans, Kennedy went to the Berlin Wall in 1963 and made a famous speech, the most famous line of which contains an also-famous grammatical error. (Instead of declaring *"Ich bin Berliner,"* which translates to "I am a Berlin native (or Berliner)," he said, *"Ich bin ein Berliner,"* which translates to "I am a popular pastry, which is called a Berliner.") As the rhetorical war between the antagonists increased, so too did fears of a military confrontation somewhere in the indefinite future.

Then, in 1962 the United States and the Soviet Union came the closest they had yet to a military (and perhaps nuclear) confrontation. The focus of the conflict was once again Cuba. In October, American spy planes detected missile sites in Cuba. Kennedy immediately decided that those missiles had to be removed at any cost; he further decided on a policy of brinksmanship to confront the **Cuban missile crisis**. He imposed a naval quarantine on Cuba to prevent any further weapons shipments from reaching the island, and then went on national television and demanded that the Soviets withdraw their missiles. By refusing to negotiate secretly, Kennedy backed the Soviets into a corner; if they removed the missiles, their international stature would be diminished. Therefore, in return, the Soviets demanded that the United States promise never again to invade Cuba and that the U.S. remove its missiles from Turkey (which is as close to the U.S.S.R. as Cuba is to the U.S.). When Kennedy rejected the second condition, he gambled that the Soviets would not attack in response. Fortunately, behind-the-scenes negotiations defused the crisis, and the Soviets agreed to accept America's promise not to invade Cuba as a pretext for withdrawing the missiles. In return, the U.S. secretly agreed to remove its missiles from Turkey.

Anti-Communism even motivated such ostensibly philanthropic programs abroad as the **Peace Corps**. The Peace Corps' mission was to provide teachers and specialists in agriculture, health care, transportation, and communications to the Third World, in the hopes of starting these fledgling communities down the road to American-style progress. The government called this process "**nation building**." The Peace Corps had many successes, although the conflict between its humanitarian goals and the government's foreign policy goals often brought about failures as well. Furthermore, many countries did not want American-style progress and resented having it forced upon them.

The greatest theater for American Cold War policy during this era, however, was **Vietnam**. We'll discuss the history of American involvement in Vietnam up through the Johnson administration on page 143.

KENNEDY AND DOMESTIC POLICY

Kennedy began the presidency with the promise that America was about to conquer a **New Frontier**. He promised a series of programs that would increase government aid to the elderly, combat racism, improve American education, assist the many farmers who were facing business failure, and halt the recession that had dogged the American economy throughout the fifties. Kennedy's domestic programs aimed high, but his domestic legacy was, in fact, meager. His greatest successes were in the space program which received a great boost from Cold War fears and the Soviets' early accomplishments in space flight. During his three years in office, Kennedy never learned how to rally Congress to his domestic agenda, and it was only during the Johnson administration that New Frontier ideals were realized.

Kennedy's civil rights agenda produced varied results. Kennedy did support **women's rights**, establishing a presidential commission that in 1963 recommended removing all obstacles to women's participation in all facets of society. However, it was only late in his presidency that Kennedy openly embraced the black civil rights movement. After almost two years of near inaction, in September 1962 Kennedy enforced desegregation at the University of Mississippi. In the summer of 1963, he asked Congress for legislation that would outlaw segregation in all public facilities. After his assassination in November, Lyndon Johnson was able to push that legislation—the **Civil Rights Act of 1964**—through Congress on the strength of the late president's popularity.

Still, Kennedy's presidency proved an active period for the civil rights movement as a number of nongovernmental organizations mobilized to build on the gains of the previous decade. Martin Luther King, Jr. led the **Southern Christian Leadership Conference** (**SCLC**), which staged numerous sit-ins and other peaceful demonstrations. The **Congress of Racial Equality** (**CORE**) organized the **Freedom Riders** movement; the Freedom Riders basically staged sit-ins on buses, sitting in sections prohibited to them by segregationist laws. The Freedom Riders were initially an integrated group, as was the **Student Non-Violent Coordinating Committee** (**SNCC**), which did grass-roots work in the areas of voter registration and antisegregationist activism. Such groups met considerable resistance. In 1963 Mississippi's NAACP director **Medger Evers** was shot to death by an anti-integrationist. Not long after, demonstrators in Montgomery, Alabama, were assaulted by the police and fire department who used attack dogs and firehoses against the crowd. News reports of both events horrified millions of Americans and thus helped bolster the movement. So too, for reasons mentioned above, did Kennedy's assassination.

LYNDON JOHNSON'S SOCIAL AGENDA

Like Kennedy, Lyndon Johnson made an early commitment to the civil rights movement, but unlike Kennedy, Johnson took immediate action to demonstrate that commitment. From the time he took office, Johnson started to lobby hard for the **Civil Rights Act of 1964**, which outlawed discrimination based on a person's race, color, religion, or gender. The law prohibited discrimination in employment as well as in public facilities (thus increasing the scope of Kennedy's proposed civil rights act). Not long after, Johnson oversaw the establishment of the **Equal Employment Opportunity Commission** (**EEOC**) to enforce the employment clause of the Civil Rights Act. During his second term, Johnson signed the **Voting Rights Act**, which cracked down on those states that denied blacks the right to vote. He also signed another civil rights act banning discrimination in housing, and yet another that extended voting rights to Native Americans living under tribal governments.

Johnson believed that social justice stemmed from economic equality; hence, his advocacy of civil rights in employment. Toward the same end, he lobbied for and won the **Economic Opportunity Act**, which appropriated nearly $1 billion for poverty relief. After his landslide victory in the 1964 presidential election, Johnson greatly expanded his antipoverty program. A number of programs combined to form Johnson's **War on Poverty**. **Project Head Start** prepared underprivileged children for early schooling; **Upward Bound** did the same for high school students. **Job Corps** trained the unskilled so they could get better jobs, while **Volunteers in Service to America** (**VISTA**) acted as a domestic Peace Corps. In addition, **Legal Services for the Poor** guaranteed legal counsel to those who could not afford their own lawyer. To further assist the poor, Johnson founded the **Department of Housing and Urban Development** (HUD), increased federal aid to low-income apartment renters, and built more federal housing projects.

The legislation passed during 1965 and 1966 represented the most sweeping change to United States' government since the New Deal. Johnson's social agenda even got a New Deal-like name, the **Great Society**. Best of all, taxpayers did not feel much pain: Increased tax revenues from a quickly expanding economy funded the whole package. Not everyone liked Johnson's agenda, however; many objected to any increase in government activity, and the extension of civil rights met with bigoted opposition, especially in the South. Thus, ironically, the huge coalition that had given Johnson his victory and his mandate for change started to fall apart because of his successes (and were hastened by a bitter national debate over American involvement in Vietnam).

THE CIVIL RIGHTS MOVEMENT

In the early sixties the civil rights movement made a number of substantial gains. Legislative successes such as those passed under Johnson's Great Society program provided government support. The movement also won a number of victories in the courts, particularly in the Supreme Court. Under Chief Justice **Earl Warren**, the Court was for a brief moment in history extremely liberal. The **Warren Court** worked to enforce voting rights for blacks and forced states to redraw congressional districts so that minorities would receive greater representation. (The Warren Court expanded civil rights in other areas as well. Among its landmark rulings are those that prohibited school prayer and protected the right to privacy. The Warren Court also made several decisions concerning the rights of the accused. In *Gideon v. Wainwright*, the Court ruled that a defendant in a felony trial must be provided a lawyer for free if he or she could not afford one. In the **Miranda case**, the Court ruled that, upon arrest, a suspect must be advised of his or her right to remain silent and the right to consult with a lawyer.)

Civil rights victories did not come easily. Resistance to change was strong, as evidenced by the opposition of state governments, police, and white citizens. In Selma, police prevented blacks from registering to vote; in Birmingham, police and firemen attacked civil rights protesters. All over the South, the **Ku Klux Klan** and other racists bombed black churches and the homes of civil rights activists with seeming impunity. In Mississippi, three civil rights workers were murdered by a group that included members of the local police department.

With news reports of each event, outrage in the black community grew. Some activists abandoned Martin Luther King's strategy of nonviolent protest. Among the leaders who advocated a more aggressive approach was **Malcolm X**, a minister of the **Nation of Islam**. Malcolm X urged blacks to claim their rights "by any means necessary." (His autobiography is an essential and extremely interesting document of the history of racism in America.) Later, two groups that previously had preached integration—the **SNCC** and **CORE**—expelled their white members and advocated the more separatist, radical program of **Black Power**. By 1968, when King was assassinated, the civil rights movement had fragmented, with some continuing to advocate integration and peaceful change, while others argued for empowerment through segregation and aggression.

THE NEW LEFT, FEMINISM, AND THE COUNTERCULTURE

Black Americans were not the only ones challenging the status quo in the sixties. Young whites, particularly those in college, also rebelled. For these young adults, the struggle was one against the hypocrisy, complacency, and conformity of middle-class life.

In 1962 the **Students for a Democratic Society** (SDS) formed. Its leftist political agenda, laid out in a platform called the **Port Huron Statement**, set the agenda for other progressive groups on college campuses; these groups collectively became known as the **New Left**. New Left ideals included the elimination of poverty and racism and an end to Cold War politics. One particularly active branch of the New Left formed at University of California at Berkeley. In 1964 students there protested when the university banned civil rights and antiwar demonstrations on campus. These protests grew into the **Free Speech movement**, which in turn fostered a number of leftist and radical political groups on the Berkeley campus.

Most New Left groups, however, were male-dominated and insensitive to the cause of women's rights. Eventually women got tired of being treated as second-class citizens within a liberation movement and started their own political groups. Also, in 1963, Betty Friedan's book *The Feminine Mystique* openly challenged many people's assumptions about women's place in society, and its popularity gave the feminist movement a boost. In 1966 the **National Organization of Women (NOW)** formed to fight for legislative changes, including the ill-fated **Equal Rights Amendment (ERA)** to the Constitution. Feminists fought against discrimination in hiring, pay, and college admissions, and financial aid. They also fought for control of reproductive rights, a battle that reached the Supreme Court in the 1971 case *Roe v. Wade*, which decriminalized abortion.

Rebellion against "the establishment" also took the form of nonconformity. **Hippies** grew their hair long, wore tie-dyed shirts and ripped jeans, and advocated drug use, communal living, and "free love." Their way of life came to be known as the **counterculture** because of its unconventionality and its total contrast to the staid mainstream culture, typified by big band music and banal television variety shows. By the end of the sixties, the counterculture became more widely accepted, and artists such as Andy Warhol, Bob Dylan, Jimi Hendrix, and the Rolling Stones were among the biggest money makers in the arts.

The New Left, the feminists, the counter culture, and others on the growing left wing of American politics almost uniformly opposed American participation in the Vietnam War. These groups' vocal protests against the war and the fierce opposition they provoked from the government and pro war Americans created a huge divide in American society by 1968. Before we discuss that fateful year, let's summarize the Vietnam situation up to that point.

AMERICAN INVOLVEMENT IN VIETNAM, 1950–1963

From the Eisenhower administration until the fall of Soviet Communism in 1991, United States foreign policy leaders believed that the country had the right to intervene anywhere in the world to stop the spread of Communism and to protect American interests. Nowhere did that policy fail more miserably than in Vietnam, where the U.S. maintained a military presence for almost 25 years. The Vietnam War divided America as no war before had.

American involvement in the Vietnam War began in 1950. From the 1890s until World War II, Vietnam was a French colony. France exported the country's resources—rice, rubber, and metals—for French consumption. This foreign exploitation of Vietnam helped foster a nationalist Vietnamese resistance called the **Vietminh**, led by **Ho Chi Minh**. Ho had been schooled in France and had joined the French Communist Party before returning home. During World War II, the Vietminh took control of the northern part of the country and declared Vietnamese independence. The United States did not recognize the legitimacy of Ho's government, in part because of America's alliance with France (which wanted its colony back), and in part because Ho was a Communist, who therefore had to be stopped. Instead, the U.S. recognized the government of **Bao Dai**, the Vietnamese emperor whom the French had installed in the south, which France still controlled. Vietnam was divided thus in two; Ho Chi Minh controlled North Vietnam, and Bao Dai ruled South Vietnam. A civil war began as both halves fought to reunite the country.

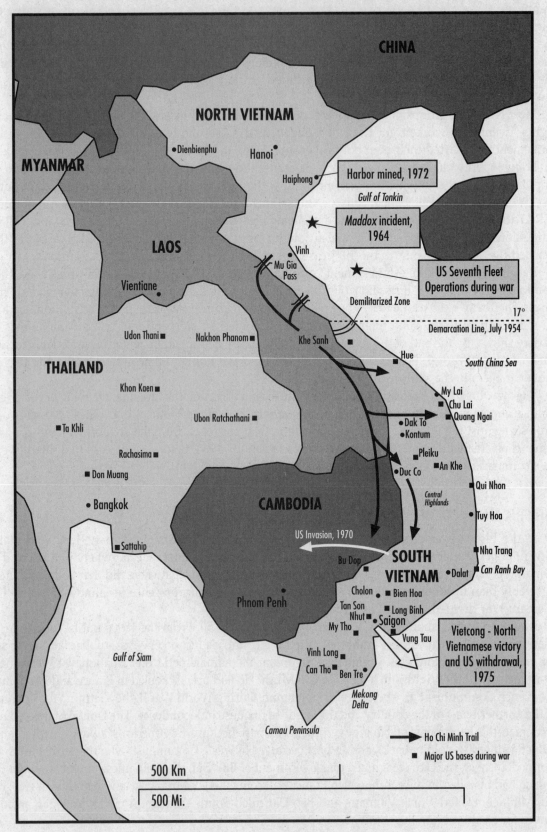

CHINA

NORTH VIETNAM

MYANMAR

• Dienbienphu   Hanoi •

Haiphong •   Harbor mined, 1972

Gulf of Tonkin

★   *Maddox* incident, 1964

LAOS

Vinh •

Mu Gia Pass

★   US Seventh Fleet Operations during war

Vientiane •

Demilitarized Zone

17°

Demarcation Line, July 1954

Udon Thani ■   Nakhon Phanom ■   Khe Sanh   ■

THAILAND   Hue •   South China Sea

Khon Kaen ■   My Lai ■

Chu Lai ■

Ubon Ratchathani ■   Quang Ngai ■

Dak To •

■ Ta Khli   Kontum •

Pleiku •

Rachasima ■   An Khe ■

Duc Co •

■ Don Muang   Qui Nhon ■

CAMBODIA

Central Highlands

Tuy Hoa •

• Bangkok

Nha Trang ■

■ Sattahip   US Invasion, 1970   Bu Dop ■   SOUTH   • Dalat   ■ Can Ranh Bay

VIETNAM

Cholon •   ■ Bien Hoa

Phnom Penh •   Tan Son   ■ Long Binh
Nhut •

My Tho •   Saigon •   Vietcong - North
Vung Tau   Vietnamese victory
and US withdrawal,
1975

Gulf of Siam   Vinh Long •

Can Tho •   Ben Tre •

Mekong Delta

Camau Peninsula

→ Ho Chi Minh Trail

■ Major US bases during war

500 Km

500 Mi.

Southeast Asia During Vietnam War

President Truman immediately began sending military aid and military advisers to the French in Vietnam. Meanwhile, the French moved to extricate themselves from the country, as Vietnam was becoming a political liability for them. In 1954 all the involved parties met in Geneva and agreed to Vietnamese elections in 1956, which would decide who would rule a unified Vietnam. The elections never took place, however. The United States, certain that Ho Chi Minh would win an election, sabotaged the peace agreement. First, the U.S. made an alliance with another South Vietnamese leader named **Ngo Dinh Diem** and helped him oust Bao Dai (whom the U.S. felt was too weak to control the country). Then, the CIA organized commando raids across the border in North Vietnam to provoke a Communist response (which the South Vietnamese could then denounce). Diem pronounced South Vietnam an autonomous country and refused to participate in the agreed-upon national election. The U.S. rallied Britain, France, Thailand, Pakistan, the Philippines, New Zealand and Australia to form the NATO-like **SEATO** (Southeast Asian Treaty Organization) to provide for South Vietnam's defense against Communist takeover.

Unfortunately, the situation continued its downward spiral. Diem, it turned out, was a vicious leader. He took despotic control of South Vietnam, imprisoning political enemies and closing newspapers that criticized his government. As a result, many South Vietnamese citizens joined the North Vietnamese side. These South Vietnamese insurgents were called the **Vietcong**. Rather than cut its losses, the United States fully committed to Diem. Kennedy sent in even more troops, and the U.S. military helped the government relocate non-Vietcong (supposedly for their protection) in detention camps that were virtually prisons. This move, you might well imagine, angered the Vietnamese even more and resulted in even more people joining the Vietcong. Finally, in 1963 the CIA helped the South Vietnamese military stage a coup to overthrow Diem's government. A few weeks later, Kennedy was assassinated, and Johnson took control of America's war efforts.

American Involvement in Vietnam, 1964–1968

Upon taking office, Johnson had the opportunity to withdraw American forces in a way that would not have embarrassed his administration. The United Nations, backed by France and the Vietcong, would have intervened and set up a coalition government to rule South Vietnam. Johnson, however, remained convinced that U.S. forces could overwhelm any opposition in the region. He determined to use those forces to achieve "total victory."

In 1964 the United States supported a second coup in South Vietnam; apparently, the U.S. was not terribly selective as to who ran the country, so long as it was not the Communists. The U.S. Army also started bombing the neighboring country of **Laos**, through which the North Vietnamese were shipping weapons to the Vietcong. Then, in August of the same year, reports stated that the North Vietnamese had fired on two American destroyer ships in the **Tonkin Gulf**. (However, the North Vietnamese attack was never confirmed.) Johnson used the event to get Congress to pass the **Tonkin Gulf resolution**, which allowed the president to take any measures he deemed necessary to protect American interests in the region. The Tonkin Gulf resolution gave Johnson carte blanche to escalate U.S. participation in the war. It also is the closest Congress ever came to an official declaration of war in the Vietnam "police action."

Soon, Johnson had flooded the region with American troops. He also authorized massive Air Force bombing raids into North Vietnam. Throughout Johnson's administration, the United States essentially took over the war effort from the South Vietnamese; hence, the "**Americanization**" of the Vietnam War. As the military draft claimed more Americans, opposition to the war grew. Protest rallies grew larger and more frequent, and more and more young men either ignored their draft notices or fled to a foreign country (more than 30,000 went to Canada) to avoid military service.

Johnson continued to believe that the war was "winnable" until January 1968, when the North Vietnamese launched the **Tet Offensive** (named after the Vietnamese holiday celebrating the New Year). In conjunction with the Vietcong, the North Vietnamese made major gains and inflicted tremendous damage on American forces; the Vietcong nearly captured the American embassy in the South Vietnamese capital of Saigon. The Tet Offensive convinced Johnson's advisers and many American citizens that Vietnam was a lost cause. Protests to the war grew angrier and more frequent. In response, Johnson announced that he would begin peace negotiations with the North Vietnamese government. He also announced, to everyone's surprise, that he would not run for reelection. It was the beginning of the very tumultuous summer of 1968.

THE SUMMER OF 1968 AND THE 1968 ELECTION

Johnson withdrew from the presidential race, in part, because his association with the Vietnam War had turned many Americans against him including many within his own party. Johnson's renomination would not have been easy; both Eugene McCarthy and **Robert Kennedy,** John F. Kennedy's brother and former Attorney General, were poised to challenge him. Johnson's withdrawal opened the field to a third candidate, vice-president **Hubert Humphrey**.

Early in April 1968 a white assassin killed **Martin Luther King Jr.** The murder ignited black riots in more than 150 towns and cities. Arson, looting, and even murder were committed by the outraged mobs. In Chicago, where the Democratic convention would later be held, the mayor ordered the police to shoot arsonists on sight. To say that King's assassination heightened the already considerable tension surrounding race relations would be a huge understatement.

Then, in June, frontrunner for the Democratic nomination, **Robert Kennedy,** was assassinated. Kennedy had come to represent the last bastion of hope for many Americans. Young, handsome, and vital (like his adored older brother), Kennedy was also an aggressive advocate for the poor and a harsh critic of the war in Vietnam. Together, the two assassinations convinced many that peaceful change from within the political system was impossible.

Many disenchanted young Americans came to Chicago in August to demonstrate at the Democratic Convention against government policy. The police were ordered to break up the crowds of protesters, which they did with tear gas, billy clubs, and rifles. Images of American policemen in gas masks clubbing American citizens reached millions of living rooms across the country through television and the newspapers, presenting a picture eerily reminiscent of the police states *against* which America supposedly fought. When the convention chose prowar vice-president Humphrey over the antiwar McCarthy *and* refused to condemn the war effort, the Democrats alienated many of their core constituency on the left.

Meanwhile, the Republicans handed their nomination to former vice-president **Richard Nixon** at a strife-free convention. Then, a third candidate entered the national election, Alabama governor **George Wallace**, who ran a segregationist third-party campaign. Wallace was popular in the South, which traditionally voted Democratic. Thus, Humphrey was twice cursed: He had alienated his progressive urban base in the North and Wallace was siphoning his potential support in the South. Humphrey denounced the Vietnam War late in the campaign, but it was too little, too late. In one of the closest elections in history, Richard Nixon won.

NIXON, THE END OF THE VIETNAM WAR, AND DÉTENTE

Nixon entered office promising to end American involvement in Vietnam. He soon began withdrawing troops; however, he also increased the number and intensity of air strikes. Like his predecessors, Nixon was a veteran Cold Warrior who believed that the U.S. could, and must, win in Vietnam. He ordered bombing raids and ground troops into Cambodia, in hopes of rooting out Vietcong strongholds and weapons supplies. Because of these new incursions, American involvement in Vietnam dragged on into 1973, when Secretary of State **Henry Kissinger** completed negotiations for a peace treaty with the North Vietnamese.

There are a couple of postscripts to the Vietnam story. First, the negotiated peace crumbled almost as soon as American troops started to vacate the country. In 1975 Saigon fell to the North Vietnamese Army, and Vietnam was united under Communist rule. Second, Congress passed the **War Powers Resolution** in 1973 in order to prevent any future president from involving the military in another Vietnam-type situation. The War Powers Resolution requires the president to obtain Congressional approval for any troop commitment lasting longer than sixty days.

Nixon did have success, however, in his other foreign policy initiatives, especially those concerning the world's two other "superpowers," the U.S.S.R. and China. During Nixon's first term, the United States increased trade with the Soviets, and the administration negotiated the first of a number of arms treaties between the two countries. Results were even more dramatic with China. After a series of secret negotiations, Nixon traveled to Communist China, whose government the U.S. had previously refused to acknowledge. Nixon's trip eased tensions and opened trade relations between the two countries. It also allowed Nixon to use his friendship with the Chinese as leverage against the U.S.S.R., and vice versa. (The Chinese and the Soviets, despite both being Communist, hated each other.)

The Nixon years added two new terms to the vocabulary of foreign policy. Together, Nixon and Kissinger formulated an approach called **détente**, which called for countries to respect each other's differences and cooperate more closely, even while they competed to gain power throughout the world and advantages over one another. The **Nixon Doctrine** announced that the U.S. would withdraw from many of its overseas troop commitments, relying instead on alliances with local governments to check the spread of Communism.

NIXON'S DOMESTIC POLICY

Nixon could not match his successes overseas at home. During Nixon's presidency, the economy worsened, going through a period of combined recession-inflation that economists called **stagflation**. Nixon attempted to combat the nation's economic woes with a number of interventionist measures, including a price-and-wage freeze and increased federal spending. None of his efforts produced their intended results.

Politically, American society remained divided among the haves and have-nots, the progressives and the conservatives. Much of the political rhetoric on both sides painted the opposition as enemies of the "American way." Several confrontations on college campuses heightened political tensions, most notably when national guardsmen shot and killed four protesters at **Kent State University**. Meanwhile, urban crime levels rose, causing many to flee to the apparent tranquillity of the suburbs.

Still, in 1972 Nixon won reelection in one of the great landslide victories in American political history, defeating liberal senator George McGovern. Although Nixon won the election easily, both houses of Congress remained under Democratic control, an indication of the mixed feelings many Americans felt toward Republican politics.

WATERGATE AND NIXON'S RESIGNATION

In the summer of 1971, two major newspapers published the **Pentagon Papers**, a top-secret government study of the history of U.S. involvement in Vietnam. The study covered the period from World War II to 1968, and it was not complimentary. It documented numerous military miscalculations and flat-out lies the government had told the public. Even though the documents contained nothing about the Nixon administration, Nixon fought aggressively to prevent their publication. The United

States was involved in secret diplomatic negotiations with North Vietnam, the U.S.S.R., and China at the time, and Nixon and Kissinger both believed that the revelation of secret government dealings in the past might destroy their credibility in the present.

Nixon lost his fight to suppress the Pentagon Papers, a loss that increased Nixon's already considerable paranoia. In an effort to prevent any further "leaks" of classified documents, Nixon put together a team of investigators called the **Plumbers**. The Plumbers undertook such disgraceful projects as burglarizing a psychiatrist's office in order to gather incriminating information on the government official who had turned the Pentagon Papers over to the press. During the 1972 elections, the Plumbers sabotaged the campaigns of several Democratic hopefuls and then botched a **burglary** of Democratic headquarters in the **Watergate** Hotel.

When the Plumbers were arrested at the Watergate Hotel, the White House began an all-out effort to cover up the scandal. A Senate hearing into the matter began in early 1973 and dragged on, keeping the story alive in the news for the next year and a half. Information was slowly revealed that incriminated the president's closest advisers, who began dropping off like flies. They would resign, then most would be tried and convicted of felonies. (Perjury and destruction of evidence were two popular and successful charges against them.) At last, it was discovered that Nixon had secretly taped all conversations in the White House, including many concerning Watergate. For the next year, a legal battle over the tapes raged; the Senate demanded them, and Nixon refused to turn them over, claiming executive privilege. All the while, more damning evidence came to light and more former Nixon associates were jailed. When the president lost the battle over the tapes—the Supreme Court ordered Nixon to turn them over to the Senate—he knew his days were numbered as the tapes revealed a number of unsavory aspects of Nixon's character. Rather than face impeachment proceedings, Nixon resigned in August 1974. His vice-president, **Gerald Ford**, took office and almost immediately granted Nixon a presidential **pardon**, thereby preventing a trial.

... And the Rest

Please note that, according to The College Board's AP U.S. History Web page:

> The multiple choice section may include a few questions on the period since 1970, but neither the DBQ nor the essay questions in Parts B and C deal exclusively with this period.

Translation: If you know nothing about the period after 1970, the worst that can happen is that you might miss a few multiple choice questions. Accordingly, we are not going to spend much time reviewing this period. Below are a few things you ought to know about U.S. history since Nixon's resignation.

The Ford and Carter Presidencies

Gerald Ford became president when Nixon resigned. Ford had been chosen to replace Nixon's first vice-president, **Spiro Agnew**, who resigned in the face of impending criminal charges (not related to Watergate, oddly enough). When Ford selected his vice-president (Nelson Rockefeller), it was the first time that neither the president nor the vice-president had been elected by the public.

Ford's **pardon** of Nixon brought the Watergate era to a close. It also cost Ford politically, as it raised suspicions that Nixon and Ford had struck a deal. Ford's political fortunes were further undermined by a weak economy. An oil embargo organized by Arab nations (under the leadership of **OPEC**) against the U.S. increased fuel prices which in turn caused the price of almost everything else to rise. Inflation, coupled with an increasing unemployment rate, sealed Ford's fate. In 1976 he was defeated by Democrat **Jimmy Carter**.

Carter inherited a weakening economy. During his presidency, inflation exceeded 10 percent, and interest rates on loans approached 20 percent. Carter enjoyed some foreign policy successes. He negotiated a peace treaty between Israel and Egypt and also concluded an arms agreement with the Soviets. However, Carter also suffered some major setbacks. When the U.S.S.R. invaded Afghanistan, Carter's efforts proved powerless in forcing a withdrawal. Carter also flip-flopped in Nicaragua, where first he befriended the revolutionary **Sandinista** government and then turned against them as they allied themselves more closely with the U.S.S.R. and Cuba. Carter's worst crisis involved Iran when American hostages were taken in retaliation for America's decades-long support of the repressive, deposed Shah. Held for more than a year, the hostages were not released until after Ronald Reagan took office.

Ronald Reagan tried to revive the economy by applying the theory of **supply-side economics**. Reagan believed that if he cut taxes for the wealthy, they would invest in the economy. Their increased wealth would "**trickle down**," creating more jobs and more wealth. Reagan coupled this approach with large-scale deregulation, particularly in the areas of banking, industry, and the environment. Although inflation subsided, the unemployment rate continued to rise, lending credence to the criticism that, under Reagan, the rich were getting richer while the poor were getting poorer.

In foreign policy, Reagan was a full-fledged Cold War hawk. He supported repressive regimes and right-wing insurgents in El Salvador, Nicaragua, Panama, the Philippines, and Mozambique, all simply because they opposed Communism. The Reagan administration also sent marines to **Lebanon** as part of a United Nations peacekeeping force. A suicide bomb killed 240 servicemen, marking one of the low points of Reagan's foreign policy record. Another came during his second term, when it was revealed that administration officials had concocted a bizarre scheme to supply arms to Nicaraguan insurgents called the **contras**. Prevented by Congress from using tax money to supply the contras, the government secretly sold weapons to Iran, then used the income to buy guns for the contras. In short, the government had set up an illegal little side-business as it involved both arms sales to a terrorist state and a usurpation of Congress' power of appropriation. Reagan denied knowledge of the operation, now known as the **Iran-contra affair**, and the consequences for the government's actions seemed few. In fact, despite the scandal, Oliver North, the military leader in charge of the operation, today has his own talk show.

Reagan's vice-president, **George Bush**, won the 1988 election. His administration is much too recent to be the subject of a question on the AP test. However, you should be aware that during his administration, the Soviet Union first lost control of its satellite states before dissolving into a number of independent countries.

part 3

The Test and Explanations

10

The Princeton Review
AP U.S. History
Diagnostic Test

UNITED STATES HISTORY

Three hours and five minutes are allotted for this examination: 55 minutes for Part A, which consists of multiple-choice questions; one hour for Part B, which consists of the document-based question; and 70 minutes for part C, which consists of the free response questions. The time allotted for Part B includes a mandatory 15 minute reading period and a 45 minute writing period. The document-based question and the free response questions are essay questions. Part B is printed in this examination booklet; Parts B and C are printed in a separate green booklet. The multiple-choice section counts for 50 percent of your final grade; the document-based question, 22 1/2 percent; and the free response questions, 27 1/2 percent.

PART A

Time – 55 minutes

Number of questions – 80

Percent of total grade – 50

This examination contains 80 multiple-choice questions. Therefore, please be careful to fill in only the ovals that are preceded by numbers 1 through 80 on your answer sheet.

General Instructions

DO NOT OPEN THIS BOOKLET UNTIL YOU ARE INSTRUCTED TO DO SO.

INDICATE ALL YOUR ANSWERS TO QUESTIONS IN PART A ON THE SEPARATE ANSWER SHEET. No credit will be given for anything written in this examination booklet, but you may use the booklet for notes or scratchwork. After you have decided which of the suggested answers is best, COMPLETELY fill in the corresponding oval on the answer sheet. Give only one answer to each question. If you change an answer, be sure that the previous mark is erased completely.

Example: Sample Answer

The first president of the United States was

(A) Millard Fillmore
(B) George Washington
(C) Benjamin Franklin
(D) Andrew Jackson
(E) Harry Truman

Many candidates wonder whether or not to guess the answers to questions about which they are not certain. In this section of the examination, as a correction for haphazard guessing, one-fourth of the number of questions you answer incorrectly will be subtracted from the number of questions you answer correctly. It is improbable, therefore, that mere guessing will improve your score significantly; it may even lower your score, and it does take time. If, however, you are not sure of the best answer but have some knowledge of the questions and are able to eliminate one or more answer choices as wrong, your chance of getting the right answer is improved, and it may be to your advantage to answer such a question.

Use your time effectively, working as rapidly as you can without losing accuracy. Do not spend too much time on questions that are too difficult. Go on to other questions and come back to the difficult ones if you have time. It is not expected that everyone will be able to answer all the multiple-choice questions.

SECTION I

Time—55 minutes

80 questions

Directions: Each of the following questions or incomplete statements below is followed by five suggested answers or completions. Select the one that is best in each case and then blacken the corresponding space on the answer sheet.

1. A major weakness of the Articles of Confederation was that they

   (A) created a too-powerful chief executive
   (B) did not include a mechanism for their own amendment
   (C) made it too difficult for the government to raise money through taxes and duties
   (D) denied the federal government the power to mediate disputes between states
   (E) required the ratification of only a simple majority of states

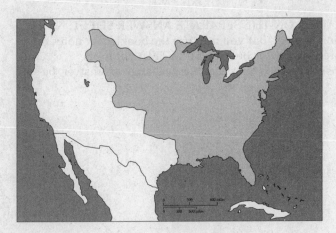

2. The shaded region in the map above shows the land held by the United States immediately following the

   (A) American Revolution
   (B) passage of the Northwest Ordinance
   (C) negotiation of the Treaty of Greenville
   (D) Louisiana Purchase
   (E) War of 1812

3. Which of the following states the principle of Manifest Destiny?

   (A) The colonists were destined to leave the British empire because of the distance between the New World and England.
   (B) Women are biologically predestined to lives of child rearing and domestic labor.
   (C) America's expansion to the West Coast was inevitable and divinely sanctioned.
   (D) The abolition of slavery in the United States was certain to come about, because slavery was immoral.
   (E) American entry into World War I was unavoidable and was in America's long-term interests.

4. In his opinion on the case *Dred Scott v Sanford*, Chief Justice Roger Taney ruled that

   (A) the Supreme Court had the right to rule on the constitutionality of any federal law
   (B) "separate but equal" facilities for people of different races was constitutional
   (C) corporations were entitled to the same protections guaranteed individuals under the Fourteenth Amendment
   (D) school prayer violated the principle of "separation of church and state"
   (E) Congress had no right to regulate slavery in United States territories

GO ON TO THE NEXT PAGE

5. Following the Civil War, most freed slaves

(A) stayed in the South and worked as sharecroppers
(B) joined the pioneering movement as it headed West
(C) moved to the North and learned professions
(D) took work building the nation's growing railroad system
(E) moved to Liberia with the aid of the American Colonial Society

6. Of the following policies pursued by President Theodore Roosevelt, which was NOT a main objective of American progressives?

(A) Passage of the Pure Food and Water Act
(B) Creation of national forests and protected wildlife reserves
(C) Initiation of antitrust law suits against various corporate monopolies
(D) Intervention in the affairs of Central American governments
(E) Expansion of the power of the Interstate Commerce Commission

7. Which of the following statements about the Treaty of Versailles is true?

(A) The United States Senate rejected it because it treated Germany too leniently.
(B) The United States Senate rejected it because it required increased American involvement in European affairs.
(C) The United States Senate approved it, with reservations concerning the division of Eastern Europe.
(D) The United States Senate approved it without reservations.
(E) It was never voted on by the United States Senate.

8. Senator Joseph McCarthy gained national prominence with his accusation that

(A) American meat packers disregarded fundamental rules of sanitation
(B) the Federal Bureau of Investigation was violating many innocent citizens' right to privacy
(C) some congressmen were taking bribes in return for pro-business votes
(D) massive voter fraud was common throughout the Southwest
(E) the State Department had been infiltrated by communist spies

9. The 1956 boycott of the Montgomery bus system

(A) was led by Malcolm X
(B) started because the city doubled bus fares
(C) was instigated by the arrest of Rosa Parks
(D) lasted for three weeks and failed to achieve its goal
(E) resulted from the assassination of Martin Luther King, Jr.

10. The Puritans believed that the freedom to practice religion should be extended to

(A) Puritans only
(B) all Protestants only
(C) all Christians only
(D) all Jews and Christians only
(E) all inhabitants of the New World, including Africans and Native Americans

11. The Sugar Act of 1764 represented a major shift in British policy toward the colonies in that, for the first time, the British

(A) allowed all proceeds from a tax to stay in the colonial economy
(B) attempted to control colonial exports
(C) offered the colonists the opportunity to address Parliament with grievances
(D) required the colonies to import English goods exclusively
(E) levied taxes aimed at raising revenue rather than regulating trade

GO ON TO THE NEXT PAGE

12. The Industrial Revolution had which of the following effects on slavery in the South?

   (A) The creation of numerous labor-saving machines vastly reduced the need for slave labor.
   (B) Rapid growth in the textile industry encouraged Southern planters to grow cotton, thereby making slavery more important to the economy.
   (C) The government bought and freed Southern slaves, then transported them to the North, where factories were experiencing a major labor shortage.
   (D) The Industrial Revolution began as the Civil War was ending and it provided work for many former slaves.
   (E) New farm machinery required slaves and masters to work more closely together, with a resulting reduction of mutual hostility.

13. The Know-Nothing Party focused its efforts almost exclusively on the issue of

   (A) religious freedom
   (B) the right to bear arms
   (C) the prohibition of alcohol
   (D) women's rights
   (E) immigration

14. Someone who emigrated to the United States during the nineteenth century probably chose his or her new hometown based on where

   (A) jobs were most plentiful
   (B) relatives already lived
   (C) premiums were paid to new settlers
   (D) the climate was most healthful
   (E) passage by boat was available at the time

15. The "Ghost Dancer" movement among Western Native Americans stressed all of the following EXCEPT

   (A) the belief that the world would soon come to an end
   (B) rejection of alcohol and other trappings of white society
   (C) unity among Native Americans of different tribes
   (D) non-violence
   (E) the use of magic to neutralize the effectiveness of whites' weaponry

16. In response to several unfavorable Supreme Court rulings concerning New Deal programs, Franklin Roosevelt

   (A) urged the voting public to write letters of protest to Supreme Court justices
   (B) submitted four separate Constitutional amendments broadening the powers of the presidency
   (C) abandoned the New Deal and replaced it with a laissez-faire policy
   (D) instructed both the legislative and executive branches to ignore the rulings
   (E) proposed legislation that would allow him to appoint new federal and Supreme Court judges

GO ON TO THE NEXT PAGE

Strike-Breaking

17. The 1933 political cartoon shown above makes the point that

(A) infighting within and among unions prevented their rise to economic power
(B) government inspectors turned their backs to illegal repression of labor unions
(C) attacks on unions were so well concealed that the government did not know where to begin its investigations
(D) from their beginnings, labor unions were controlled by organized crime
(E) the government moved too hastily in investigating misbehavior in labor unions

18. In which decision did the Supreme Court invalidate the practice of "separate but equal" facilities for blacks and whites?

(A) *Marbury v. Madison*
(B) *Bradwell v. Illinois*
(C) *Plessy v. Ferguson*
(D) *Brown v. Board of Education of Topeka, Kansas*
(E) *Holden v. Hardy*

19. The Bay of Pigs invasion of Cuba, in 1961, was carried out by

(A) Caribbean mercenaries hired by the United States
(B) American soldiers
(C) the Soviet Navy
(D) Cuban exiles trained by the Central Intelligence Agency
(E) Cuban Communist rebels led by Fidel Castro

20. Roger Williams was banished from Massachusetts Bay in 1636 for advocating

(A) the separation of church and state
(B) women's suffrage
(C) bigamy
(D) the export of tobacco
(E) independence from England

21. All of the following influenced the United States' decision to declare war against Great Britain in 1812 EXCEPT

(A) the impressment of American sailors
(B) British control of the Atlantic and resulting interference in United States trade with Europe
(C) the American government's certainty that its navy was more powerful than Great Britain's
(D) Great Britain's alliances with American Indian tribes, which curtailed United States westward expansion
(E) the failure of the Embargo Act

22. Which of the following does NOT accurately describe the Missouri Compromise of 1820?

(A) It provided a method for counting slaves among state populations when determining the size of the states' Congressional delegations.
(B) It allowed Missouri to be admitted to the Union as a slave state.
(C) It created the free state of Maine from territory that belonged to Massachusetts.
(D) One of its purposes was to maintain the equal representation of free states and slave states in the Senate.
(E) It included a northern border in the Louisiana Territory above which slavery was prohibited.

GO ON TO THE NEXT PAGE

23. Between 1820 and 1854, the greatest number of immigrants to the United States came from

(A) France
(B) Russia
(C) Spain
(D) England
(E) Ireland

24. Congress brought impeachment proceedings against Andrew Johnson primarily because

(A) Johnson sought to block the punitive aspects of Congressional Reconstruction
(B) Johnson's Republican policies had fallen out of favor with the Democratic majority
(C) the Johnson administration was riddled with corruption
(D) Johnson's pro-North bias was delaying the readmission of southern states to the Union
(E) many Congressmen personally disliked Johnson, although they agreed with his policies

25. The "Open Door policy" in 1899 primarily concerned

(A) independence movements in Africa
(B) Mexican immigration to the United States
(C) the removal of trade tariffs from United States-European trade
(D) trade with Asia
(E) the United States's colonies in Central America

26. Which of the following was NOT a major contributing factor to the onset of the Great Depression?

(A) Technological advances had allowed farmers and manufacturers to overproduce, creating large inventories.
(B) The federal government interfered too frequently with the economy, causing investors to lose confidence.
(C) The average wage earner was not earning enough money to afford the many consumer goods new technology had made available.
(D) Stock investors had been allowed to speculate wildly, creating an unstable and volatile stock market.
(E) Major businesses were controlled by so few producers that the failure of any one had a considerable effect on the national economy.

27. The Truman Doctrine declared the government's commitment to assist

(A) Japanese families affected by the atomic bomb blasts in Hiroshima and Nagasaki
(B) any nation facing widespread poverty as a result of World War II
(C) free nations in danger of takeover by repressive governments, especially Soviet-style Communism
(D) American farmers, who suffered through major price drops after World War II ended
(E) American families who could not afford to build homes without government aid

28. Which of the following best summarizes the United States's primary reason for participating in the war in Vietnam?

(A) The United States was required to fight under the terms of its military alliance with Japan.
(B) Vietnamese leader Ho Chi Minh requested American military assistance.
(C) The United States was hoping to promote Asian autonomy and anti-colonialism.
(D) American foreign policy experts believed that, without intervention, Communism would spread from Vietnam throughout Southeast Asia.
(E) The government felt obliged to protect the United States's considerable business interests in Vietnam.

29. The "First Great Awakening" can be seen as a direct response to which of the following?

(A) Puritanism
(B) the Enlightenment
(C) Transcendentalism
(D) existentialism
(E) post-modernism

GO ON TO THE NEXT PAGE

30. Which of the following states the principle of "virtual representation," as it was argued during the eighteenth century?

(A) Paper money has value even though it is inherently worth very little.
(B) Slave populations must be counted when figuring Congressional apportionment, even though slaves may not vote.
(C) American property-holding colonists may, if they so desire, join their state legislatures.
(D) All English subjects, including those who are not allowed to vote, are represented in Parliament.
(E) All English subjects are entitled to a trial before a jury of their peers.

31. By the first decade of the nineteenth century, American manufacturing had been revolutionized by the advent of

(A) interchangeable machine parts
(B) the electric engine
(C) transcontinental railroads
(D) labor unions
(E) mail-order catalogues

32. The principle of "popular sovereignty" stated that

(A) whenever a new area was settled, all United States citizens were required vote on the slave status of that area
(B) slavery would not be permitted in any area after 1848
(C) the President, after meeting with public interest groups, was to decide on whether slaves would be allowed in a given territory
(D) settlers in the Western territories, not Congress, would decide whether to allow slavery in their territory
(E) any settlers disagreeing with federal laws governing slavery were free to ignore those laws

"Society everywhere is in conspiracy against the manhood of every one of its members…The virtue in most request is conformity. Self-reliance is its aversion."

33. The passage above was written by

(A) Ralph Waldo Emerson
(B) Jonathan Edwards
(C) Harriet Beecher Stowe
(D) Charles G. Finney
(E) Andrew Carnegie

34. The majority of those who voted Republican in the 1854 elections were

(A) either Northern businessmen or Southern farmers
(B) settlers in the Western territories
(C) Northern abolitionists
(D) merchants and businessmen in the Middle Atlantic states
(E) recent immigrants

35. Which of the following is NOT a requirement set by the Reconstruction Act of 1867 for Southern states's readmission to the Union?

(A) Blacks had to be allowed to participate in state conventions and state elections.
(B) The state had to ratify the Fourteenth Amendment to the Constitution.
(C) The state had to pay reparations and provide land grants to all former slaves.
(D) The state had to rewrite its constitution and ratify it.
(E) Congress had to approve the new state constitution.

36. Which of the following is true of the American rail system in the nineteenth century?

(A) Government subsidies and land grants played a major role in its expansion.
(B) The entire national system was planned before the first railway was constructed.
(C) Transcontinental rail travel was not possible at any time during the century.
(D) The development of the rails had little effect on the development of American industry.
(E) A more highly developed rail system gave the Confederacy a decided advantage in the Civil War.

GO ON TO THE NEXT PAGE ⟶

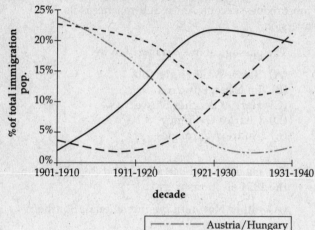

Percent of U.S. immigration total per decade, by nationality

%of total immigration pop.

25%
20%
15%
10%
5%
0%

1901-1910   1911-1920   1921-1930   1931-1940

decade

Legend:
— · — · — Austria/Hungary
———— Canada
— — — Germany
- - - - - Italy

37. Which of the following best explains the changes in immigration patterns reflected in the chart above?

(A) The Depression resulted in a massive wave of Canadian emigration.
(B) After World War I ended, the Austrian and Hungarian economies improved.
(C) Between 1920 and 1930, Congress passed immigration restrictions prejudicial. against southern and eastern Europeans
(D) During the years represented on the chart, relations between the United States and Germany improved greatly.
(E) Between the years 1900 and 1910, the Italian government instituted a number of measures restricting emigration.

38. All of the following contributed to the spirit of isolationism in the United States during the 1930s EXCEPT

(A) disclosures that munitions manufacturers had lobbied for American involvement in World War I, then profited heavily from the war
(B) a foreign policy tradition that could be traced to Washington's Farewell Address
(C) a universal lack of awareness of the goals of the Third Reich
(D) memories of the cost, both in financial terms and in human life, of participation in World War I
(E) the desire to focus resources on recovery from the Depression rather than on strengthening the military

39. Jack Kerouac's *On the Road* and *The Dharma Bums* articulated the ideals of

(A) the silent majority
(B) the "lost generation"
(C) Middle America
(D) the Beat generation
(E) conservative academics

40. Legislation and executive orders associated with the Great Society created all of the following EXCEPT

(A) the Works Progress Administration
(B) the Equal Employment Opportunity Commission
(C) Medicare
(D) the Department of Housing and Urban Development
(E) Project Head Start

41. Which of the following most accurately describes the system of indentured service in the Chesapeake settlement during the seventeenth century?

(A) Indentured servants were slaves for life; however, their children were born free and could own property.
(B) Most indentured servants were lured by the promise of freedom and property upon completion of their service.
(C) Most indentured servants were convicted criminals sentenced to servitude in the New World.
(D) The vast majority of indentured servants died within two years of arriving in the New World.
(E) Indentured servant were not protected under colonial law.

GO ON TO THE NEXT PAGE

42. The Northwest Ordinance of 1787 was a significant achievement because it

   (A) laid claim to the all of North America east of the Mississippi River
   (B) represented one of the rare successes of diplomacy between the United States government and American Indians
   (C) defined the process by which territories could become states
   (D) opened all territories west of the states to slavery
   (E) was the only piece of legislation to pass through Congress under the Articles of Confederation

43. All of the following were elements of Henry Clay's American System EXCEPT

   (A) protective tariffs on imports
   (B) the establishment of the Second Bank of the United States
   (C) the construction of the National Road and other roadways
   (D) the creation of large numbers of federal jobs in areas with unemployment problems
   (E) incentives to develop manufacturing and interstate trade

44. Reform movements during the first half of the nineteenth century attempted to accomplish all of the following EXCEPT

   (A) convince people not to drink alcohol
   (B) widen the division between church and state
   (C) rehabilitate criminals
   (D) induce humane treatment for the insane
   (E) bring about an end to slavery

"The price which society pays for the law of competition... is great; but the advantages of this law are also greater...[W]hether the law be benign or not, we must say of it: It is here; we cannot evade it; ...it is best for the race, because it ensures the survival of the fittest in every department."

45. The above passage is characteristic of

   (A) Calvinism
   (B) Social Darwinism
   (C) Progressivism
   (D) cultural pluralism
   (E) egalitarianism

46. The United States army supported Panama's 1903 war of independence against Colombia primarily because

   (A) the United States was sympathetic to the rebels' democratic ideals
   (B) the Monroe Doctrine required the United States to support all wars of independence in the Western hemisphere
   (C) Colombia was asking too high a price for control of the projected Atlantic-Pacific canal
   (D) the success of Panama's rebellion would have lowered sugar prices in the United States considerably
   (E) the Colombian government was guilty of numerous human rights violations in Panama

47. The rapid growth of American towns in the 1920s and 1930s was made possible primarily by the

   (A) invention of the steam locomotive
   (B) greater access to information provided by radio and television
   (C) mass production of automobiles
   (D) end of open-range cattle ranching
   (E) advent of electric lighting

48. Which of the following is true about the internment of those Japanese living in the United States during World War II?

   (A) The majority of those confined were native-born Americans.
   (B) Many of those relocated were known dissidents.
   (C) Only 2,000 Japanese Americans were relocated.
   (D) Congress passed a law requiring the relocation of all aliens during the war.
   (E) Those who were relocated eventually recovered their homes and possessions.

GO ON TO THE NEXT PAGE

49. Anglo-American women in colonial times

   (A) could own property or execute legal documents only if they were widowed or unmarried
   (B) enjoyed more liberties and rights than did Native American women
   (C) attended church less frequently than did Anglo-American men
   (D) were more likely than men to do agricultural work
   (E) were required by law to learn to read and write, in order to teach their children

50. In the seventeenth century, the Chesapeake Bay settlement expanded its territorial holdings more quickly than did the Massachusetts Bay settlement primarily because

   (A) Massachusetts settlers were entirely uninterested in expansion
   (B) a high birth-rate and healthy environment resulted in a population boom in the Chesapeake region
   (C) no Native Americans lived in the Chesapeake Bay area, and the colonists were free to expand their settlements at will
   (D) farm land in the Chesapeake area was less fertile, and so more of it was needed to support sustenance farming
   (E) farming of the chief Chesapeake export, tobacco, required a great deal of land

51. The debate over the First Bank of the United States was significant because it raised the issue of

   (A) whether the new government should issue paper currency
   (B) how strictly the Constitution should be interpreted
   (C) whether the United States should pay back its war debt to France
   (D) how to finance the construction of the railroads
   (E) whether the president had the power to act unilaterally on important economic issues

52. The "Lowell System" of early nineteenth-century textile manufacturing was noteworthy for its

   (A) practice of hiring only adult males at a time when textiles was considered "women's work"
   (B) commitment, in the face of the Industrial Revolution, to maintaining the old, "by-hand" method of manufacture
   (C) efforts to minimize the dehumanizing effects of industrial labor
   (D) pioneering advocacy of such issues as parental leave, vacation time, and health insurance for employees
   (E) particularly harsh treatment of employees

53. The election of 1824 marked a turning point in presidential politics because, for the first time,

   (A) the presidency was won by someone who was not a member of the Federalist Party
   (B) a presidential and vice-presidential candidate ran together on one ticket
   (C) all the candidates campaigned widely throughout the states
   (D) political parties officially participated in the election
   (E) the system of choosing nominees by congressional caucus failed

54. In the late nineteenth century, political machines such as Tammany Hall were successful primarily because

   (A) federal legislation sanctioned their activities
   (B) they operated primarily in rural areas, where the government could not monitor their activities
   (C) they focused on accomplishing only a narrow set of human rights objectives
   (D) they championed the suffragettes and received their support in return
   (E) machine politicians provided needed jobs and services to naturalized citizens in return for their votes

GO ON TO THE NEXT PAGE

55. The disagreement between W.E.B. Du Bois and Booker T. Washington regarding the status of African-Americans in the early twentieth century is best summed up as a debate over

(A) what social injustices federal legislation should correct first
(B) whether African-Americans should emigrate to Africa
(C) whether state governments or the federal government should be the primary vehicle of social change
(D) how prominent a role African-American churches should play in the struggle for civil rights
(E) whether African-Americans should first seek legal or economic equality with white Americans

56. One of the unintended effects of Prohibition was that it

(A) caused a national epidemic of alcohol withdrawal
(B) brought about a decrease in alcoholism and an increase in worker productivity
(C) resulted in a substantial increase in the abuse of hard drugs, particularly heroin
(D) lowered the cost of law enforcement by decreasing the incidence of drunkenness
(E) provided organized crime syndicates with a means to gain both wealth and power

57. The 1927 motion picture *The Jazz Singer* was the first major commercial film to feature

(A) color images
(B) the illusion of three dimensions
(C) synchronous sound
(D) special effects
(E) a dramatic plot

58. Which of the following was LEAST likely a factor in the decision to drop atomic bombs on Hiroshima and Nagasaki?

(A) Hope that a quick victory in the Pacific would hasten an Allied victory in Europe
(B) Fear that the Soviet Union would soon enter the war with Japan.
(C) Concern that a land war in Japan would result in massive American casualties
(D) Awareness that Japanese forces were numerous and spread throughout Asia
(E) Desire to demonstrate to other world powers the potency of America's new weapon

59. The failed Equal Rights Amendment to the Constitution was intended to prevent discrimination against

(A) African-Americans
(B) Native Americans
(C) children and adolescents
(D) legal immigrants
(E) women

60. Which of the following statements about the Stamp Act is NOT true?

(A) Because it most affected lawyers and writers, the Stamp Act fostered a particularly eloquent opposition to the Crown.
(B) Colonial legislatures sent letters of protest to Parliament threatening secession from England if the Stamp Act was not repealed.
(C) Opposition to the Stamp Act built upon colonial resentment of the Sugar and Currency Acts.
(D) Among the colonists' reactions to the Stamp Act was an effective boycott of British goods.
(E) According to the Stamp Act, those who violated the law were not entitled to a jury trial.

61. The doctrine of nullification stated that

(A) legal immigrants may be deported when they fall into a state of destitution
(B) Congress may override an executive order with a two-thirds majority vote
(C) the government may take control of a bank if its cash reserves fall below a certain percentage of its total deposits
(D) municipal and county governments may rescind licenses granted by the state
(E) a state may repeal any federal law that it deems unconstitutional

GO ON TO THE NEXT PAGE

62. Alexis de Tocqueville attributed American social mobility to

(A) the continuation of European traditions in the New World
(B) Americans' rights to speak freely and to bear arms
(C) the government's tolerance of labor unions and progressive organizations
(D) the lack of an aristocracy and the availability of frontier land
(E) mandatory public education

63. Which of the following changes in westward migration occurred in 1848?

(A) The number of pioneers headed for the Oregon territory decreased while the number headed for California greatly increased.
(B) The first great wave of migration ended, and the number of migrants remained extremely low until after the Civil War.
(C) For the first time, pioneers began to settle areas west of the Mississippi River.
(D) Large numbers of free blacks, unwelcome in the East, began to resettle in the West.
(E) The government began to enforce quotas limiting the number of people who could migrate each year.

64. The "free silver" campaign of 1896 received its greatest popular support from

(A) New England businessmen, who were discriminated against under the existing banking system
(B) Southern women, who incorporated it into a larger campaign for economic equality
(C) bankers, who had run out of paper currency to invest
(D) gold miners, who stood to profit from the movement's success
(E) farmers, who hoped that a more generous money supply would ease their debt burdens

65. The United States took control of the Philippines in 1898

(A) by purchasing it from China
(B) as a result the Spanish-American War
(C) after conquering the autonomous Philippine government
(D) when Japan exchanged it for a promise of non-aggression
(E) as the leader of a multinational coalition called in to suppress a revolution there

"Free speech would not protect a man falsely shouting fire in a theater and causing panic."

66. The excerpt above is from a 1919 Supreme Court ruling prohibiting speech that represented a "clear and present danger." The defendant in the case had

(A) given a speech urging black residents of Chicago to demand equal rights
(B) written a magazine article in support of the Russian revolution
(C) sent letters to military draftees arguing that conscription was illegal
(D) given a speech suggesting that Texas should be returned to Mexico
(E) posted fliers denouncing a department store in St. Louis

GO ON TO THE NEXT PAGE

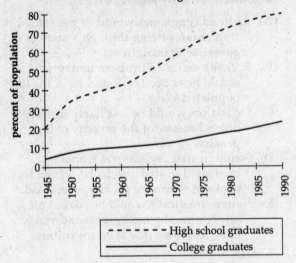

Percent of U.S. population completing high school and college

- - - - - - High school graduates
———— College graduates

67. Which of the following best accounts for the trend illustrated in the chart above?

(A) Increased affluence beginning in the post-War era allowed people the opportunity to stay in school longer.
(B) The Supreme Court decision *Brown v. the Board of Education* led to increased enrollment in colleges and universities.
(C) During the 1960s, increasing numbers of high school graduates rejected the notion that a college education was desirable.
(D) The first state passed a compulsory education law in 1946, and others quickly followed.
(E) Jobs in advanced technical and medical industries generally require post-graduate degrees.

68. The 1968 George Wallace presidential campaign, on the American Independence ticket, probably helped Richard Nixon win the election because

(A) Wallace's racism directed voters' attention away from the Watergate scandal
(B) Wallace won several traditionally Democratic Southern states
(C) Wallace's participation sent the election to the House of Representatives, where Nixon was more popular
(D) in the final week, Wallace withdrew from the race and threw his support to Nixon
(E) Wallace and Humphrey, the Democratic candidate, held similar views on all the major issues

69. The English colonists who settled Virginia and the neighboring Indian tribes had widely different attitudes about all of the following subjects EXCEPT

(A) whether property could be privately owned
(B) what type of work was appropriate for men and women
(C) how best to utilize the earth's resources
(D) the centrality of religion in daily life
(E) the means by which leaders should receive and exercise power

70. Puritan emigration from England came to a near-halt between the years 1649 and 1660 because, during that period,

(A) most English Puritans were imprisoned for heresy
(B) most Puritans converted to Catholicism
(C) the New England settlement had become too overcrowded, and colonial legislatures strongly discouraged immigration
(D) the Puritans controlled the English government
(E) Parliament outlawed travel to the New World

71. The Monroe Doctrine stated that the United States had legitimate reason to fear European intervention in the Western Hemisphere because

(A) Europe's militaries were considerably more powerful than was the United States's
(B) the overpopulation of Europe made future incursions in the New World a real possibility
(C) Europe's forms of government were fundamentally different from those of the United States and newly liberated South American countries
(D) the United States anticipated reprisals for its frequent interference in European affairs
(E) the United States ultimately intended to annex all of the Western Hemisphere

GO ON TO THE NEXT PAGE

72. Supreme Court decisions concerning Native Americans in 1831 and 1832

(A) reinforced the rights of states to remove Native Americans from disputed lands

(B) denied them the right to sue in federal court but affirmed their rights to land that was traditionally theirs

(C) voided previous treaties between Native Americans and the United States on the grounds that the treaties were unfair

(D) granted tribes official status as foreign nations

(E) ruled that the federal government had a unilateral right to relocate Native Americans to lands west of the Mississippi

73. In the 1830s, Southern states passed a number of laws regarding the behavior of free blacks. These laws were intended to

(A) encourage free blacks to migrate to the North

(B) impose a uniform procedure regarding the retrieval of fugitive slaves

(C) increase the pool of available black skilled laborers in the growing Southern economy

(D) guarantee the rights of free blacks traveling through slave states

(E) create an official set of guidelines concerning "acceptable" treatment of slaves

74. By what means did the United States take possession of the Oregon Territory?

(A) The United States was granted the territory in a post-war treaty with France.

(B) The United States bought it from the Native Americans who lived there.

(C) United States settlers were the first to arrive in the region; they claimed it for their country.

(D) Great Britain ceded it to the United States as part of a negotiated treaty.

(E) The French sold it to the United States as part of the Louisiana Purchase.

75. Which of the following was the intended result of the Dawes Severalty Act of 1887?

(A) Railroad companies would be persuaded to stop unfair pricing through a number of government incentives.

(B) Recently arrived European immigrants would be enticed into settling in the less populated West.

(C) Legislators would be less likely to accept bribes because of the severity of the penalty.

(D) Southern state legislatures would be motivated to strike racist laws from their books in return for greater federal aid.

(E) Native Americans would be coaxed off reservations by land grants and would thus assimilate into Western culture.

76. During the decade following passage of the Sherman Antitrust Act, most courts applied the rule to break up

(A) railroad monopolies
(B) utility companies
(C) telegraph cartels
(D) labor unions
(E) political machines

GO ON TO THE NEXT PAGE

"Wot'd I care about the price of coal?"

77. The main point of the 1902 political cartoon above is that

(A) rural populations of different ethnic backgrounds did not get along together
(B) because farmers lived in warm climates, they had no need for coal
(C) rural dwellers had little sympathy for the problems of city dwellers
(D) corn was the major American cash crop at the turn of the century
(E) farmers were entirely unaware of the high cost of coal in the East

78. The term "welfare capitalism" refers to the corporate practice of

(A) providing social services for the unemployed poor who live near a factory
(B) offering workers incentives, such as pensions and profit-sharing, to dissuade them from joining unions
(C) marketing only to those potential customers who earn considerably below the national average wage
(D) raising prices in stores whenever AFDC checks are sent
(E) selling inventories to the government at highly inflated prices

79. The Agricultural Adjustment Act of 1933 sought to lessen the effects of the Depression by

(A) paying farmers to cut production and, in some cases, destroy crops
(B) purchasing farms and turning them into government collectives
(C) instituting an early retirement program for farmers over the age of 50
(D) encouraging farmers to increase production
(E) subsidizing food processing plants in order to lower food prices

80. During the 1960s, the Student Nonviolent Coordinating Committee (SNCC) shifted its political agenda in which of the following ways?

(A) Although it started as an anti-war organization, by the mid-1960s the SNCC was solely pursuing a civil rights agenda.
(B) The SNCC, initially a Christian organization, officially allied itself with the Nation of Islam in 1963.
(C) Although initially integrationist, by 1966 the SNCC advocated black separatism.
(D) The SNCC originally concerned itself exclusively with political issues on college campuses; over the years, the organization broadened its agenda.
(E) The SNCC initially sought to achieve its goals through litigation; later, it pursued it agenda through peaceful demonstrations.

STOP
END OF SECTION I

IF YOU FINISH BEFORE TIME IS CALLED, YOU MAY CHECK YOUR WORK ON THIS SECTION.
DO NOT GO ON TO SECTION II UNTIL YOU ARE TOLD TO DO SO.

UNITED STATES HISTORY

SECTION II

PART A

(Suggested writing time—40 minutes)

Directions: The following question requires you to construct a coherent essay that integrates your interpretation of Documents A-I and your knowledge of the period referred to in the question. High scores will be earned only by essays that both cite key pieces of evidence from the documents and draw on outside knowledge of the period.

1. When World War I broke out, the United States declared its policy of neutrality. Was the United States ever neutral in the conflict, and if so, when did it change to a policy favoring the Allies?

    Use the documents and your knowledge of history in the 1910s to construct your response.

Document A

Source: President Woodrow Wilson, message to Congress (August 19, 1914):

The effect of the war upon the United States will depend upon what American citizens say and do. Every man who really loves America will act and speak in the true spirit of neutrality, which is the spirit of impartiality and fairness and friendliness to all concerned.

The people of the United States are drawn from many nations, and chiefly from the nations now at war. It is natural and inevitable that there should be the utmost variety of sympathy and desire among them with regard to the issues and circumstances of the conflict.

Such divisions amongst us would be fatal to our peace of mind and might seriously stand in the way of the proper performance of our duty as the one great nation at peace, the one people holding itself ready to play a part of impartial mediation and speak the counsels of peace and accommodation, not as a partisan, but as a friend.

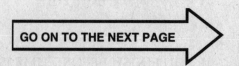

Source: Hugo Munsterberg, Harvard University professor, letter to Woodrow Wilson (November 19, 1914)

Dear Mr. President:

[I] ask your permission to enter into some detail with regard to the neutrality question. But let me assure you beforehand that I interpret your inquiry as referring exclusively to the views which are expressed to me by American citizens who sympathize with the German cause or who are disturbed by the vehement hostility to Germany on the part of the American press. My remarks refers in no way to the views of official Germany....

First, all cables sent by and received by wire pass uncensored, while all wireless news is censored. This reacts against Germany, because England sends all her news by cable, whereas Germany alone uses the wireless...

Second, the policy of the administration with regard to the holding up, detaining and searching of Germans and Austrians from neutral and American vessels is a reversal of the American policy established in 1812. It has excited no end of bitterness.

Third, the United States permitted the violation by England of the Hague Convention and international law in connection with conditional and unconditional contraband. ...[O]n former occasions the United States has taken a spirited stand against one-sided interpretations of international agreements. The United States, moreover, [previously] insisted that conditional contraband can be sent in neutral or in American [ships] even to belligerent nations, provided it was not consigned to the government, the military or naval authorities... By permitting this new interpretation the United States practically supports the starving out policy of the Allies [and seriously handicapping] Germany and Austria in their fight for existence....

Many of the complaints refer more to the unfriendly spirit than to the actual violation of the law. Here above all belongs the unlimited sale of ammunition to the belligerents...

Document C

Source: Robert Lansing, War Memoirs (1935)

The author was Acting Secretary of State during the period described below.

The British authorities...proceeded with their policy [of blockading American ships headed for mainland Europe] regardless of protests and complaints. Neutral ships were intercepted and, without being boarded or examined at sea, sent to a British port, where their cargoes were examined after delays, which not infrequently lasted for weeks. Even a vessel which was finally permitted to proceed on her voyage was often detained so long a time that the profits to the owners or charterers were eaten up by the additional expenses of lying in port and by the loss of the use of the vessels during the period of detention.

GO ON TO THE NEXT PAGE

Source: Secretary of State William Jennings Bryan, letter to the Chairman of the Senate Committee on Foreign Relations: (January 20, 1915)

Dear Mr. Stone:

I have received your letter...referring to frequent complaints or charges made...that this Government has shown partiality to Great Britain, France, and Russia against Germany and Austria during the present war... I will take them up...

(1) Freedom of communication by submarine cables versus censored communication by wireless.

The reason that wireless messages and cable messages require different treatment by a neutral government is as follows: Communications by wireless can not be interrupted by a belligerent. With a submarine cable it is otherwise. The possibility of cutting the cable exists... Since a cable is subject to hostile attack, the responsibility falls upon the belligerent and not upon the neutral to prevent cable communication.

A more important reason, however, at least from the point of view of a neutral government is that messages sent out from a wireless station in neutral territory may be received by belligerent warships on the high seas. If these messages...direct the movements of warships...the neutral territory becomes a base of naval operations, to permit which would be essentially unneutral.

(4) Submission without protest to British violations of the rules regarding absolute and conditional contraband as laid down in the Hague conventions, the Declaration of London, and international law.

There is no Hague convention which deals with absolute or conditional contraband, and, as the Declaration of London is not in force, the rules of international law only apply. As to the articles to be regarded as contraband, there is no general agreement between nations...

The United States has made earnest representations to Great Britain in regard to the seizure and detention by the British authorities of all American ships... It will be recalled, however, that American courts have established various rules bearing on these matters.

(9) The United States has not interfered with the sale to Great Britain and her allies of arms, ammunition, horses, uniforms, and other munitions of war, although such sales prolong the conflict.

There is no power in the Executive to prevent the sale of ammunition to the belligerents.

The duty of a neutral to restrict trade in munitions of war has never been imposed by international law...

(20) General unfriendly attitude of Government toward Germany and Austria. If any American citizens, partisans of Germany and Austria-Hungary, feel that this administration is acting in a way injurious to the cause of those countries, this feeling results from the fact that on the high seas the German and Austro-Hungarian naval power is thus far inferior to the British. It is the business of a belligerent operating on the high seas, not the duty of a neutral, to prevent contraband from reaching an enemy...

I am [etc.]

W.J. Bryan

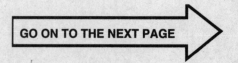
GO ON TO THE NEXT PAGE

Document E

Source: New York Times, notice (May 1, 1915)

NOTICE!

TRAVELLERS intending to embark on the Atlantic voyage are reminded that a state of war exists between Germany and her allies; that the zone of her waters includes the waters adjacent to the British Isles; that, in accordance with formal notice given by the Imperial German Government, vessels flying the flag of Great Britain, or of any of her allies, are liable to destruction in those waters and that travellers sailing in the war zone on ships of Great Britain or her allies do so at their own risk.

IMPERIAL GERMAN EMBASSY

Document F

Source: Report from the American Customs Inspector in New York (1915)

Q: Did the Lusitania have on board on said trip 5400 cases of ammunition? If so, to whom were they consigned?

A: The Lusitania had on board, on said trip, 5468 cases of ammunition. The Remington Arms-Union Metallic Cartridge Co. shipped 4200 cases of metallic cartridges, consigned to the Remington Arms Co., London, of which the ultimate consignee was the British Government. G. W. Sheldon & Co. shipped three lots of fuses of 6 cases each, and 1250 cases of shrapnel, consigned to the Deputy Director of Ammunition Stores, Woolwich, England.

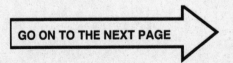
GO ON TO THE NEXT PAGE

Document G

Source: Woodrow Wilson, speech to Congress (March 24, 1916)

...I have deemed it my duty, therefore, to say to the Imperial German Government, that if it is still its purpose to prosecute relentless and indiscriminate warfare against vessels of commerce by the use of submarines, notwithstanding the now demonstrated impossibility of conducting that warfare in accordance with what the Government of the United States must consider the sacred and indisputable rules of international law and the universally recognized dictates of humanity, the Government of the United States is at last forced to the conclusion that there is but one course it can pursue; and that unless the Imperial German Government should now immediately declare and effect an abandonment of its present methods of warfare against passenger and freight carrying vessels this Government can have no choice but to sever diplomatic relations with the Government of the German Empire altogether.

This decision I have arrived at with the keenest regret; the possibility of the action contemplated I am sure all thoughtful Americans will look forward to with unaffected reluctance But we cannot forget that we are in some sort and by the force of circumstances the responsible spokesmen of the rights of humanity, and that we cannot remain silent while those rights seem in process of being swept utterly away in the maelstrom of this terrible war. We owe it to a due regard to our own rights as a nation, to our sense of duty as a representative of the rights of neutrals the world over, and to a just conception of the rights of mankind to take this stand now with the utmost solemnity and firmness....

Document H

Source: Arthur Zimmerman, confidential telegram to German Ambassador Johann von Bernstoff (January 1917)

On the first of February we intend to begin unrestricted submarine warfare. In spite of this, it is our intention to endeavor to keep the United States of America neutral.

If this attempt is not successful, we propose an alliance with Mexico, on the following terms: that we shall make war together and together make peace. We shall give general financial support, and it is understood that Mexico is to reconquer the lost territory in New Mexico, Texas, and Arizona. The details are left to you regarding settlement.

You are instructed to inform the President of Mexico of the above in the greatest confidence as soon as the outbreak of war with the United States is certain. You will also suggest that Japan be requested to take part at once and that he also mediate between ourselves and Japan.

Please call to the attention of the President of Mexico that the employment of ruthless submarine warfare now promises to compel England to make peace in a few months.

Foreign Minister Zimmerman

GO ON TO THE NEXT PAGE

Document I

Source: Des Moines Register, 1917

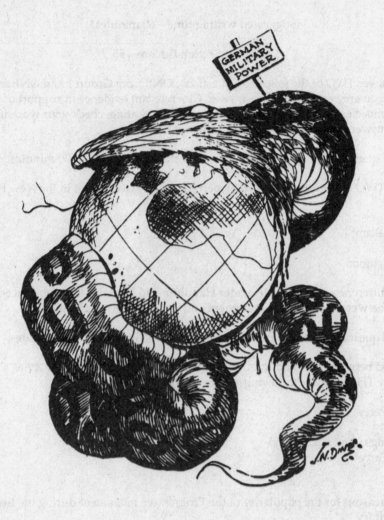

GERMAN MILITARY POWER

The Python

END OF DOCUMENTS FOR QUESTION 1.

GO ON TO THE NEXT PAGE

UNITED STATES HISTORY

Section II

Part B

(Suggested writing time—60 minutes)

Percent of Section II score—55

Directions: You are to answer TWO of the following questions, ONE from Group 1 and ONE from Group 2. Carefully choose the question that you are best prepared to answer. Cite relevant evidence in support of your generalizations and present your arguments clearly and logically. When you finish writing, check your work if time permits. Make certain to number your answers as the questions are numbered below.

Group 1: Choose ONE question from this group. The suggested writing time is 30 minutes.

2.   Discuss any TWO of the following as they pertain to self-government in the New England settlements prior to 1650:

Constitutionalism
Democracy
Freedom of religion

3.   Discuss the differences between Alexander Hamilton and Thomas Jefferson concerning the ideal relationship between the federal government and the states' governments.

Group 2: Choose ONE question from this group. The suggested writing time is 30 minutes.

4.   For the period between 1844 and the Civil War, evaluate the impact of slavery as a political issue on the history of any THREE of the following parties:

Democratic Party
Free-Soil Party
Know-Nothings (American Party)
Republican Party
Whig Party

5.   Analyze the reasons for the popularity of the Progressive movement during the first two decades of the twentieth century.

END OF EXAMINATION

11

Answers and Explanations

MULTIPLE-CHOICE SECTION EXPLAINED

1. A major weakness of the Articles of Confederation was that they

   (A) created a too-powerful chief executive
   (B) did not include a mechanism for their own amendment
   (C) made it too difficult for the government to raise money through taxes and duties
   (D) denied the federal government the power to mediate disputes between states
   (E) required the ratification of only a simple majority of states

(C) is correct. After fighting a war of liberation against the English monarchy, the colonists were leery of establishing a too-powerful national government. They erred on the side of caution, however; by severely limiting the government's ability to levy taxes and duties, the framers of the Articles essentially hobbled the fledgling government. The Articles also curtailed the government's ability to regulate international trade, enforce treaties, and perform other tasks necessary to international relations. Havoc ensued. The British refused to abandon military posts in the States, and the government was powerless to expel them. Furthermore, the British, French, and Spanish began to restrict U.S. trade with their colonies. That, coupled with the government's reluctance and inability to tax its citizens, nearly destroyed the country's economy.

Answer choice (A) is incorrect because the Articles did not create an executive, just a unicameral legislature. (B) is incorrect because the Articles could be amended, but only by unanimous approval of the states. (D) is incorrect; the Articles gave the government the power to mediate such disputes, on appeal raised by the states. The Articles required unanimous approval by the 13 states, not a simple majority, as (E) states.

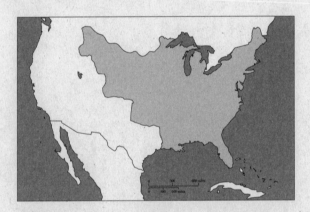

2. The shaded area of the map above shows the land held by the United States immediately following the

   (A) American Revolution
   (B) passage of the Northwest Ordinance
   (C) negotiation of the Treaty of Greenville
   (D) Louisiana Purchase
   (E) War of 1812

(D) is correct. In 1802, Spain ceded New Orleans to the French. This caused considerable unease in the Jefferson administration; while Spain had never taken advantage of New Orleans's strategic location (it controls access to the Mississippi River from the Gulf of Mexico, and vice versa), France seemed much more likely to exploit the advantage. Jefferson sent James Monroe to France to offer to buy New Orleans for $2 million. What the Americans did not know, however, was that Napoleon had decided to withdraw from the New World entirely in order to deploy his troops in Europe, which he hoped to conquer. Thus Monroe received a pleasant surprise when he arrived in Paris: the French offered to sell the entire territory for $15 million.

3. Which of the following states the principle of Manifest Destiny?

   (A) The colonists were destined to leave the British empire because of the distance between the New World and England.
   (B) Women are biologically predestined to lives of child rearing and domestic labor.
   (C) America's expansion to the West Coast was inevitable and divinely sanctioned.
   (D) The abolition of slavery in the United States was certain to come about, because slavery was immoral.
   (E) American entry into World War I was unavoidable and was in America's long-term interests.

(C) is correct. The idea of Manifest Destiny was originally advanced by a newspaper editor in the 1840s, and it quickly became a part of the public's and government's vocabulary. Part and parcel with the doctrine of Manifest Destiny was the notion that Europeans, especially English-speaking Europeans, were culturally and morally superior to those whom they supplanted, and so were entitled to the land even if others were already living on it. Manifest Destiny was later invoked as a justification for the Spanish-American War.

Knowing that AP questions appear in chronological order would have helped you eliminate answer choices (A) and (E). For an explanation of how chronological order works on the AP, see pp. 20-22.

4. In his opinion on the case *Dred Scott v. Sanford*, Chief Justice Roger Taney ruled that

   (A) the Supreme Court had the right to rule on the constitutionality of any federal law
   (B) "separate but equal" facilities for people of different races was constitutional
   (C) corporations were entitled to the same protections guaranteed individuals under the Fourteenth Amendment
   (D) school prayer violated the principle of "separation of church and state"
   (E) Congress had no right to regulate slavery in United States territories

(E) is correct. Dred Scott was a slave whose owner had traveled with him into the free state of Illinois and also into the Wisconsin Territory, where slavery was prohibited. Scott declared himself a free man, and a series of court cases ruled variously for and against his claim. The case finally reached the Supreme Court in 1857. Taney's ruling was remarkable in that it far exceeded the scope of the case. Taney could simply have ruled on the merits of the case; instead, he decided to establish a wide-ranging precedent. Slaves, he said, were property, and as such could be transported anywhere. Because slaves were not citizens, Taney further reasoned, they could not sue in federal court (thereby eliminating the possibility of the court reviewing any such cases in the future). Taney topped his decision off by stating that Congress could neither prevent settlers from transporting their slaves to western territories nor could it legislate slavery in those areas, thus nullifying the Missouri Compromise. Taney's decision is infamous for its lack of compassion for Scott and slavery, and is significant in that it hastened the inevitable Civil War.

Answer choice (A) describes *Marbury v. Madison*; (B) describes *Plessy v. Ferguson*; (C) describes many Supreme Court cases of the 1890s; and (D) describes *Engle v. Vitale*. You should know the *Marbury*, *Plessy*, and *Dred Scott* decisions, but not *Engle*, by name.

5. Following the Civil War, most freed slaves

    (A) stayed in the South and worked as share-croppers

    (B) joined the pioneering movement as it headed West

    (C) moved to the North and learned profes-sions

    (D) took work building the nation's growing railroad system

    (E) moved to Liberia with the aid of the American Colonial Society

(A) is correct; although the Homestead Act of 1867 was designed to give former slaves the opportunity to buy land at bargain basement rates, very few had even the little amount of money necessary to become property holders. The land was subsequently bought up by the wealthy, who often turned around and rented it, at steep rates, to farmers too poor to buy their own property. The resulting system was known as "tenant farming" or "sharecropping." Tenants would work a piece of land and turn over 50 percent of their crop to their landlord. Often other expenses, such as rent for a run-down shack, overpriced groceries available only through the land owner etc., devoured all other income a sharecropper would earn.

6. Of the following policies pursued by President Theodore Roosevelt, which was NOT a main objective of American progressives?

    (A) Passage of the Pure Food and Water Act

    (B) Creation of national forests and protected wildlife reserves

    (C) Initiation of antitrust law suits against various corporate monopolies

    (D) Intervention in the affairs of Central American governments

    (E) Expansion of the power of the Interstate Commerce Commission

(D) is correct. Progressives were primarily concerned with domestic reform; their agenda was the greater empowerment of labor, women, and the poor. The successes of the Progressive Era include those mentioned in the answer choices, the beginning of direct elections for U.S. Senate, and the establishment of three popular political tools: the ballot initiative, the referendum, and the recall. The Progressives pursued no coherent foreign policy per se.

7. Which of the following statements about the Treaty of Versailles is true?

(A) The United States Senate rejected it because it treated Germany too leniently.

(B) The United States Senate rejected it because it required increased American involvement in European affairs.

(C) The United States Senate approved it, with reservations concerning the division of Eastern Europe.

(D) The United States Senate approved it without reservations.

(E) It was never voted on by the United States Senate.

(B) is correct. Many Americans supported the U.S. war effort only grudgingly, and then only after German (and, to a lesser extent, British) interference with American shipping had provoked the U.S. to action. Many argued that America should stick to the foreign policy suggested in both George Washington's farewell address and the Monroe Doctrine, and therefore (1) avoid political alliances with other countries, and (2) remain neutral regarding European conflicts. Wilson negotiated the Treaty of Versailles (the peace treaty following World War I) for the United States. He was unable to get a treaty that reflected his conciliatory Fourteen Points, as the Allies demanded a treaty that punished Germany harshly. Nonetheless, Wilson did the best he could and returned with a document he was ready to present to the Senate. The treaty included provisions for the League of Nations (which Wilson had fought hard for) and contained a clause that could have been interpreted as committing the American military to the defense of European borders. Wilson, a Democrat, tried to sell this treaty to the Republican Senate, but could not muster the two-thirds majority required for ratification, and so the treaty was never approved by the U.S.

8. Senator Joseph McCarthy gained national prominence with his accusation that

(A) American meat packers disregarded fundamental rules of sanitation

(B) the Federal Bureau of Investigation was violating many innocent citizens' right to privacy

(C) some congressmen were taking bribes in return for pro-business votes

(D) massive voter fraud was common throughout the Southwest

(E) the State Department had been infiltrated by communist spies

(E) is correct. Senator McCarthy leapt onto the national scene when he stated that he knew of 205 known Communists in the State Department. McCarthy soon changed the number, first to 57 and then to 81. That should have called his credibility into question, but somehow it didn't. The charges gained immediate national attention, and McCarthy had discovered a potent political issue: America's widespread fear of Communism, heightened by the Chinese Revolution and the USSR's successful detonation of an atomic bomb. In the years to come he would preside over numerous investigative hearings, but he would never uncover any Communist spies. He brought about his own downfall when he accused the Army of harboring Communists. During televised hearings, McCarthy came across as foolish, bullying, and occasionally drunk, and subsequently lost his credibility, even among his many devoted followers.

9. The 1956 boycott of the Montgomery bus system

   (A) was led by Malcolm X
   (B) started because the city doubled bus fares
   (C) was instigated by the arrest of Rosa Parks
   (D) lasted for three weeks and failed to achieve its goal
   (E) resulted from the assassination of Martin Luther King, Jr.

(C) is correct. Rosa Parks was arrested after she refused to give up her seat on a bus to a white man; a Montgomery ordinance required blacks to sit in the back of the bus and to surrender their seats to whites if asked to do so. Outrage over the arrest, coupled with long-term resentment over Jim Crow laws, provided the impetus for the year-long boycott.

The boycott also brought Martin Luther King, Jr. (1929-1968) to national prominence. Twenty seven years old at the time, King was pastor at Rosa Parks's church. Although clearly groomed for greatness—his grandfather had led the protests resulting in Atlanta's first black high school, his father was a minister and community leader, and King had already amassed impressive academic credentials (Morehead College, Crozier Theological Seminary, University of Pennsylvania and finally a Ph.D. from Boston University)—the year-long bus boycott gave him his first national podium. King organized peaceful protests based in principle on his studies of Thoreau and Mohandas Gandhi, and in these he saw the springboard to the national civil rights movement he would spearhead for the next decade (until his assassination).

10. The Puritans believed that the freedom to practice religion should be extended to

    (A) Puritans only
    (B) all Protestants only
    (C) all Christians only
    (D) all Jews and Christians only
    (E) all inhabitants of the New World, including Africans and Native Americans

(A) is correct. The Puritans came to the New World to escape religious and political persecution in England. Believing that theirs was the one true church, the Puritans saw no contradiction in denying others the same rights they had sought in England. In their communities, freedom of worship was solely a Puritan right. Non-Puritans were limited politically as well: only property-owning male Puritans were allowed to vote in the colonial assembly (which, oddly, were quite democratic, within the extremely limited parameters of their membership). Those who questioned the church too aggressively—as did Roger Williams and Anne Hutchinson—were banished from the community. Williams went on to found the colony of Rhode Island, which for decades was the only place in New England where religious liberty was granted.

11. The Sugar Act of 1764 represented a major shift in British policy toward the colonies in that, for the first time, the British

(A) allowed all proceeds from a tax to stay in the colonial economy
(B) attempted to control colonial exports
(C) offered the colonists the opportunity to address Parliament with grievances
(D) required the colonies to import English goods exclusively
(E) levied taxes aimed at raising revenue rather than regulating trade

(E) is correct. Throughout the colonial period, the English subscribed to the economic theory of mercantilism, which held, among other things, that a nation's wealth rested on colonial holdings, a favorable balance of trade, and a large store of precious metals. Mercantilists held that governments must regulate trade through taxes so as to preserve its self-interest. Accordingly, English taxes and levies on the colonists (prior to the Sugar Act) were proposed and accepted as acts of a mercantilist protectionism. The Sugar Act was something different. England accrued a large war debt during the French and Indian War. Since, it was argued, the war was fought to protect the colonists, the colonists should share in its expense. Revenues from the Sugar Act were earmarked toward repaying that debt. The colonists saw things differently, however. Many argued that Englishmen could not be taxed without their consent, and that since the colonists had no representatives in Parliament, they simply could not be taxed. The Sugar Act is often regarded as a major catalyst in the chain of events that led to the Revolutionary War.

12. The Industrial Revolution had which of the following effects on slavery in the South?

(A) The creation of numerous labor-saving machines vastly reduced the need for slave labor.
(B) Rapid growth in the textile industry encouraged Southern planters to grow cotton, thereby making slavery more important to the economy.
(C) The government bought and freed Southern slaves, then transported them to the North, where factories were experiencing a major labor shortage.
(D) The Industrial Revolution began as the Civil War was ending and it provided work for many former slaves.
(E) New farm machinery required slaves and masters to work more closely together, with a resulting reduction of mutual hostility.

(B) is correct. The Industrial Revolution began in earnest in the United States after the War of 1812, and the first fast-growing industry was textiles (most textile mills, by the way, were in New England). England also had a booming textile industry and, at war's end, began buying all the American cotton it could. Farmers started expanding to the west, buying land and planting cotton wherever possible.

All these new plantations required lots of labor; hence, an increase in demand for slaves. It's worth noting that other major Southern crops—tobacco, for instance—were not wildly profitable under the slave system. The growth of the textile industry and its voracious need for cotton, however, solidified the role of slavery in antebellum Southern agriculture.

13. The Know-Nothing Party focused its efforts almost exclusively on the issue of

    (A) religious freedom
    (B) the right to bear arms
    (C) the prohibition of alcohol
    (D) women's rights
    (E) immigration

(E) is correct. The Know-Nothings were a nativist group formed in response to the growing concentration of immigrants—particularly Italian and Irish Catholics—in Eastern cities. The party grew out of a number of secret societies whose members were instructed to tell outsiders nothing, hence the party's name: when asked anything about their groups, Know-Nothings would respond, "I know nothing." Their program included a 25-year residency requirement for citizenship; they also wanted to restrict all public offices to only those who were native-born Americans. By 1855 they had changed their name to the American party and, in 1856, fielded a presidential candidate (former president Millard Fillmore). Within a few years the party had disbanded, destroyed by their disagreements over slavery. Most Northern Know-Nothings joined the Republican party.

14. Someone who emigrated to the United States during the nineteenth century probably chose his or her new hometown based on where

    (A) jobs were most plentiful
    (B) relatives already lived
    (C) premiums were paid to new settlers
    (D) the climate was most healthful
    (E) passage by boat was available at the time

(B) is correct. The majority of immigrants during the nineteenth century came from places in which family concerns were of primary and sometimes solitary importance. Those who left their homelands usually did so in order to create greater opportunities for their families, and they usually headed for a location in which family had already settled. The same, by the way, is pretty much true today.

15. The "Ghost Dancer" movement among western Native Americans stressed all of the following EXCEPT

    (A) the belief that the world would soon come to an end
    (B) rejection of alcohol and other trappings of white society
    (C) unity among Native Americans of different tribes
    (D) non-violence
    (E) the use of magic to neutralize the effectiveness of whites' weaponry

(D) is correct. The Ghost Dancers arose in the late 1800s when the sad fate awaiting the great Native American tribes of the era was becoming all too apparent. Wovoka, a Paiute Indian, started the Ghost Dance movement, which resembled a religious revival. It centered on a dance ritual that enabled participants to envision a brighter future, one in which whites no longer dominated North America. Wovoka preached unity among Native Americans and the rejection of white culture and its trappings, especially alcohol. He also preached the imminent end of the world, at which point the Indian dead would rise to reclaim the land that was rightfully theirs. Sioux Ghost Dancers believed in the power of "ghost shirts," garments blessed by medicine men that were capable of stopping bullets. This belief led to a rise in Sioux militancy and ultimately contributed to their massacre at Wounded Knee in 1890.

16. In response to several unfavorable Supreme Court rulings concerning New Deal programs, Franklin Roosevelt

    (A) urged the voting public to write letters of protest to Supreme Court justices
    (B) submitted four separate Constitutional amendments broadening the powers of the presidency
    (C) abandoned the New Deal and replaced it with a laissez-faire policy
    (D) instructed both the legislative and executive branches to ignore the rulings
    (E) proposed legislation that would allow him to appoint new federal and Supreme Court judges

(E) is correct. The question refers to Roosevelt's notorious "court packing" plan. Unhappy with the Supreme Court and the federal judiciary, whose conservatism several times resulted in the nullification of New Deal programs, Roosevelt proposed that he be allowed to name a new federal judge for every sitting judge who had reached the age of 70 and not retired. The plan would have allowed Roosevelt to add six new Supreme Court justices and more than 40 other federal judges. The proposal was not at all popular and was roundly defeated in the Senate. It also helped fuel the arguments of those who contended that FDR had grown too powerful. Not long after the 'court packing' incident, several conservative justices retired and FDR replaced them with liberals, so that he achieved his goal despite the failure of his plan.

Strike-Breaking

17. The 1933 political cartoon above makes the point that

(A) infighting within and among unions prevented their rise to economic power

(B) government inspectors turned their backs to illegal repression of labor unions

(C) attacks on unions were so well concealed that the government did not know where to begin its investigations

(D) from their beginnings, labor unions were controlled by organized crime

(E) the government moved too hastily in investigating misbehavior in labor unions

(B) is correct. Although it's hard to imagine today, labor unions had a very rough go of it for many decades. At first, government policy and law was directed only at the protection of corporations and their property. Eventually, legislatures passed bills protecting the rights of workers to organize and to bargain collectively. Enforcement of those protections, however, was lax to nonexistent; as a result, many union workers were subject to all sorts of harassment. The use of scabs and strike-breaking thugs was common; workers who dared to organize could lose their jobs and even their lives. The cartoon depicts the government conducting a misdirected fact-finding mission at a time when abuses against labor unions are obvious.

18. In which decision did the Supreme Court invalidate the practice of "separate but equal" facilities for blacks and whites?

(A) *Marbury v. Madison*
(B) *Bradwell v. Illinois*
(C) *Plessy v. Ferguson*
(D) *Brown v. Board of Education of Topeka, Kansas*
(E) *Holden v. Hardy*

(D) is correct. In 1954, the Supreme Court ruled invalid the "separate but equal" standard approved by the court in *Plessy v. Ferguson* (1896). In a 9 to 0 decision, the court ruled that "separate educational facilities are inherently unequal." The suit was brought on behalf of Linda Brown, a black school-age child, by the NAACP. Then-future Supreme Court justice Thurgood Marshall argued the case. About the other cases mentioned here: *Marbury v. Madison* is the case that established the principle of judicial review. *Bradwell v. Illinois* is an 1873 decision in which the court upheld the state of Illinois' right to deny a female attorney the right to practice law simply on the basis of gender. The case represented a setback for both women's rights and the Fourteenth Amendment. In *Holden v. Hardy*, the Court ruled that states could pass laws regulating safety conditions in privately owned workplaces.

19. The Bay of Pigs invasion of Cuba, in 1961, was carried out by

(A) Caribbean mercenaries hired by the United States
(B) American soldiers
(C) the Soviet Navy
(D) Cuban exiles trained by the Central Intelligence Agency
(E) Cuban Communist rebels led by Fidel Castro

(D) is correct. The Cuban Revolution, led by Fidel Castro, ousted the government of Fulgencio Batista in 1959. Not long after, Castro began nationalizing American-owned property (United States companies owned 40 percent of Cuba's sugar industry and practically all of its telephone and electricity services). Eisenhower broke off diplomatic relations with Cuba as he was leaving office and suggested an invasion of Cuba to incoming President Kennedy. The CIA presented Kennedy with its plan: Cuban exiles, trained by the CIA, would land at the Bay of Pigs and fight the Communists. According to the CIA scenario, the Cuban people would then rise up in support of the American-backed rebels, resulting in a new revolution and the ouster of Castro. To say the plan didn't work is an understatement. The invasion was poorly planned, poorly executed, and did not receive any support from the Cuban people. After two days it was over, and the new administration had suffered a major embarrassment.

20. Roger Williams was banished from Massachusetts Bay in 1636 for advocating

(A) the separation of church and state
(B) women's suffrage
(C) bigamy
(D) the export of tobacco
(E) independence from England

(A) is correct. Williams was quite a radical thinker for his time and place. After accepting a position as teacher in the Salem Bay settlement, Williams both taught and published a number of controversial principles. He believed, for example, that the king of England had no power to give away land that clearly belonged to the Native Americans. He also felt that the state was an imperfect vehicle for the imposition of God's will on Earth, and therefore advocated religious tolerance and the separation of church and state. Such ideas were pure anathema to the Puritans, who had settled Massachusetts Bay to establish precisely the type of state that Williams preached against. Neither easygoing nor good sports, the Puritans eventually banished Williams. Williams moved to what is now Rhode Island, received a charter and founded a new colony. Rhode Island's charter allowed for the free exercise of religion; it did not require voters in its legislature to be church members.

21. All of the following influenced the United States's decision to declare war against Great Britain in 1812 EXCEPT

    (A) the impressment of American sailors
    (B) British control of the Atlantic and resulting interference in United States trade with Europe
    (C) the American government's certainty that its navy was more powerful than Great Britain's
    (D) Great Britain's alliances with American Indian tribes, which curtailed United States westward expansion
    (E) the failure of the Embargo Act

(C) is correct. Nobody in the U.S. government was so foolish as to believe that America's navy was superior to England's, then the greatest in the world. In fact, had the American navy been so powerful, the war would never have been necessary, because American naval vessels could have accompanied merchant ships and ensured their safe passage across the Atlantic. However, England had the dominant navy and exploited its advantage throughout the beginning of the nineteenth century. Strapped for soldiers—England was at war with Napoleon, among others—the British confiscated American ships and forced their crews (some of whom, incidentally, were British deserters) to join the British navy. England also interfered with U.S.- European trade, in an effort to gain the upper hand on France (by denying the French American goods and commerce). The U.S. retaliated by imposing a national ban on many British goods, an act which provoked Great Britain to exploit even further its advantage on the seas. An intensification of the boycott, called the Embargo Act, failed miserably, causing a near-collapse of New England's economy. Meanwhile, southern and western settlers were anxious for expansion; their desires were thwarted by powerful alliances between the British and American Indians. Southerners, rallying behind Henry Clay, called for war.

22. Which of the following does NOT accurately describe the Missouri Compromise of 1820?

   (A) It provided a method for counting slaves among state populations when determining the size of the states' Congressional delegations.
   (B) It allowed Missouri to be admitted to the Union as a slave state.
   (C) It created the free state of Maine from territory that belonged to Massachusetts.
   (D) One of its purposes was to maintain the equal representation of free states and slave states in the Senate.
   (E) It included a northern border in the Louisiana Territory above which slavery was prohibited.

(A) is correct. The provision for counting slaves when determining apportionment in the House of Representatives is part of the body of the Constitution. All the other answer choices describe aspects of the Missouri Compromise, negotiated by Speaker of the House Henry Clay. The compromise forestalled the Civil War for decades. It also brought about the demise of the first Republicans (not the current Republican party, which gained prominence in the 1850s) by driving a wedge between the Northern and Southern factions. The slavery issue would continue to be the cause of regional division in the United States until after the Civil War.

23. Between 1820 and 1854, the greatest number of immigrants to the United States came from

   (A) France
   (B) Russia
   (C) Spain
   (D) England
   (E) Ireland

(E) is correct. Overpopulation and poor harvests in Ireland fueled a steady stream of immigration to the United States. Between the years 1820 and 1854, the Irish made up the single largest immigrant group for all but two of the years. The peak immigration period was between 1847 and 1854, when the potato famine struck Ireland; during those years, well over one million Irish left for America. In 1854, German immigrants began to outnumber the Irish, although Irish immigration remained at such a level that, by 1900, there were more Irish in the United States than in Ireland.

24. Congress brought impeachment proceedings against Andrew Johnson primarily because

(A) Johnson sought to block the punitive aspects of Congressional Reconstruction
(B) Johnson's Republican policies had fallen out of favor with the Democratic majority
(C) the Johnson administration was riddled with corruption
(D) Johnson's pro-North bias was delaying the readmission of southern states to the Union
(E) many Congressmen personally disliked Johnson, although they agreed with his policies

(A) is correct. Johnson, a Southern Democrat whom Lincoln had chosen as a vice-presidential candidate to balance the ticket in 1864, became president upon Lincoln's assassination. Although a vocal opponent to secession, Johnson nonetheless was sympathetic to the South and hoped to effect a quick reconciliation after the war. His Reconstruction plan was implemented during a recess of Congress; its intent was to gently shift the Southern power base from the aristocracy to the region's many small farmers and craftsmen. When Congress reconvened, Northern legislators were shocked to find that Johnson had allowed Southern states to elect former Confederate soldiers and government officials as their representatives. Led by Radical Republicans, Congress first refused to seat the Southern delegations, then proceeded to draft a more far-reaching Reconstruction, which included punitive measures. From then on, Johnson and Congress waged open war. Twice the House Judiciary committee considered impeachment proceedings. The third time was the charm; the official reason was that Johnson had violated the Tenure of Office Act (through which Congress had usurped Johnson's power to fire Cabinet members), but the real reason was their constant disagreements over the course of Reconstruction. Impeachment failed by one vote, after which Johnson served the last few months of his term and retired.

25. The "Open Door policy" in 1899 primarily concerned

(A) independence movements in Africa
(B) Mexican immigration to the United States
(C) the removal of trade tariffs from United States-European trade
(D) trade with Asia
(E) the United States' colonies in Central America

(D) is correct. The United States formed its "Open Door policy" in response to Europe's aggressive colonization of China. Fearful that the stronger European imperial forces would partition China, the U.S. called for guaranteed free trade in the region and the preservation of China's traditional borders. Europe might have disregarded the policy had not Chinese insurrections (e.g., the Boxer Rebellion in 1900) made it extremely difficult for Europe to control China. European imperialists had to band together, and accept help from the U.S. military, in order to avoid expulsion. The U.S. pursued the Open Door policy because policymakers had come to believe in the necessity of trading in as many regions as possible, maintaining a favorable trade balance, and expanding the U.S. economy on a continual basis.

26. Which of the following was NOT a major contributing factor to the onset of the Great Depression?

(A) Technological advances had allowed farmers and manufacturers to overproduce, creating large inventories.

(B) The federal government interfered too frequently with the economy, causing investors to lose confidence.

(C) The average wage earner was not earning enough money to afford the many consumer goods new technology had made available.

(D) Stock investors had been allowed to speculate wildly, creating an unstable and volatile stock market.

(E) Major businesses were controlled by so few producers that the failure of any one had a considerable effect on the national economy.

(B) is correct. In fact, the federal government did almost nothing to regulate the economy even though many within the government foresaw the potential for economic disaster. Many possible remedies—an income tax to redistribute wealth, a tighter money supply to discourage speculation, aggressive enforcement of antitrust regulations—were rejected. Meanwhile, manufacturers were overproducing, causing them to stockpile large inventories and lay off workers; consumers weren't making enough money to buy what, in some cases, they built at work; and the wealth of the nation was concentrating in a very few, often irresponsible hands. The system was too fragile, and when it started to tumble, it fell entirely to pieces very quickly.

27. The Truman Doctrine declared the government's commitment to assist

(A) Japanese families affected by the atomic bomb blasts in Hiroshima and Nagasaki

(B) any nation facing widespread poverty as a result of World War II

(C) free nations in danger of takeover by repressive governments, especially Soviet-style Communism

(D) American farmers, who suffered through major price drops after World War II ended

(E) American families who could not afford to build homes without government aid

(C) is correct. In 1947, the United States received word from London that the British could no longer afford to support Greece, at the time a client state. Both Greece and Turkey were in danger of falling to Communist insurgents, a result Truman was intent on preventing. In a speech before Congress in which he asked for almost $500 million in aid to allies in the two countries, Truman declared what came to be known as the Truman Doctrine: "I believe it must be the policy of the United States to support free peoples who are resisting attempted subjugation by armed minorities or outside pressures." Truman got the aid, Greece and Turkey remained allied with the West, and the Cold War intensified.

28. Which of the following best summarizes the United States's primary reason for participating in the war in Vietnam?

(A) The United States was required to fight under the terms of its military alliance with Japan.
(B) Vietnamese leader Ho Chi Minh requested American military assistance.
(C) The United States was hoping to promote Asian autonomy and anti-colonialism.
(D) American foreign policy experts believed that, without intervention, Communism would spread from Vietnam throughout Southeast Asia.
(E) The government felt obliged to protect the United States's considerable business interests in Vietnam.

(D) is correct. Answer choice (D) sums up the "domino theory," first articulated by President Eisenhower. In a speech explaining America's interest in Vietnam, Eisenhower said, "You have a row of dominoes set up; you knock over the first one, and what will happen to the last one is that it will go over very quickly."

Some of the incorrect answers are noteworthy. Ho Chi Minh was leader of the North Vietnamese, who were Communists; Ho had been a U.S. ally during World War II and had even received CIA assistance, but ultimately the U.S. opposed him for political reasons. The U.S. first came to assist France, the colonial power in Vietnam, so U.S. policy was hardly anti-colonial. Finally, the U.S. had few business interests in the area at the time, although the government was interested in the Vietnamese rice market, which fed America's strongest ally in the region, Japan.

29. The "First Great Awakening" can be seen as a direct response to which of the following?

(A) Puritanism
(B) the Enlightenment
(C) Transcendentalism
(D) existentialism
(E) post-modernism

(B) is correct. The term "First Great Awakening" refers to a period of resurgence of religious fundamentalism that took place between the 1730s and the 1760s. Its most prominent spokesmen were the Congregationalist preacher Jonathan Edwards and the Methodist preacher George Whitefield. From 1739 until his death in 1770, Whitefield toured the colonies preaching what has since come to be known as "revivalism." The period was marked by the creation of a number of evangelical churches, emphasis on the emotional power of religion, and, briefly, a return of the persecution of witches. Whitefield was a native of England, where the Enlightenment was in full swing; it's effects were also beginning to be felt in the colonies.

The Enlightenment was a natural outgrowth of the Renaissance, during which Europe rediscovered the great works of the ancient world and began to assimilate some of its ideals. While European thinkers of the time did not turn their backs on religion, they also entertained ideas about the value of empirical thought and scientific inquiry that were not entirely consonant with contemporary religious beliefs. Further, they began to view humanity as more important, and God as less important, a force in shaping human history. The First Great Awakening is usually characterized as a response to the threats posed by the intellectual trends of the Enlightenment.

30. Which of the following states the principle of "virtual representation," as it was argued during the eighteenth century?

(A) Paper money has value even though it is inherently worth very little.
(B) Slave populations must be counted when figuring Congressional apportionment, even though slaves may not vote.
(C) American property-holding colonists may, if they so desire, join their state legislatures.
(D) All English subjects, including those who are not allowed to vote, are represented in Parliament.
(E) All English subjects are entitled to a trial before a jury of their peers.

(D) is correct. The debate over "virtual representation" arose during the 1760s in the wake of English tax hikes imposed on the colonies. Anti-tax colonists argued that, because the colonists were not represented in Parliament, they could not justly be taxed; this argument was based on the widely held belief that the government could not tax a citizen without his consent. The English responded with the concept of "virtual representation," which, as answer choice (D) correctly states, holds that all English subjects are "virtually" represented in Parliament, even if they have not voted for a specific representative or, indeed, have not voted at all.

31. By the first decade of the nineteenth century, American manufacturing had been revolutionized by the advent of

(A) interchangeable machine parts
(B) the electric engine
(C) transcontinental railroads
(D) labor unions
(E) mail-order catalogues

(A) is correct. In 1798, Eli Whitney patented a process for manufacturing interchangeable parts. Several years later, at a demonstration before John Adams and Thomas Jefferson, Whitney took apart a number of guns he had built, scrambled the parts, and then assembled guns. Whitney's audience was astonished; previously, manufacturers had custom-fitted parts, and so guns, machines, etc., could only be assembled from their own, specifically fitted parts. The idea took national manufacturing by storm. Whitney's innovation brought about the end of cottage industries and gave rise to an American Industrial Revolution so successful that, by 1850, Europe was sending delegations to the U.S. to study its manufacturing systems. As a side note: the innovation also made Whitney rich, something his cotton gin had failed to do because that invention was so widely pirated.

32. The principle of "popular sovereignty" stated that

(A) whenever a new area was settled, all United States citizens were required vote on the slave status of that area
(B) slavery would not be permitted in any area after 1848
(C) the President, after meeting with public interest groups, was to decide on whether slaves would be allowed in a given territory
(D) settlers in the Western territories, not Congress, would decide whether to allow slavery in their territory
(E) any settlers disagreeing with federal laws governing slavery were free to ignore those laws

(D) is correct. In the election of 1848, the Democrats realized that their party was crumbling because its members could not agree on whether to allow slavery in the Western territories. They sought a policy to appease both abolitionists and slave-holders; the result of that search was the concept of "popular sovereignty." By allowing the settlers to decide the slave status of an area, popular sovereignty took some pressure off Congress, which was growing increasingly divided over the issue. It also took pressure off the political parties, which were coming apart due to the irreconcilable regional differences of their members. Henry Clay invoked the notion of popular sovereignty in the Compromise of 1850, but the compromise contained a purposefully ambiguous interpretation of what popular sovereignty meant. While the ambiguous wording was necessary to make the Compromise of 1850 possible, it also made future disagreements over the issue inevitable.

> "Society everywhere is in conspiracy against the manhood of every one of its members...The virtue in most request is conformity. Self-reliance is its aversion."

33. The passage above was written by

(A) Ralph Waldo Emerson
(B) Jonathan Edwards
(C) Harriet Beecher Stowe
(D) Charles G. Finney
(E) Andrew Carnegie

(A) is correct. The term "self-reliance" should have been your tip-off here; it's the title of one of Emerson's most famous essays (in which this quote appears). Emerson was a leader of the influential Transcendentalist movement, which preached non-conformity, individualism, and the belief that God was tangible and merciful, unlike the Calvinists, who described God as a distant, unforgiving judge of humanity. Transcendentalism is often seen as a rebellion against Calvinism and other forms of American fundamentalism.

34. The majority of those who voted Republican in the 1854 elections were

    (A) either Northern businessmen or Southern farmers
    (B) settlers in the Western territories
    (C) Northern abolitionists
    (D) merchants and businessmen in the Middle Atlantic states
    (E) recent immigrants

(C) is correct. The Republican Party was formed in 1854 as a party for those who opposed slavery, including abolitionists within the Whig and Democratic parties—almost all of them Northerners—as well as those who had belonged to the Free Soil Party. (The Free Soil Party had formed in 1848 over the issue of slavery in the Western territories. It dissolved because it appeared that the Compromise of 1850 had settled the issue.) The party was an immediate success in the North; in its very first election, it won over half the North's Congressional seats.

35. Which of the following is NOT a requirement set by the Reconstruction Act of 1867 for Southern states's readmission to the Union?

    (A) Blacks had to be allowed to participate in state conventions and state elections.
    (B) The state had to ratify the Fourteenth Amendment to the Constitution.
    (C) The state had to pay reparations and provide land grants to all former slaves.
    (D) The state had to rewrite its constitution and ratify it.
    (E) Congress had to approve the new state constitution.

(C) is correct. The Reconstruction Act of 1867, Congress's plan for the rehabilitation of the South, was much harsher than President Johnson's plan. Johnson, like Lincoln (who began planning the method for readmitting southern states before his assassination) wanted a reconciliatory plan that punished only the most prominent leaders of the secession. Radical Republicans in Congress wanted something much tougher, and the Johnson's plan was so lenient (in the first post-War Congress, Johnson's plan would have allowed the former president of the Confederacy to take a seat in Senate) that it drove many moderates into the radical's camp. The result was the Reconstruction Act, a punitive measure that imposed a number of strict requirements on southern states as preconditions for their readmission to the Union. Answer choices (A), (B), (D), and (E) list all of those preconditions; the fact that Congress did not impose any requirements such as the one described in answer choice (C) pretty much doomed post-War southern blacks to poverty.

36. Which of the following is true of the American rail system in the nineteenth century?

(A) Government subsidies and land grants played a major role in its expansion.
(B) The entire national system was planned before the first railway was constructed.
(C) Transcontinental rail travel was not possible at any time during the century.
(D) The development of the rails had little effect on the development of American industry.
(E) A more highly developed rail system gave the Confederacy a decided advantage in the Civil War.

(A) is correct. During the century, the federal government gave over 180 million acres to railroad companies; state and local governments gave away another 50 million. For the federal government, the goal was the completion of a national rail system in order to promote trade. Local governments often wanted the railroad to come to a specific town, since a rail station was a great boon to growth.

The incorrect answers are all entirely false. The nation's railroads grew haphazardly, and frequently different lines could not be joined because the tracks were of different gauges (B). The transcontinental railroad was completed in 1869 (C) and was the single greatest factor in the growth of the American steel industry (D). The North had a much more sophisticated rail system than the South, which gave the Union a great advantage in the Civil War (E).

**Percent of U.S. immigration total
per decade, by nationality**

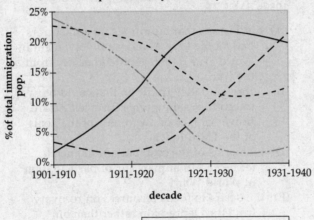

Austria/Hungary
Canada
Germany
Italy

37. Which of the following best explains the changes in immigration patterns reflected in the chart above?

(A) The Depression resulted in a massive wave of Canadian emigration.

(B) After World War I ended, the Austrian and Hungarian economies improved.

(C) Between 1920 and 1930, Congress passed immigration restrictions prejudicial against southern and eastern Europeans

(D) During the years represented on the chart, relations between the United States and Germany improved greatly.

(E) Between the years 1900 and 1910, the Italian government instituted a number of measures restricting emigration.

(C) is correct. The "Second Wave" of immigration starting in 1890 brought fewer northern and western Europeans and more southern and eastern Europeans. The result was increased ethnic tensions in the U.S. and, eventually, calls to limit immigration. Congress' first measure, the Emergency Quota Act of 1921, limited annual immigration levels to 3 percent of the number of people from that country living in the U.S. in 1910. In 1924 Congress tightened restrictions further, lowering the quota to 2 percent and changing the reference date to 1890, thereby dramatically lowering quotas for southern and eastern Europeans. A third law, in 1927, loosened restrictions a little (but not much). As a result, Canadians and others from the Americas soon became, proportionally, the greater share of U.S. immigrants.

38. All of the following contributed to the spirit of isolationism in the United States during the 1930s EXCEPT

(A) disclosures that munitions manufacturers had lobbied for American involvement in World War I, then profited heavily from the war
(B) a foreign policy tradition that could be traced to Washington's Farewell Address
(C) a universal lack of awareness of the goals of the Third Reich
(D) memories of the cost, both in financial terms and in human life, of participation in World War I
(E) the desire to focus resources on recovery from the Depression rather than on strengthening the military

(C) is correct. Hitler made little secret of either his totalitarian inclinations or his expansionist goals. He had written about both in his autobiography *Mein Kampf* while in prison in 1925; the book was widely circulated in the 1930s. Furthermore, news reporters, government officials, and many others witnessed firsthand the transformation of Germany under Hitler. While Americans may not have known the full extent of the Nazis' plans, they certainly had a good general idea.

However, Senate hearings conducted between 1934 and 1936 by Senator Gerald Nye revealed unwholesome activities by American arms manufacturers; many had lobbied intensely for entry into World War I, others had bribed foreign officials, and others still were supplying Fascist governments. This, coupled with the great losses the country had suffered in World War I, created a strong anti-war sentiment in the U.S. Liberal pacifists argued further that intervention in Europe would require a costly military build-up at a time when money might be better spent pulling the nation out of the Depression. Finally, there was the America's traditional neutrality, which dated back to Washington's admonition to avoid permanent alliances with other nations.

39. Jack Kerouac's *On the Road* and *The Dharma Bums* articulated the ideals of

(A) the silent majority
(B) the "lost generation"
(C) Middle America
(D) the Beat generation
(E) conservative academics

(D) is correct. The Beat generation rose in reaction to the growing complacency and materialism of 1950s America, particularly as it was manifested in the suburbs. Kerouac's characters are the antithesis of the typical suburbanite: they hop freight trains, drink and take drugs, engage in extra-marital sex, write poetry, and study Eastern mysticism. Other Beat writers include Allen Ginsberg, Lawrence Ferlinghetti, William Burroughs, and Gary Snyder. "Silent majority" is the term Richard Nixon used to describe those who supported his policy in Vietnam (as opposed to the vocal critics who protested it). The "lost generation" is the group of 1920s writers such as Ernest Hemingway who spent much of their creative lives in Europe. Middle America is, according to the *American Heritage Dictionary*, "That part of the U.S. middle class thought of as being average in income and education and moderately conservative in values and attitudes." Although many academics teach Kerouac's works, those works do not express the ideals of conservatives among anybody's ranks.

40. Legislation and executive orders associated with the Great Society created all of the following EXCEPT

(A) the Works Progress Administration
(B) the Equal Employment Opportunity Commission
(C) Medicare
(D) the Department of Housing and Urban Development
(E) Project Head Start

(A) is correct. The WPA was created in 1935 as part of the New Deal. Its purpose was twofold; to improve the U.S. through large-scale building and arts projects, and to provide work for the unemployed. The EEOC was created to police discriminatory hiring practices. Medicare insures that the elderly do not go without health care. HUD develops government projects to revitalize inner-city residential areas and polices discriminatory housing practices. Project Head Start helps insure that low-income pre-schoolers receive adequate food, health care, and other preparation for schooling.

41. Which of the following most accurately describes the system of indentured service in the Chesapeake settlement during the eighteenth century?

(A) Indentured servants were slaves for life; however, their children were born free and could own property.
(B) Most indentured servants were lured by the promise of freedom and property upon completion of their service.
(C) Most indentured servants were convicted criminals sentenced to servitude in the New World.
(D) The vast majority of indentured servants died within two years of arriving in the New World.
(E) Colonial law provided no protection for indentured servants.

(B) is correct. A population boom, political unrest, and hard economic times are the main factors that motivated many Englishmen and women—nearly 100,000—to go to the New World as indentured servants. Most were young farmers (not criminals), between the ages of 15 and 24, who were attracted by the promise of ultimate liberty and, until, 1670, a parcel of land upon completion of their period of service (usually between four and seven years). Compared with conditions at home, indenture represented real opportunity. Disease and hard work conspired to kill over one-third of those who came, but the rest survived to make up the majority of the European populations of Maryland and Virginia. Colonial law offered indentured servants some protections: masters were required to feed, clothe, and house servants, and were prohibited from beating them excessively.

42. The Northwest Ordinance of 1787 was a significant achievement because it

(A) laid claim to the all of North America east
of the Mississippi River
(B) represented one of the rare successes of
diplomacy between the United States
government and American Indians
(C) defined the process by which territories
could become states
(D) opened all territories west of the states to
slavery
(E) was the only piece of legislation to pass
through Congress under the Articles of
Confederation

(C) is correct. The Northwest Ordinance of 1787, along with ordinances of 1784 and 1785, created a process for distributing land to settlers. The Northwest Ordinance was the most important of them, because it also provided settlers with a number of civil rights (trial by jury, freedom of religion, freedom from excessive punishment), abolished slavery in the territories, and set specific regulations concerning the conditions under which territory could apply for statehood. The ordinance covered the territories northwest of the Ohio River and east of the Mississippi River, up to the Canadian border. This area was inhabited by a number of American Indian tribes, none of whom were consulted before the government started giving their homes to settlers. Violence ensued, and peace did not come until 1795, when the U.S. gained a military advantage over the Miami Confederacy, their chief opponent in the area. The Northwest Ordinance remained important long after the northwest territory was settled, because of its pertinence to the statehood process and to the issue of slavery.

43. All of the following were elements of Henry
Clay's American System EXCEPT

(A) protective tariffs on imports
(B) the establishment of the Second Bank of the
United States
(C) the construction of the National Road and
other roadways
(D) the creation of large numbers of federal
jobs in areas with unemployment prob-
lems
(E) incentives to develop manufacturing and
interstate trade

(D) is correct. Clay's American System was initiated during the Madison administration. A Republican, Madison believed in a limited role for the federal government; in fact, he sanctioned only those road and waterway projects that were truly interstate, arguing that intra-state travel should be the responsibility of the states. At the time, the government's suggestion to the unemployed was "Move where there's work!"; the feasibility of a federal jobs program was still over a century away. However, in the period following the War of 1812, the country and its leaders experienced increased feelings of nationalism, and Republicans felt that some federal action, if it served the national interest, could be beneficial. Poor roadways had hurt the U.S. during the war, and everyone agreed that the routes of long-distance travel needed improvement. A shortage of capital during the war convinced everyone that a National Bank was necessary (even though many still continued to distrust banks and blame them for the nation's financial woes). Finally, the American System sought to develop U.S. commercial capacities through protective tariffs and incentives for American merchants and manufacturers.

44. Reform movements during the first half of the nineteenth century attempted to accomplish all of the following EXCEPT

(A) convince people not to drink alcohol
(B) widen the division between church and state
(C) rehabilitate criminals
(D) induce humane treatment for the insane
(E) bring about an end to slavery

(B) is correct. The many reform movements of the early nineteenth century were the result of a combination of factors. Religious fervor grew during the Second Great Awakening, which began in the post-Revolutionary War period. With that fervor came the desire of many to do good works. Also contributing was the industrial boom that occurred after the War of 1812. Rapid industrialization had several unwholesome effects. One was the growth of cities, which was accompanied by urban poverty and despair. Another was the widening gulf between the commercial and moral realms: as businesses became larger and competition more keen, the ethical treatment of employees became less of a concern for many businessmen.

The memberships of many reform societies were made up almost exclusively of middle-class women. They formed benevolent groups, ministered to the sick, visited shut-ins, and preached the gospel. Through their contact with the less fortunate, these women saw the ill effects of industrialization and looked for ways to remedy them. In time their goals broadened to include emancipation of the slaves.

"The price which society pays for the law of competition...is great; but the advantages of this law are also greater...[W]hether the law be benign or not, we must say of it: It is here; we cannot evade it; ...it is best for the race, because it ensures the survival of the fittest in every department."

45. The above passage is characteristic of

(A) Calvinism
(B) Social Darwinism
(C) Progressivism
(D) cultural pluralism
(E) egalitarianism

(B) is correct. Social Darwinism took its cue from Darwin's theory of evolution, which states that natural selection determines the survival and demise of living beings. Many of the wealthy in the late nineteenth century used Darwin's theories as a justification for their phenomenal wealth in the face of widespread poverty (much of which they had created through low wages and poor work conditions). The quote above is taken from Andrew Carnegie's book *The Gospel of Wealth*. The applicability of Darwin's theory, which treats phenomena that occur over millennia, to the effects of the Industrial Revolution in the late nineteenth century is certainly questionable.

About the incorrect answers: Calvinism is the theological doctrine of John Calvin; it stresses the predetermination of the soul's status in the afterlife. Progressivism was a political movement in the early twentieth century; it championed labor unions, women's suffrage, and the direct election of senators. Cultural pluralism is a fancy way of expressing the idea that America is a melting pot. Egalitarianism is the belief that all individuals should have equal political, social, and economic rights.

46. The United States army supported Panama's 1903 war of independence against Colombia primarily because

(A) the United States was sympathetic to the rebels' democratic ideals
(B) the Monroe Doctrine required the United States to support all wars of independence in the Western hemisphere
(C) Colombia was asking too high a price for control of the projected Atlantic-Pacific canal
(D) the success of Panama's rebellion would have lowered sugar prices in the United States considerably
(E) the Colombian government was guilty of numerous human rights violations in Panama

(C) is correct. The U.S. desperately wanted a canal somewhere on the Latin American isthmus so that American ships could travel from coast to coast without circumnavigating South America. Nicaragua was Washington's first choice, but powerful American businessmen with investments in Panama convinced (or bribed, in many cases) Congress to adapt the Panama Canal plan. At the time, Panama was part of Colombia. Unable to cut a favorable deal with the Colombian government, the U.S. saw an opportunity in Panama's political instability. Roosevelt encouraged Panamanian rebels, sent military aid when they revolted, and then cut a much sweeter deal with the new Panamanian government for control of the canal. The creation of the Panama Canal raised the stakes in Central America considerably. American interest in the smooth operation of the canal was such that, in the first two decades of the twentieth century, U.S. troops intervened in the region six times. The idea that any threat to regional stability was a threat to U.S. interests was known as the Roosevelt Corollary to the Monroe Doctrine.

47. The rapid growth of American towns in the 1920s and 1930s was made possible primarily by the

(A) invention of the steam locomotive
(B) greater access to information provided by radio and television
(C) mass production of automobiles
(D) end of open-range cattle ranching
(E) advent of electric lighting

(C) is correct. In order for working people to move away from urban centers (where most of the jobs were), they needed a means of getting to and from work. By the early 1920s, the automobile provided just that. Mass production had lowered production costs and thus transformed the auto from a luxury item to an affordable convenience. Automobiles remained status symbols and were thus doubly sought after.

About the incorrect answers: the steam locomotive was invented at the turn of the nineteenth century. Televisions were not widely owned until the mid-1950s. Open-range cattle ranching took place on the open stretches of the Great Plains, far away from any cities (close to which suburbs must, by definition, be). The availability of electricity certainly made life more convenient for those who could afford it, but electric lighting, by itself, had little impact on the growth rate of suburbia.

48. Which of the following is true about the internment of those Japanese living in the United
   States during World War II?

   (A) The majority of those confined were native-
       born Americans.
   (B) Many of those relocated were known
       dissidents.
   (C) Only 2,000 Japanese Americans were
       relocated.
   (D) Congress passed a law requiring the
       relocation of all aliens during the war.
   (E) Those who were relocated eventually
       recovered their homes and possessions.

(A) is correct. More than 110,000 Japanese Americans were relocated during World War II. Most lost their homes and possessions, to the tune of an estimated $40 million. The relocation was mandated by Presidential order; Congress was compliant in that it never acted to stop it, but that was the extent of Congressional participation. There were not 100,000 Japanese American dissidents in the U.S. before the war, nor even half that many, making answer choice (B) incorrect. A question about this shameful episode in U.S. history appears on almost every AP U.S. History exam.

49. Anglo-American women in colonial times

   (A) could own property or execute legal
       documents only if they were widowed or
       unmarried
   (B) enjoyed more liberties and rights than did
       Native American women
   (C) attended church less frequently than did
       Anglo-American men
   (D) were more likely than men to do agricul-
       tural work
   (E) were required by law to learn to read and
       write, in order to teach their children

(A) is correct. Those few women who reached the age of majority and remained unmarried had the same legal standing as men, except that they were denied the right to vote in colonial legislatures. Widows had the same legal rights as unmarried women; however, married women forfeited nearly all rights to their husbands. Married women could neither sue nor be sued; sign contracts, deeds, or a will; buy, sell, or own property. Anything a woman owned prior to marriage became her husband's property.

Answer choice (B) is incorrect: although the role of women in Native American societies varied greatly from tribe to tribe, many women played a much more active role than Anglo-American women were permitted. (C), too, is wrong: church attendance was essentially mandatory in New England, although when attendance slacked off toward the end of the seventeenth century, it was mostly men, not women, who were skipping church. Indoors was considered women's domain; they were expected to keep house while the men did agricultural work (thus, (D) is incorrect). Answer choice (E) is wrong: there was no law such as the one it describes.

50. In the seventeenth century, the Chesapeake Bay settlement expanded its territorial holdings more quickly than did the Massachusetts Bay settlement primarily because

(A) Massachusetts settlers were entirely uninterested in expansion
(B) a high birth rate and healthy environment resulted in a population boom in the Chesapeake region
(C) no Native Americans lived in the Chesapeake Bay area, and the colonists were free to expand their settlements at will
(D) farm land in the Chesapeake area was less fertile, and so more of it was needed to support sustenance farming
(E) farming of the chief Chesapeake export, tobacco, required a great deal of land

(E) is correct. Area Indians introduced the Chesapeake settlers to tobacco, and its export to England proved an immediate success. Tobacco farming requires abundant acreage, since the crop drains nutrients from the soil and therefore cannot be grown repeatedly in the same fields. Accordingly, Chesapeake area settlers sought and received large land grants from the Virginia Company (prior to 1624) or the Crown (from 1624, when Virginia became a royal colony) until there was no more land to acquire.

The other answers to this question are flat-out wrong. (A): Massachusetts settlers certainly were interested in expansion, but at a slower rate. Unlike Chesapeake settlers, Massachusetts colonists built permanent, sturdy houses and settled in towns. (B): The birth rate and life expectancy was higher in the Massachusetts Bay colony; the Chesapeake region was more conducive to epidemic, and the English settlers, used to more temperate weather, found its climate inhospitable. Furthermore, whereas many Massachusetts settlers arrived with their entire families intact, most Chesapeake settlers arrived alone. Men greatly outnumbered women in the Chesapeake region, and so marriage and family life were less common there than in Massachusetts. (C): Both areas were populated by Indians when the colonists arrived; indeed each group would have starved to death had it not been for the Indians' assistance. (D): Land in the Chesapeake region was more fertile, not less, than land in the Massachusetts Bay region.

51. The debate over the First Bank of the United States was significant because it raised the issue of

(A) whether the new government should issue paper currency
(B) how strictly the Constitution should be interpreted
(C) whether the United States should pay back its war debt to France
(D) how to finance the construction of the railroads
(E) whether the president had the power to act unilaterally on important economic issues

(B) is correct. As the United States's first secretary of the treasury, Alexander Hamilton had to handle the nation's considerable war debt. His solution included the formation of a national bank, modeled on the Bank of England. Through the bank, Hamilton hoped to consolidate and manage the nation's debt and provide an agency through which a national currency could be circulated. He also wished to broaden the powers of the federal government (Hamilton, a Federalist, favored a strong central government). Both houses of Congress approved Hamilton's plan, but Washington (then president) was reluctant to sign the bill because he was uncertain of its constitutionality (Note: Washington performed very conservatively as president, aware that any action he took would set a precedent for his followers. Accordingly, he used his veto only when he was certain that a bill was unconstitutional).

The debate that followed defined the two main schools of thought on constitutional law. On one side were the strict constructionists, led by Jefferson and Madison. Both were wary of a strong central government and interpreted the Constitution accordingly. The strict constructionists argued that the Constitution allowed Congress only those powers specifically granted it or those "necessary and proper" to the execution of its enumerated powers. While a bank might be convenient and perhaps beneficial, they argued, it was not necessary, and thus its creation was beyond the powers of the national government. Hamilton, not surprisingly, disagreed. In his Defense of the Constitutionality of the Bank, he proposed what has come to be known as the broad-constructionist view. He argued that the creation of a bank was an implied power of the government, because it already had explicit power to coin money, borrow money, and collect taxes. Hamilton argued that the government could do anything in the execution of those enumerated powers—including creating a bank—that was not explicitly forbidden it by the Constitution. Washington agreed with Hamilton and signed the bill.

52. The "Lowell System" of early nineteenth-century textile manufacturing was noteworthy for its

    (A) practice of hiring only adult males at a time when textiles was considered "women's work"
    (B) commitment, in the face of the Industrial Revolution, to maintaining the old, "by-hand" method of manufacture
    (C) efforts to minimize the dehumanizing effects of industrial labor
    (D) pioneering advocacy of such issues as parental leave, vacation time, and health insurance for employees
    (E) particularly harsh treatment of employees

(C) is correct. The Lowell System is named after the town of Lowell, Massachusetts, where it originated. In their effort to recruit workers from outlying farmlands, Lowell manufacturers offered a number of incentives that, together, constituted one of the most humanitarian packages available to factory workers at the time. The workers—practically all of whom were women—were offered cash bonuses up front, housing in company boarding houses, and access to a wide range of cultural events. Owners' motivations were economic—they were suffering from a shortage of labor and so were trying to entice workers—but they were also partly humanitarian; horror stories of the effects of the Industrial Revolution in England were reaching, and frightening, Americans. Massive immigration in the following decades, and with it, the arrival of a large source of cheap labor, brought the Lowell System to its end.

53. The election of 1824 marked a turning point in presidential politics because, for the first time,

(A) the presidency was won by someone who was not a member of the Federalist Party
(B) a presidential and vice-presidential candidate ran together on one ticket
(C) all the candidates campaigned widely throughout the states
(D) political parties officially participated in the election
(E) the system of choosing nominees by congressional caucus failed

(E) is correct. Between 1800 and 1820, party nominees to the presidency were chosen by congressional caucus, then approved by state electors (delegates to a state nominating convention). Before 1824, electors were chosen by a variety of methods. Many electors were chosen by state legislatures, which chose electors who agreed with the choices of the caucus (often they were the same men who had participated in the caucus). By 1824, however, a majority of states allowed voters to choose their presidential electors directly. When the Republican caucus chose William H. Crawford in 1824, others, among them John Quincy Adams, Henry Clay, and Andrew Jackson, decided to challenge the nomination. Their opposition, along with their accusations that the caucuses were undemocratic, brought about the demise of the caucus system.

A couple of the incorrect answers are noteworthy. Answer choice (B) refers to an early constitutional problem remedied by the 12th Amendment. Prior to 1804, the person with the most votes in the electoral college became president; the one who received the second-most votes became vice-president. In 1796, this created an administration in which the two highest office holders, Adams and Jefferson, were of different parties. In 1800, it caused confusion when Jefferson and his running mate, Burr, received an equal number of votes in the electoral college. The election was thrown to the House of Representatives, who chose Jefferson on the 35th (!) ballot. Answer choice (C) refers to the election of 1840, sometimes referred to as "the first modern election" because candidates wooed the electorate directly during the campaign.

54. In the late nineteenth century, political machines such as Tammany Hall were successful primarily because

(A) federal legislation sanctioned their activities
(B) they operated primarily in rural areas, where the government could not monitor their activities
(C) they focused on accomplishing only a narrow set of human rights objectives
(D) they championed the suffragettes and received their support in return
(E) machine politicians provided needed jobs and services to naturalized citizens in return for their votes

(E) is correct. Waves of European immigration throughout the nineteenth century swelled cities' populations. Governments of the time were nowhere near as activist as they are today, and only a very few provided even minimal services to immigrants as they accommodated themselves to their new homeland; ethic communities and churches were expected to provide such services. A number of enterprising, unscrupulous men recognized in these immigrants the opportunity for great political power. Such men, known as political bosses, helped immigrants find homes and jobs, and acquire citizenship and voting rights. In essence, these bosses created entire communities, then provided them with all sorts of services: food and loans for the poor, parks and protection for the community. In return, the communities were expected to provide loyal political support, which they did, originally out of loyalty, and later, as the machines became extremely powerful, out of both loyalty and fear. The bosses could then hand an election to a politician of their choice, in return for favors. Political machines filled a need, albeit in an expensive and unethical way. They fell from power when governments started to provide many of the services machines had provided.

55. The disagreement between W.E.B. Du Bois and Booker T. Washington regarding the status of African-Americans in the early twentieth century is best summed up as a debate over

(A) what social injustices federal legislation should correct first

(B) whether African-Americans should immigrate to Africa

(C) whether state governments or the federal government should be the primary vehicle of social change

(D) how prominent a role African-American churches should play in the struggle for civil rights

(E) whether African-Americans should first seek legal or economic equality with white Americans

(E) is correct. Booker T. Washington was a famous agricultural scientist and the founder of the Tuskegee Institute in Alabama; W.E.B. Du Bois was a noted sociologist and the founder of the National Negro Committee, which later became the NAACP. Washington is often characterized as an assimilationist; indeed, he stressed that the best method for blacks to achieve equality in the U.S. was to gain economic power and integrate (or assimilate) into white society. In his most famous speech, delivered at the Atlanta Cotton Exposition of 1895, Washington stressed these views and also suggested that blacks would withdraw from Southern politics in return for guarantees of educational opportunity. Du Bois strongly disagreed; he viewed Washington's plan as one in which blacks would be required to earn the equality that should already rightfully be theirs. Du Bois argued instead for full equality for blacks before the law. Many historians explain the differences between these two men by pointing to their backgrounds: Washington, the son of slaves and a thoroughly self-made man, valued self-reliance. He lived his life in the South and had few illusions about how receptive Southern whites would be to black equality. Du Bois was a Northerner who studied at Harvard and in Germany, which may explain why he was more receptive to idealistic goals.

56. One of the unintended effects of Prohibition was that it

(A) caused a national epidemic of alcohol withdrawal
(B) brought about a decrease in alcoholism and an increase in worker productivity
(C) resulted in a substantial increase in the abuse of hard drugs, particularly heroin
(D) lowered the cost of law enforcement by decreasing the incidence of drunkenness
(E) provided organized crime syndicates with a means to gain both wealth and power

(E) is correct. The Eighteenth Amendment to the Constitution (1919) prohibited the manufacture or sale of alcoholic beverages in the U.S.. At first it worked fairly well; World War I had given Americans a sense of purpose and self-sacrifice, and the concept of abstinence was popular with Northern religious conservatives and fundamentalists elsewhere. The law did lower the incidence of public drunkenness and increase productivity (the law's intended effect, which is why answer choice (B) is incorrect). Eventually, however, a large enough contingent wanted to drink that it couldn't be contained. Especially in the cities, a massive underground industry arose to serve drinkers. That industry was controlled by organized crime, which became much more powerful as a result. Crime enforcement costs rose dramatically with the level of illegal activity, and soon it was clear that Prohibition had failed. In 1933 the Twenty-first Amendment, repealing Prohibition, was passed.

57. The 1927 motion picture *The Jazz Singer* was the first major commercial film to feature

(A) color images
(B) the illusion of three dimensions
(C) synchronous sound
(D) special effects
(E) a dramatic plot

(C) is correct. Prior to *The Jazz Singer*, movies were silent. Dialogue appeared on title cards on the film, and music was provided by a live accompanist or ensemble. Much of *The Jazz Singer* is silent, but it contains a number of scenes with synchronous dialogue and singing. It was a huge hit, and within a few years the majority of Hollywood movies were "talkies."

58. Which of the following was LEAST likely a factor in the decision to drop atomic bombs on Hiroshima and Nagasaki?

(A) Hope that a quick victory in the Pacific would hasten an Allied victory in Europe
(B) Fear that the Soviet Union would soon enter the war with Japan.
(C) Concern that a land war in Japan would result in massive American casualties
(D) Awareness that Japanese forces were numerous and spread throughout Asia
(E) Desire to demonstrate to other world powers the potency of America's new weapon

(A) is correct. The Axis powers surrendered months before the bombing of Hiroshima and Nagasaki, so speeding the end of war in Europe could not have been a consideration. The U.S. was primarily concerned with the difficulty of defeating the Japanese forces; they were both powerful and tenacious. Earlier land battles with the Japanese had resulted in heavy casualties for both sides. But the U.S. was also concerned about the Soviet Union; with the war in Europe over, the Cold War was beginning. Harry Truman was anxious to finish the war in Japan before the USSR could enter the fray and establish a greater presence in the region. He also hoped that, by demonstrating the power of the atomic bomb, he could intimidate the Soviets and other potential enemies.

59. The failed Equal Rights Amendment to the Constitution was intended to prevent discrimination against

    (A) African-Americans
    (B) Native Americans
    (C) children and adolescents
    (D) legal immigrants
    (E) women

(E) is correct. The first Equal Rights Amendment was introduced in Congress in 1923. It failed a floor vote every year thereafter until 1948, at which point it stopped clearing the Judiciary Committee in order to get a floor vote. It finally emerged from Judiciary in 1970, passed both houses with overwhelming majorities, and seemed on its way to ratification. At that point, a considerable coalition of fundamentalists and other social conservatives (including many women) rose up against it. It failed to win ratification in the necessary three-quarters of state legislatures, despite Congress granting its supporters a three-year extension on the ratification deadline. The amendment proscribed, in general terms, discrimination on the basis of gender.

60. Which of the following statements about the Stamp Act is NOT true?

    (A) because it most effected lawyers and writers, the Stamp Act fostered a particularly eloquent opposition to the Crown
    (B) colonial legislatures sent letters of protest to Parliament threatening secession from England if the Stamp Act was not repealed
    (C) opposition to the Stamp Act built upon colonial resentment of the Sugar and Currency Acts
    (D) among the colonists' reactions to the Stamp Act was an effective boycott of British goods
    (E) according to the Stamp Act, those who violated the law were not entitled to a jury trial

(B) is correct. The colonists objected strongly to the Stamp Acts (1765-1766), but still considered themselves loyal English subjects. The separation movement didn't begin to gather significant momentum until the Boston Massacre (1770).

The Stamp Act required that all printed matter—including all legal documents, licenses, pamphlets and newspapers—bear a government stamp, on which a duty was to be paid (in hard currency, which, because of the Currency Act and an unfavorable trade balance, was very rare). Violators were tried in vice-admiralty courts (basically military courts, so that the accused was denied the right of a trial before sympathetic peers). The law particularly affected lawyers, writers, and other elites and intellectuals, who in turn immediately began to eloquently publicize their opposition. The Sugar and Currency Acts had raised the rankles of the colonists, but because they had never protested before, their opposition was weak and poorly organized; however, those protests laid the groundwork for more effective opposition to the Stamp Act. Ultimately, the colonists settled on a three-tiered attack on the Stamp Act: raise public consciousness on the issue (through meetings, held by the Sons of Liberty), petition Parliament (none of these petitions included threats of rebellions), and boycott British imports. The last strategy effectively brought British merchants into political mix; they lobbied Parliament for a repeal because many depended on colonial commerce.

61. The doctrine of nullification stated that

(A) legal immigrants may be deported when they fall into a state of destitution
(B) Congress may override an executive order with a two-thirds majority vote
(C) the government may take control of a bank if its cash reserves fall below a certain percentage of its total deposits
(D) municipal and county governments may rescind licenses granted by the state
(E) a state may repeal any federal law that it deems unconstitutional

(E) is correct. The doctrine is a central tenet of the radical wing of the state's rights movement. It grows out of the principle that the main purpose of the Constitution is to protect the states against the potential tyranny of the national government; thus, the states have the right to nullify any federal law. The doctrine first appears in the Kentucky Resolutions, in which Jefferson argued (as he also would in the debate over the First Bank of the United States) that the Tenth Amendment prohibits federal government from exercising powers not explicitly given it by the Constitution.

The doctrine played a central role in a dispute between President Andrew Jackson and the state of South Carolina. The state declared its right to nullification in response to the Tariff of 1828, popularly known as the Tariff of Abominations. The state did not actually nullify any federal laws until 1832, when it nullified a different tariff. A potentially violent confrontation was averted when Henry Clay negotiated a compromise Tariff of 1833, in response to which South Carolina repealed its nullification law. The concept of nullification remained a powerful one up through the Civil War, when it was invoked by secessionists, and is, in fact, argued today by many so-called "patriot" militias and groups.

62. Alexis de Tocqueville attributed American social mobility to

(A) the continuation of European traditions in the New World
(B) Americans' rights to speak freely and to bear arms
(C) the government's tolerance of labor unions and progressive organizations
(D) the lack of an aristocracy and the availability of frontier land
(E) mandatory public education

(D) is correct. Tocqueville arrived in the United States in the 1830s; his assignment from the French government was to study U.S. prisons. He was immediately impressed by the level of interest the general public took in politics, and later came to admire the relative impermanence of the social hierarchy, especially compared with Europe's rigid social order. In his popular and influential *Democracy in America*, he argues that the absence of an aristocracy, along with the seemingly limitless amount of land available to the west, allowed Americans tremendous opportunities for self-advancement.

Some of the incorrect answers are noteworthy. (C) is quite wrong: there were few unions to speak of at this early stage in American economic development, and when the government took sides in labor-management disputes, it was invariably to side with management. (E) also is chronologically inaccurate: mandatory education and public schools were not widespread phenomena in the U.S. until after the Civil War.

63. Which of the following changes in westward migration occurred in 1848?

    (A) the number of pioneers headed for the Oregon territory decreased while the number headed for California greatly increased
    (B) the first great wave of migration ended, and the number of migrants remained extremely low until after the Civil War
    (C) for the first time, pioneers began to settle areas west of the Mississippi River
    (D) large numbers of free blacks, unwelcome in the East, began to resettle in the West
    (E) the government began to enforce quotas limiting the number of people who could migrate each year

(A) is correct. In January 1848, a carpenter discovered gold at Sutter's Mill, California. Word spread quickly, and soon the Gold Rush was on. Western migrants continued to travel west on the Oregon Trail until they reached Fort Hall (in modern Idaho), but then they turned south on the California Trail and headed for where the gold was supposed to be. Most wound up disappointed, as only a very few found much gold. In seven years, California's population went from 15,000 to 300,000. One observer noted that, by 1849, the western section of the Oregon Trail (which led into the Oregon Territory) "bore no evidence of having been much traveled."

64. The "free silver" campaign of 1896 received its greatest popular support from

    (A) New England businessmen, who were discriminated against under the existing banking system
    (B) Southern women, who incorporated it into a larger campaign for economic equality
    (C) bankers, who had run out of paper currency to invest
    (D) gold miners, who stood to profit from the movement's success
    (E) farmers, who hoped that a more generous money supply would ease their debt burdens

(E) is correct. The "free silver" campaign aimed to increase the money supply through the free coinage of silver. It was the great cause of the Populist party, which argued that the existing monetary practices favored the wealthy and elite, particularly in the Northeast. Free coinage of silver, the party argued, would cause inflation but would also put more money in circulation, making it easier for farmers to pay off their debts. Furthermore, Populists felt that a larger money supply was appropriate to the United States' tremendous growth rate at that time. The policy was naturally quite popular with farmers, but not with bankers, who would have had their loans repaid with devalued currency.

65. The United States took control of the Philippines in 1898

    (A) by purchasing it from China
    (B) as a result the Spanish-American War
    (C) after conquering the autonomous Philippine government
    (D) when Japan exchanged it for a promise of non-aggression
    (E) as the leader of a multinational coalition called in to suppress a revolution there

(B) is correct. The Spanish took control of the Philippines early in the sixteenth century (the country is named after the Spanish king Philip II). The United States recognized the nation's value as a port for Pacific trade, and during the Spanish-American War attacked and destroyed the Spanish fleet, effectively ending Spanish control there. Spain granted ownership of the nation to the United States in the treaty that followed the war. You should know that the Filipinos had been waging a war of independence against the Spanish and continued to fight the U.S. for years. In the 1930s, the U.S. allowed the Philippines to govern its internal affairs and was preparing to grant it full independence when World War II broke out. The Japanese captured the Philippines, forestalling Filipino independence until the island was liberated by the United States.

66. "Free speech would not protect a man falsely shouting fire in a theater and causing panic."

    The excerpt above is from a 1919 Supreme Court ruling prohibiting speech that represented a "clear and present danger." The defendant in the case had

    (A) given a speech urging black residents of Chicago to demand equal rights
    (B) written a magazine article in support of the Russian revolution
    (C) sent letters to military draftees arguing that conscription was illegal
    (D) given a speech suggesting that Texas should be returned to Mexico
    (E) posted fliers denouncing a department store in St. Louis

(C) is correct. The case was *Schenck v. United States* and it tested the validity of the Espionage Act of 1917, which forbade "false" statements intended to obstruct the draft or foment rebellion in the military; it also forbade the use of the mail to send any treasonous material. Schenck and his codefendants had sent fliers arguing against the draft to conscripts, for which he was tried and convicted in a lower court. The Supreme Court upheld the conviction. Oliver Wendell Holmes wrote the majority opinion, which included the passages in the question as well as this: "When a nation is at war many things that might be said in times of peace are such a hindrance to its effort that their utterance will not be endured so long as men fight."

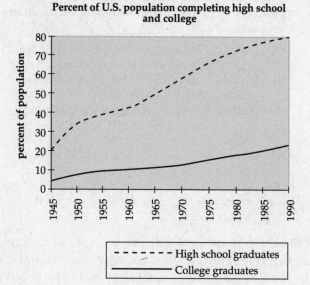

Percent of U.S. population completing high school and college

67. Which of the following best accounts for the trend illustrated in the chart above?

(A) Increased affluence beginning in the post-War era allowed people the opportunity to stay in school longer.

(B) The Supreme Court decision *Brown v. the Board of Education* led to increased enrollment in colleges and universities.

(C) During the 1960s, increasing numbers of high school graduates rejected the notion that a college education was desirable.

(D) The first state passed a compulsory education law in 1946, and others quickly followed.

(E) Jobs in advanced technical and medical industries generally require post-graduate degrees.

(A) is correct. America's economic recovery during World War II continued through the post-war years. When the war ended, the Depression-era generation found that it finally had money for luxuries and the leisure time in which to enjoy them. This new level of comfort meant that, in growing numbers of American families, children no longer had to drop out of school to get jobs as a matter of survival. Furthermore, many of those who lived through the Depression believed that education was a hedge against bad economic periods, and they strongly encouraged their children to study further. The result was steadily increasing graduation rates.

About the wrong answers: (B) *Brown v. the Board of Education* concerned school segregation. The chart clearly indicates that college enrollments increased during the 1960s, so (C) is incorrect. Massachusetts passed a compulsory education law in 1852; by World War II, most states had some form of compulsory education. And while (E) is true, it addresses post-graduate study, which is not represented in the chart, and it discusses career choices that relatively few people pursue.

68. The 1968 George Wallace presidential campaign, on the American Independence ticket, probably helped Richard Nixon win the election because

(A) Wallace's racism directed voters' attention away from the Watergate scandal
(B) Wallace won several traditionally Democratic Southern states
(C) Wallace's participation sent the election to the House of Representatives, where Nixon was more popular
(D) in the final week, Wallace withdrew from the race and threw his support to Nixon
(E) Wallace and Humphrey, the Democratic candidate, held similar views on all the major issues

(B) is correct. George Wallace was governor of Alabama and a staunch segregationist. Unhappy with the direction his national party, the Democrats, was taking, Wallace mounted a third-party candidacy in 1968. Wallace knew he could never win a national election, but he hoped to win enough states in the South to throw the election to the House of Representatives, where his chances would be better. Wallace garnered 10,000,000 votes and took 46 electoral votes. In some states where he didn't win, he gathered enough potential Democratic votes to throw the state to Nixon. In the end, Nixon was able to win enough states to take the electoral college.

69. The English colonists who settled Virginia and the neighboring Indian tribes had widely different attitudes about all of the following subjects EXCEPT

(A) whether property could be privately owned
(B) what type of work was appropriate for men and women
(C) how best to utilize the earth's resources
(D) the centrality of religion in daily life
(E) the means by which leaders should receive and exercise power

(D) is correct. The English settlers who arrived in Virginia in 1607 would almost certainly have starved to death had it not been for assistance they received from the Powhatan Confederacy, a group of six area Algonkian tribes. The Algonkians traded with the colonists, providing food in return for weapons and tools, in hopes that an alliance with the Europeans would provide them with an advantage against enemy tribes. The alliance was an uneasy one at best, however; despite their sometimes pathetic reliance on the Algonkians, the English settlers refused to consider seriously the legitimacy of Algonkian culture. Some of these areas of difference are enumerated in the answer choices. (A): The English not only claimed the right to private property—an alien notion to the Algonkians—but they also refused to acknowledge the Algonkians' right to their hunting grounds, on the basis that the land was not cultivated. (B): In Algonkian society, women worked the fields and men hunted; the English found this barbaric, as they considered farming to be work and hunting a leisure activity. (C): The English certainly considered their society superior, and the Algonkians certainly did not agree. (E): the English came from a monarchical society, in which leadership positions were inherited and power was nearly absolute; in Algonkian society, authority was conferred by fellow tribe members and could be revoked. The two groups were both deeply religious, making (D) the correct answer.

70. Puritan emigration from England came to a near-halt between the years 1649 and 1660 because, during that period,

    (A) most English Puritans were imprisoned for heresy

    (B) most Puritans converted to Catholicism

    (C) the New England settlement had become too overcrowded, and colonial legislatures strongly discouraged immigration

    (D) the Puritans controlled the English government

    (E) Parliament outlawed travel to the New World

(D) is correct. The period between 1649 and 1660 is often referred to as the "Interregnum," Latin for "between kings," because during that brief period England had no king. Rather, it was governed as a republican Commonwealth, with it's leader, Oliver Cromwell named "lord protector."

The English Civil Wars, between 1642 and 1648, are often called the Puritan Revolution, because they pitted the Puritans against the Crown. Royalists fought for the divine right of the king to rule and the maintenance of the Church of England (the Episcopal church) as the official church of state. The Puritans fought for a republican Commonwealth and a greater level of state tolerance for freedom of religion. The Puritans won and, for a little over a decade, ruled England. The death of Cromwell (1658) robbed the Puritans of their best-known and most respected leader, and by 1660 the Stuarts were restored to the throne. During the Interregnum, Puritans had little motive to move to the free world. Everything they wanted—freedom to practice their religion, representation in the government—was available to them in England. With the restoration of the Stuarts, many Puritans sought the opportunities and freedoms of the New World, bringing with them the republican ideals of the revolution.

71. The Monroe Doctrine stated that the United States had legitimate reason to fear European intervention in the Western Hemisphere because

    (A) Europe's militaries were considerably more powerful than was the United States's

    (B) the overpopulation of Europe made future incursions in the New World a real possibility

    (C) Europe's forms of government were fundamentally different from those of the United States and newly liberated South American countries

    (D) the United States anticipated reprisals for its frequent interference in European affairs

    (E) the United States ultimately intended to annex all of the Western Hemisphere

(C) is correct. The Monroe Doctrine basically declares the United States' prerogative over the Western Hemisphere, with an accompanying promise by the U.S. not to interfere in matters in the Eastern Hemisphere. Monroe's declaration followed a period in which a number of Latin American colonies fought and won wars of independence. After carefully considering the pros and cons, the U.S. decided to recognize the new governments (Europe had not yet done so). Fear that Spain, France, or even England might try to conquer these new countries led Monroe and his Secretary of State, John Quincy Adams, to devise a policy of mutual non-interference. That policy was completed and announced at a time when France was occupying Spain, further validating American fears that European governments did not respect others' autonomy. Monroe declared the United States' willingness to recognize and respect sovereign governments, and pointed out that difference between the U.S. and Europe in justifying his doctrine. He further declared the United States' right to intercede in the Americas when U.S. interests were threatened. Europe basically ignored the Monroe Doctrine, because the U.S. military lacked the power to enforce it. However, no one intervened in the Western Hemisphere because England wouldn't let them, which made the Monroe Doctrine look like a big success. It was invoked with greater success by later administrations, most notably Teddy Roosevelt's.

72. Supreme Court decisions concerning Native Americans in 1831 and 1832

    (A) reinforced the rights of states to remove Native Americans from disputed lands
    (B) denied them the right to sue in federal court but affirmed their rights to land that was traditionally theirs
    (C) voided previous treaties between Native Americans and the United States on the grounds that the treaties were unfair
    (D) granted tribes official status as foreign nations
    (E) ruled that the federal government had a unilateral right to relocate Native Americans to lands west of the Mississippi

(B) is correct. In the 1831 case *Cherokee Nation v. Georgia*, Chief Justice John Marshall ruled that American Indian tribes were neither foreign nations nor states, and as such had no standing in federal court: in short, he ruled they had no right to sue. He argued further, however, that the tribes had a right to their land and could not be forced to give them up by anyone, including the federal government. The 1832 case *Worcester v. Georgia* reaffirmed that position. When the state of Georgia tried to relocate the Cherokees, Marshall ruled that only the federal government, not the states, had authority over Native Americans within the boundaries of the United States. President Jackson didn't like Marshall's rulings and simply ignored them, pursuing an aggressive policy aimed at pushing tribes farther and farther west. The result was the Trail of Tears, the involuntary westward migration of the Cherokees. Over one-quarter died of disease and exhaustion during the 3–4 month forced march (supervised by the U.S. Army).

73. In the 1830s, Southern states passed a number of laws regarding the behavior of free blacks. These laws were intended to

    (A) encourage free blacks to migrate to the North

    (B) impose a uniform procedure regarding the retrieval of fugitive slaves

    (C) increase the pool of available black skilled laborers in the growing Southern economy

    (D) guarantee the rights of free blacks traveling through slave states

    (E) create an official set of guidelines concerning "acceptable" treatment of slaves

(A) is correct. These laws or "black codes" pertained to those few free blacks in the South. (Do not confuse them with the more widespread, better-known black codes imposed by Southern legislatures in the period between the end of the Civil War and the beginning of military Reconstruction.) As slavery became a more divisive issue both nationally and locally, Southern slave owners began to fear the presence of free blacks. They saw such blacks as potential instigators of rebellion. Furthermore, many viewed blacks as 'inferior,' and resented their freedom. Finally, freed slaves made up the majority of skilled laborers in the South, meaning that they were competing with whites for better-paying work.

Accordingly, the Southern states sought ways to encourage free blacks to leave the South; barring that, the states sought to severely restrict their freedoms. To that end, they enacted black codes. In various states black codes required black skilled laborers to be licensed, banned blacks from specific jobs, such as river captains and pilots, forbade blacks to assemble in public, and prohibited teaching blacks to read and write. Not surprisingly, many free Southern blacks moved north. Interestingly, many Northern states tried to discourage their migration.

Southern whites (particularly large property holders) feared free blacks so much that as time passed, they placed greater and greater restrictions on the ability of slave holders to free their slaves. By the end of the 1830s, most Southern states required court and/or legislative approval of a manumission (a fancy word for "freeing slaves"). By the 1850s, some states had entirely outlawed manumission.

74. By what means did the United States take possession of the Oregon Territory?

    (A) the United States was granted the territory in a post-war treaty with France

    (B) the United States bought it from the Native Americans who lived there

    (C) United States settlers were the first to arrive in the region; they claimed it for their country

    (D) Great Britain ceded it to the United States as part of a negotiated treaty

    (E) the French sold it to the United States as part of the Louisiana Purchase

(D) is correct. The United States almost fought a war over the Oregon Territory, which consisted of present-day Oregon, Washington, and parts of Montana and Idaho. Originally, American expansionists and settlers demanded all the territory up to the 54°40' boundary, and were willing to fight the British (who held it as part of their Canadian territories) to get it. Contemporaneous conflicts near Mexico caused President Polk to reconsider war with Great Britain; he feared that two wars would spread forces dangerously thin, as well as damage his popularity with voters. Therefore, Polk decided to negotiate a settlement with the British—the U.S. accepted a boundary at the 49th parallel —and directed his military activities southward. The U.S. subsequently entered a war with Mexico which netted them much of the territory that makes up the southwest states.

75. Which of the following was the intended result of the Dawes Severalty Act of 1887?

  (A) Railroad companies would be persuaded to stop unfair pricing through a number of government incentives.
  (B) Recently arrived European immigrants would be enticed into settling in the less populated West.
  (C) Legislators would be less likely to accept bribes because of the severity of the penalty.
  (D) Southern state legislatures would be motivated to strike racist laws from their books in return for greater federal aid.
  (E) Native Americans would be coaxed off reservations by land grants and would thus assimilate into Western culture.

(E) is correct. In the 1860s, the government initiated its "reservation policy," by which Native Americans were granted (usually less desirable) portions of the lands they inhabited. The policy failed on many fronts, and by the 1880s the government was searching for a different tack. Congress struck on the Dawes Severalty Act, which offered individual Native Americans 160 acre plots in return for leaving their reservations; through this program Congress hoped to hasten the assimilation of Native Americans, whose cultures most congressmen held in contempt. The results were not good: most American Indians preferred to remain among their tribes and did not accept the offer. Those who did usually ended up selling their land to whites, who often placed considerable pressure on them to do so.

76. During the decade following passage of the Sherman Antitrust Act, most courts applied the rule to break up

  (A) railroad monopolies
  (B) utility companies
  (C) telegraph cartels
  (D) labor unions
  (E) political machines

(D) is correct. Although supporters of antitrust legislation had hoped to create a law that would break up corporate monopolies, the only law they could get through Congress was the vaguely worded Sherman Antitrust Act (1890). It clearly forbade "every contract, combination in the form of trust or otherwise, or conspiracy in the restraint of trade"; however, it did not define these terms, leaving their interpretation up to the business-friendly courts. In a number of cases, judges made ludicrous rulings in favor of business (in 1895, eight of nine Supreme Court justices ruled that a sugar company controlling 98 percent of the refining process did not violate the law). Many courts were quick to determine that labor unions represented "a conspiracy in the restraint of trade," and until the beginning of the twentieth century the law was most often used to harass and break unions. All that changed in 1901, when Teddy Roosevelt gained the presidency and pursued a number of successful antitrust suits against business monopolies.

"Wot'd I care about the price of coal?"

77. The main point of the 1902 political cartoon above is that

(A) rural populations of different ethnic backgrounds did not get along together
(B) because farmers lived in warm climates, they had no need for coal
(C) rural dwellers had little sympathy for the problems of city dwellers
(D) corn was the major American cash crop at the turn of the century
(E) farmers were entirely unaware of the high cost of coal in the East

(C) is correct. The cartoon depicts a city dweller peering over the fence at a farmer; we can tell he is from the city because he wears a stylish, urbane hat (compare it with the one worn by the farmer). The city dweller has a look of distress on his face because the high price of coal is making his life miserable, a situation for which the farmer hasn't the slightest concern (hence the caption "Wot'd I care about the price of coal?"). The farmer is shown living a life of comparative ease, living off the bounty of the land and enjoying his work and surroundings. This pro-farming cartoon ran in the Kansas City Journal. It illustrates the growing tensions among the nation's different populations as each pursued its own agenda.

78. The term "welfare capitalism" refers to the corporate practice of

(A) providing social services for the unemployed poor who live near a factory
(B) offering workers incentives, such as pensions and profit-sharing, to dissuade them from joining unions
(C) marketing only to those potential customers who earn considerably below the national average wage
(D) raising prices in stores whenever AFDC checks are sent
(E) selling inventories to the government at highly inflated prices

(B) is correct. On this question, the chronological arrangement of questions on the AP should have helped you. Question 77 asks about events in 1902; question 79 asks about a 1933 piece of legislation. Thus, question 78 asks about something that happened between 1902 and 1933. That should help you eliminate (D), since the AFDC was formed in 1960. It should also point you in the direction of (B), because the period in question was one in which businesses actively and aggressively fought unionization.

79. The Agricultural Adjustment Act of 1933 sought to lessen the effects of the Depression by

(A) paying farmers to cut production and, in some cases, destroy crops
(B) purchasing farms and turning them into government collectives
(C) instituting an early retirement program for farmers over the age of 50
(D) encouraging farmers to increase production
(E) subsidizing food processing plants in order to lower food prices

(A) is correct. As he began his first term, Roosevelt was faced with an agricultural market in which the bottom had dropped out; farmers had so overproduced that their crops were worth virtually nothing. Roosevelt's solution, the AAA, provided payments to farmers in return for their agreement to cut production by up to one-half. The money to cover this program came from increased taxes on meat packers, millers, and other food processors. The program stabilized agricultural prices and increased American income from imports, but it came to and end when the Supreme Court declared it unconstitutional in 1936. A second AAA in 1938 served much the same purpose while avoiding those aspects that voided the first AAA.

80. During the 1960s, the Student Nonviolent Coordinating Committee (SNCC) shifted its political agenda in which of the following ways?

(A) although it started as an anti-war organization, by the mid-1960s the SNCC was solely pursuing a civil rights agenda.

(B) the SNCC, initially a Christian organization, officially allied itself with the Nation of Islam in 1963

(C) although initially integrationist, by 1966 the SNCC advocated black separatism

(D) the SNCC originally concerned itself exclusively with political issues on college campuses; over the years, the organization broadened its agenda

(E) the SNCC initially sought to achieve its goals through litigation; later, it pursued it agenda through peaceful demonstrations

(C) is correct. The SNCC originated in 1960 to promote antisegregationism and black voting rights in the South. Although primarily a black organization, whites also participated in the SNCC, and in its early years the committee pursued an integrationist agenda. However, years of Southern opposition, often entailing jailings and beatings, radicalized the organization. In 1966, Stokely Carmichael took over the SNCC and expelled its white members. Proclaiming that blacks could never receive justice in the white-dominated mainstream, Carmichael advocated "black power" through separatism and violence against those who would continue to suppress blacks.

THE DBQ EXPLAINED

The document-based question begins with a mandatory fifteen-minute reading period. During these fifteen minutes, you'll want to (1) come up with some information not included in the given documents (your outside knowledge) to include in your essay; (2) get an overview of what each document means; (3) decide what opinion you are going to argue; and (4) write an outline of your essay.

This DBQ concerns U.S. neutrality prior to World War I. You will have to decide whether the U.S. started out as a neutral force or whether it was always on the side of the Allies. If you choose the former, you will have to explain when the U.S. changed its policy, and why. If you choose the latter, you will have to discuss how U.S. actions prior to the war differed from their stated policy of neutrality. On the following pages, we will talk about how you might successfully argue either position.

The first thing you want to do, BEFORE YOU LOOK AT THE DOCUMENTS, is to brainstorm for a minute or two. Try to list everything you remember about the period leading up to the United States' entry into World War I. This list will serve as your reference to the outside information you must provide in order to earn a top grade.

Next, read over the documents. As you read them, take notes in the margins and underline those passages that you are certain you are going to use in your essay. If a document helps you remember a piece of outside information, add that information to your brainstorming list. If you cannot make sense of a document or it argues strongly against your position, relax! You do not need to mention every document to score well on the DBQ.

Here is what you might see in the time you have to look over the documents:

THE DOCUMENTS

Document A

This is an excerpt from Wilson's declaration of neutrality. It makes several important points you can use.

Neutrality is defined as "impartiality and fairness and friendliness to all concerned." This standard will enable you to argue that the U.S. was, or was not, neutral

The American people come from the different nations at war. The political implication is that even if the U.S. government wanted to enter World War I, the varied national backgrounds of the electorate would make it difficult to rally the nation to one side or the other. Even before Vietnam, American politicians knew the risks of entering an unpopular war.

Wilson envisions a prominent role for the U.S. resulting from neutrality. He sees the U.S. as "the one people holding itself ready to play a part of impartial mediation and speak the counsels of peace and accommodation, not as a partisan, but as a friend." This point argues that the U.S. entered the war as a neutral force, or, at the very least, intended to.

Document B

This excerpt is from a letter a respected German-American intellectual wrote to Wilson early in the war. It describes German-American perceptions of U.S. favoritism toward the Allies.

This document persuasively argues that U.S. policies at the time favored the Allies. The details are important, but less important than the overall point; the document illustrates that an intelligent critique of U.S. policy, held up to its own definition of neutrality, is possible. In fact, when Wilson received this letter, he sent it to his Secretary of State with a note essentially saying, "This letter makes a pretty strong case."

Munsterberg's second point, regarding the detention and searching of Germans and Austrians, is not often mentioned in discussions of the events leading up to World War I, and you are not expected to have heard of this policy. However, it does provide ammunition for those arguing that the U.S. was never neutral; searching civilians is, at the very least, an act of aggressive mistrust. If Allied travellers were not being treated the same way—and the letter implies they were not—then it indicates favoritism.

The issue of contraband could lead you to discuss the British blockade. (Document C provides more evidence of the effect of the British blockade.) Contraband is illegal merchandise. During war, contraband always includes weapons and other supplies necessary to the successful execution of war. The notion that contraband is illegal does not preclude the U.S. from selling arms to Europe; this same document demonstrates that the U.S. did just that. It does mean, however, that a country executing a successful blockade has the right to confiscate contraband. Munsterberg is saying that England defined contraband very broadly, including on its list of contraband items supplies that the German civilian population needed to survive. His complains that the U.S. was not aggressive enough in protesting this practice.

The last paragraph talks about the U.S. sale of arms to belligerents. This information can be interpreted in many ways. You could argue that to sell arms is essentially un-neutral, even if you sell to both sides. To make this argument, you would have to equate neutrality with pacifism (something Wilson does in Document A) and then assert that arms sales prolong the war, and so are counterproductive to the goals of neutrality. On the other hand, you could argue that because of the successful British blockade, arms sales went predominantly to the Allies; arms shipments to Germany never made it through the blockade. Again, Document C will help bolster this position

Document C

This quote comes from the memoirs of Robert Lansing, acting Secretary of State and, later, Secretary of State under Wilson.

Lansing describes the effects of the British blockade. Note, merchants are losing profits and Americans are being terribly inconvenienced.

You might use this to argue favoritism toward the British. Since the British were interfering with U.S. trade, why didn't we go to war against them? To the contrary, you could point out that as it became clear that U.S. commercial interests were at stake, U.S. involvement in the war became more likely. In other words, the U.S. started out neutral but the British blockade and German submarine warfare slowly forced America into the war. (See Documents E, F, G, and H.) You can also use this document to further discuss the effects of the British blockade on (1) the Allies and (2) the Central Powers. As you do, ask yourself whether the United States's response to the blockade was consistent with its policy of neutrality.

Document D

This is a report from then-Secretary of State William Jennings Bryan (he would soon retire) to the Senate. It is still early in the war.

Do not be intimidated by the length of this passage! The main point is simple. The government felt that its actions were neutral. This letter can be seen as a response to the complaints voiced in Munsterberg's letter.

Bryan discusses communication, the blockade, arms sales, and perceived hostility toward the governments of the Central Powers. In almost every case, he argues that England's advantages in geographic location and naval power are causing America's perceived breaches of neutrality.

If you are arguing that the U.S. was neutral, you might mention (if you remember) that Bryan, a pacifist, was committed to neutrality. His feeling that U.S. actions were neutral could be presented as strong evidence for your case.

If you are arguing that the U.S. was not neutral, you might contend that since Bryan is reporting to the Senate, he paints the rosiest picture he can. You might also mention (if you remember) that Bryan resigned not long after because of his disagreements with U.S. policy.

Document E

This advertisement ran in 50 American newspapers just before the Lusitania sailed.

This document gives you the opportunity to discuss German submarine warfare. The British blockade was too effective for the Germans to fight it conventionally. The Germans therefore turned to the U-boat, or submarine. Submarines gave the Germans the advantage of surprise as the British had no means of detecting them. You could argue that since submarine attacks resulted in the deaths of U.S. citizens, the use of submarines constituted a hostile act that ultimately forced the neutral U.S. into war. You might mention that Wilson regarded submarines as a violation of international law (see p.122), and as such, repeatedly asked the Germans to curtail their usage.

On the contrary, you might claim that the British blockade forced Germany to use submarines, and that by not opposing the blockade more aggressively, the U.S. was essentially siding with the Allies.

This document, along with Document F, also gives you the opportunity to discuss the sinking of the Lusitania and its effects, both on U.S. policy and on anti-German sentiments in the general population. The shift in American public opinion away from neutrality is a factor you might mention in your discussion of U.S. entry into the war. Document I provides more evidence of this shift in public opinion.

Document F

This customs report provides evidence that the Lusitania carried weapons.

This document can be paired up with Munsterberg's complaint about arms sales (Document B) to support the argument that the U.S. was not neutral. Note that the shipment is headed for England. Your outside knowledge that the sinking of the Lusitania led to William Jennings Bryan's resignation as Secretary of State would also be helpful here. Remember, the U.S. protested the sinking vigorously and demanded reparations. Bryan pointed out that the ship carried arms and quietly assured the Germans that the U.S. understood why the ship was sunk. In short, Bryan was at odds with official government policy, and he resigned when he realized that his advice to the President was going unheeded. His replacement, Robert Lansing, more active in defending American interests than Bryan, was willing to trade a reduction in American commerce for peace.

If you are arguing for neutrality, it is best to mention this document only in passing. Note that in Document C Bryan explains how the U.S. reconciles arms sales and neutrality. His justification, in short, is that international law does not outlaw such sales.

Document G

Wilson gave this speech after the Germans sunk the Sussex, an unarmed French channel steamer. The document is from 1916, almost a year after the sinking of the Lusitania.

Wilson threatens to break off diplomatic relations with Germany—a first step toward war.

Wilson invokes international law. Because Wilson interpreted international law as severely restricting submarine warfare, submarine attacks by Germany particularly angered him. Wilson considered himself and the U.S. the defenders of international law.

Wilson continues to declare America's international role as a mediator and peacemaker, as he did in his 'neutrality' speech (Document A). This insistence indicates that Wilson still considers the U.S. a neutral force.

You might point out that a year after the sinking of the Lusitania and that of several other ships, the U.S. is still not at war. This fact strongly argues for neutrality through early 1916.

Document H

German Foreign Minister Arthur Zimmerman sent this telegram to German Ambassador Johann von Bernstoff.

Zimmerman instructs Bernstoff to 'cut a deal' with the Mexicans. The telegram states that if the Mexicans start a border war with the U.S., the Germans will help them. As a result, Mexico will regain much of the Southwest.

The telegram also notes that the Germans are about to resume unrestricted submarine warfare which they had renounced in a treaty with the U.S. following the sinking of the Sussex.

The telegram mentions involving Japan in the war, thus widening the conflict.

Many Americans saw this telegram, which was made public in late February 1917, as the final straw. Because it showed Germany's willingness to intervene in American affairs and to draw other parts of the world into the conflict, the telegram convinced many Americans that Germany was power-mad. The cartoon (Document I) reinforces that perception.

Document I

An editorial cartoon that appeared in 1917, just prior to U.S. entry into the war.

If you find the inclusion of this document confusing, just skip it. You have plenty to write about without it. Remember, you will do better on the DBQ writing about what you know than by taking a wild and perhaps incorrect guess at what the test writers were thinking when they included a certain document. Again, you do not need to refer to all the documents to get a high score on the DBQ.

This document illustrates the shift in America's perceptions of Germany and America's readiness to go to war. Here, Germany is clearly depicted as an evil force that must be stopped, hardly a view consistent with a policy of neutrality.

OUTSIDE INFORMATION

We have already discussed much more than you could possibly include in a 45-minute essay. Do not worry. You will not be expected to mention everything or even most of what we have covered in the section above. You will, however, be expected to include some outside information; that is, information not mentioned directly in the documents.

Here is some outside information you might have used in your essay. The information is divided into two groups: general concepts and specific events.

General Concepts

- Even before the war, the U.S. relied more on trade with the British than with Germany. After the war began, this dependence became even heavier as the British blockade decreased American trade with Germany. The war effort also resulted in an increase in British orders for American goods. This increase occurred because the war had decreased British productivity. The British had taken men out of factories and put them in the army, and they also had converted some commercial manufacturing to munitions manufacturing.

- When the war started, official U.S. policy stated that American banks should not lend money to any nation at war. However, bankers pressured the administration to change this policy because Europe did not have the money to pay for the American goods it was ordering. Also, the loans were profitable, and American banks feared losing a lucrative opportunity to banks in other neutral nations. The majority of these loans went to the Allies.

- Wilson hoped the war would end in a draw. He thought a victorious Germany "would change the course of our civilization and make the United States a military nation." He also felt that an Allied victory would shift the balance of power too favorably toward England and France. Many of Wilson's advisors, however, were both pro-British and anti-German.

- "Wilsonianism," Wilson's idealized vision of the future, included universal, non-exploitative free-market capitalism; universal political constitutionalism which would lead the disappearance of empires; and universal cooperation and peace through the offices of the League of Nations. Wilson was also anxious to create a world leadership role for the United States. Many of his actions can be explained as the pursuit of these goals.

- Wilson held very strong views concerning international law, and those views favored the British. According to international law, an attacker had to warn a passenger or merchant ship before attacking. Submarines did not do this, for the obvious reason that it would cancel the greatest advantage submarines had; namely, the element of surprise. Germany argued that submarines provided their only means of breaking British control of shipping channels, but this assertion did not persuade Wilson.

SPECIFIC EVENTS

- The British blockade—From the beginning of the war, the British used their advantage at sea. They blocked shipping channels and confiscated any contraband headed for a Central Power country. Furthermore, England defined contraband very broadly, including some food and commercial products on its contraband list. The United States lodged numerous complaints against the practice, but the British government always paid for what it confiscated. The payment satisfied merchants and took enough pressure off Washington that the U.S. government never forced the issue.

- The sinking of the Lusitania—May 7, 1915. You will lose big points if you say that this event caused the U.S. to enter the war; the U.S. waited another two years before it started to fight. The Lusitania was a luxury liner that sailed from New York to England. When it sank, it took with it 1,198 passengers, among them 128 Americans. As Document G illustrates, the Lusitania was carrying a considerable amount of contraband, including over 4 million rounds of rifle ammunition. Still, Wilson and most of his advisors considered Germany's attack on the ship barbaric. As a result of the attack, anti-German sentiments among voters grew stronger and more widespread.

- William Jennings Bryan's resignation—Bryan resigned in the aftermath of the Lusitania incident. An ardent pacifist, Bryan wanted the U.S. to respond to the incident with a strongly worded letter of protest to both the English and the Germans. Bryan also suggested that the U.S. ban American passengers from any ship flying the flag of a belligerent country. Wilson rejected both recommendations. He sent a letter of protest only to the Germans, and he refused to restrict American travel abroad. Bryan resigned in protest. In response to Wilson's letter, the Germans temporarily halted U-boat attacks on passenger ships.

- The sinking of the Arabic—In mid-August, the Germans sank another passenger liner. This time only two Americans died, but the government was furious about the breech of etiquette. The Germans pledged again never to attack a passenger liner without advance warning, a promise they did not keep.

- Gore-McLemore resolution—After the sinking of the Arabic, Congress began to seriously consider a resolution prohibiting Americans from traveling on armed merchant ships or on ships carting contraband. Wilson fought this Gore-McLemore resolution. Wilson remained adamant that neutral nations should have free access to international waters. The resolution was defeated.

- The sinking of the Sussex and the Sussex Agreement—In February 1917, the Germans sank a French channel steamer called the Sussex. No Americans died, although four were injured. However, the incident had a big impact because the Sussex was neither armed nor was it carrying contraband. In short, its sinking convinced many people that either (1) German submarines could not tell at what they were shooting, or (2) the Germans did not care that they were killing civilians. Either way, it supported the widespread sentiment that submarine warfare was barbaric. Germany again agreed not to attack passenger ships without warning. Wilson was still resolutely determined to stay out of the war, so he accepted the agreement.

- The presidential election of 1916—Despite the many quarrels with England and Germany, most Americans still wanted no part of the European hostilities. All the major candidates campaigned against entry into the war. The Republican, Hughes, courted German-American votes and depicted Wilson as partial to the Allies. Wilson campaigned on the slogan "He kept us out of war." As the campaign wore on, however, he also began to stress "preparedness" for the possibility of war. Wilson won by a narrow margin.

- More details about the Zimmerman Note—By the time this telegram was leaked to the press, Germany had already warned the U.S. of its plans to resume unrestricted submarine warfare. The reason for the shift in policy is that the Germans realized that without the submarines they would soon lose the war. The resumption of submarine warfare greatly angered Wilson. When the British intercepted the telegram, Wilson had already severed diplomatic ties with Germany and was considering his future options. Wilson received the telegram on February 24, 1917), and the newspapers received it four days later.

  The telegram represents a last-ditch effort on Germany's part to keep the U.S. out of the war. Germany knew that its resumption of submarine warfare would draw the U.S. into the war. Planning to distract the U.S. with a border skirmish, Germany hoped to buy enough time to win the war in Europe before U.S. reinforcements could arrive. Since the Mexican Revolution had just replaced a government friendly to the U.S. with one much more hostile, the U.S. government took the threat of a German-backed Mexican attack in the Southwest very seriously.

  It particularly galled the U.S. that Zimmerman sent the telegram through U.S. State Department channels. The U.S. had opened those channels to him in hopes of bringing the Germans back to the negotiating table. When he was used those same channels to plot war against the U.S., it was regarded as an act of extreme hostility and bad manners.

  The U.S. did not immediately declare war. In the weeks that followed, Wilson asked Congress for a policy of "armed neutrality," which would allow American merchant ships to mount offensive weapons. Debate was fierce, showing how strong anti-war sentiment was even at the time. The U.S. did not officially declare war until the following month on April 2, 1917.

- The Nye Commission investigations of 1933—The Nye Commission, investigating American business practices in the years leading up to World War I, revealed that American arms merchants had lobbied intensely for entry into the war. The Commission also discovered that these merchants had reaped enormous profit from arms sales, first to whomever they could get them to in Europe, then to the U.S. government.

CHOOSING A SIDE

We have just covered an intimidating amount of material. Do not worry; your essay only has to cover some of the points mentioned above. The review mentions nearly everything you might include in a successful essay, not everything that must be in a successful essay.

Your next task is to choose a position to argue and then construct a strong justification from your notes on the documents and outside information. Document-based questions are written so that there is no one "right" answer, and there are many different defensible positions to this question. There are also many different ways to argue the same point; that is, there is no one "right" way to write an essay for any given argument.

Here are some positions you might argue:

- The United States was neutral at the beginning of the war, but a combination of factors—such as economic interests, German transgressions of international law, and America's predisposition toward England—ultimately drew America into the war.

- The United States was neutral at the beginning of the war, but was provoked to fight by German aggression.

- The United States claimed neutrality, and maybe its leaders even convinced themselves that their actions were neutral, but in reality U.S. actions helped the Allies. Consequently, the U.S. was never really neutral.

- The United States was correct in claiming neutrality because its policies adhered to its standards of neutrality. However, the Central Powers legitimately accused the U.S. of acting in a way that assisted the Allies and so were justified in regarding the U.S. as un-neutral. The question is semantic; whether the U.S. was neutral depends on how you define neutrality.

- The only position you should certainly avoid is the claim that the U.S. had always sided fully with the Allies and lied about neutrality in order to help them. There is simply too much evidence of Wilson's commitment to neutrality to support that argument.

PLANNING YOUR ESSAY

Unless you read extremely quickly, you probably will not have time to write a detailed outline for your essay during the fifteen-minute reading period. However, it is worth taking several minutes to jot down a loose structure of your essay because it will actually save you time when your write! First, decide on your thesis and write it down in the test booklet. (There is usually some the blank space below the documents.) Then take a minute or two to brainstorm all the points you might put in your essay. Choose the strongest points and number them in the order you plan to present them. Lastly, note which documents and outside information you plan to use in conjunction with each point. If you organize your essay in advance of writing, the actual writing process will go much more smoothly. More important, you will not write yourself into a corner, suddenly finding yourself making a point you cannot support or heading toward a weak conclusion (or worse still, no conclusion at all).

For example, if you were going to argue that the U.S. was neutral at the start of the war, but a combination of factors eventually forced America's entry, you might write down an abbreviated version of that thesis such as:

> *Started neutral, forced into war*

Then you would brainstorm a list of ideas and events you wanted to mention in your essay such as:

> *Started neutral*
>
> *British blockade*
>
> *Business losing money from blockade*
>
> *Wilson didn't want Germany to win war*
>
> *U-boats violate international law*
>
> *U-boats kill US civilians*
>
> *Zimmerman telegram*
>
> *Lusitania*
>
> *Sussex*
>
> *American people were against war*
>
> *Americans a little more favorable to war by 1917*

Next, you would want to figure out which of your brainstorm ideas could be the main idea of a paragraph, which could be used as evidence to support a point, and which should be eliminated. You would probably want to begin your first paragraph by stating your thesis and then discussing how the US was neutral at the start of the war. Your first point, "Started neutral," could be the main idea of that paragraph. That the "American people were against the war" would help explain why the U.S. was neutral, so you could use that as evidence. At this point, your list might look this way:

> *Started neutral*   1
>
> *British blockade*
>
> *Business losing money from blockade*
>
> *Wilson didn't want Germany to win war*
>
> *U-boats violate international law*
>
> *U-boats kill US civilians*
>
> *Zimmerman telegram*
>
> *Lusitania*
>
> *Sussex*
>
> *American people were against war*   1-evidence
>
> *Americans a little more favorable to war by 1917*

What else would you want to mention in this paragraph? Certainly refer to Document A, Wilson's statement of American neutrality and his definition of neutrality. Use that definition to explain how each of America's ensuing actions was either neutral or favorable to the Allies. You might also mention Wilson's desire to turn the U.S. into a world power, and how he viewed neutrality as a means toward that end. Mentioning this point helps you fulfill the requirement to include outside information.

Next you might want to discuss the British blockade and America's response to it. That would make "British blockade" the subject of paragraph 2; "business loses money from blockade" is something you might want to mention in this paragraph. Now your list might look this way:

Started neutral	1
British blockade	2
Business losing money from blockade	2-evidence
Wilson didn't want Germany to win war	
U-boats violate international law	
U-boats kill US civilians	
Zimmerman telegram	
Lusitania	
Sussex	
American people were against war	1-evidence
Americans a little more favorable to war by 1917	

In this paragraph, you probably also want to mention Documents B, C, and D. Document D, Bryan's letter to the Senate, gives the strongest evidence of U.S. neutrality. You might want to use Documents B and C (Munsterberg's complaint to Wilson and Lansing's description of the effects of the blockade) to explain how the U.S. found itself more involved in Europe's war than it perhaps had expected to be.

Proceed in this way until you have finished planning your strategy. Try to fit as many of the documents into your argument as you can, but do not stretch too far to fit one in. An obvious, desperate stretch will only hurt your grade.

As you write, remember that you do not have to fall entirely on one side or another of this issue. History is complex, and simple explanations are rarely accurate ones. If your essay argues that the U.S. intended to remain neutral and then discusses the events referred to by the documents in the context of neutrality, you will get a "9" on your DBQ essay, even if it does not characterize each U.S. action as "neutral" or "un-neutral."

ARGUING AGAINST NEUTRALITY

If you choose to argue that the U.S. was not neutral, you should concentrate on Documents A, B, and C. Use Document A, Wilson's Congressional address, for the definition of neutrality, then use the other documents and outside knowledge to argue that the U.S. did not meet its own definition. Document B, Munserberg's letter, really helps your position as it points out how U.S. actions appeared un-neutral at the time these events were taking place. Use Document C, Lansing's criticism of the British blockade, to argue that the U.S. put up with abuses from the British at the same time they were denouncing Germany for similar abuses. Focus also on Document F which describes the substantial arms shipment aboard the Lusitania. You might then incorporate the other documents by claiming that Germany responded reasonably to its situation and that the U.S., as a neutral nation, should have understood their actions. That position, by the way, is how William Jennings Bryan felt; if you knew that and included it in your essay, you would have gotten major bonus points for outside knowledge.

WHAT YOU SHOULD HAVE DISCUSSED

Regardless of what side of the issue you argued, your essay should have discussed all of the following:

- Wilson's declaration of neutrality and his definition of neutrality
- Munsterberg's letter
- Bryan's response to Munsterberg
- the British blockade
- German submarine warfare
- the sinking of the Lusitania
- Zimmerman telegram

Give yourself very high marks for "outside knowledge" if you mentioned any three of the following:

- Wilsonianism
- U.S. balance of trade with the Allies and the Central Powers
- U.S. loans to England and France
- Wilson's cabinet and its predisposition toward England
- Wilson's interpretation of international law regarding submarine warfare
- Bryan's resignation
- the sinking of the Sussex
- the Gore-McLemore resolution
- the sinking of the Arabic
- "armed neutrality"
- the Nye Commission

FREE-RESPONSE QUESTION EXPLAINED

Because you only have thirty-five minutes to plan and write each of these essays, you will not have time to work out elaborate arguments. That's OK; nobody is expecting you to read two questions, choose one, remember all the pertinent facts about that subject, formulate a brilliant thesis, and write an essay about it, AND then repeat the process. Here is what you do. First, choose your question; brainstorm for two or three minutes; and edit your brainstorm ideas. Then, number those points you are going to include in your essay in the order you plan to present them. Last, think of a simple thesis statement that allows you to discuss the points your essay will make.

ABOUT THE FREE-RESPONSE QUESTIONS ON OUR DIAGNOSTIC TEST

Question 2—New England Before 1650

> 2. Discuss any TWO of the following as they pertain to self-government in the New England settlements prior to 1650:
>
> Constitutionalism
> Democracy
> Freedom of religion

This question is probably the more difficult of the two from which you had to choose, primarily because by the time you take the test, it has been almost a year since you have studied the colonial period. It helps to remember that the Puritans settled New England, provided you remember anything specific about the Puritans.

Below are lists of concepts and events you might have included in your essay. There is a list for each of the three subjects—constitutional government, democracy, and freedom of religion—and each list is broken into two sub-lists. The first sub-list contains that which you practically had to mention to get a decent grade, and the second sub-list consists of items whose mention would definitely have raised your score. Of course, just citing facts is not enough to get a high grade; your essay also has to make sense.

Also, to get those extra points, your essay has to show that you understand the significance of those facts and events. In other words, it does not suffice to simply mention Roger Williams; you also have to state why he was banished from Massachusetts Bay and what his exile reveals about religious tolerance in New England. So, to get a really good grade, you have to mention that he founded Rhode Island and established freedom of religion there. For maximum points, you have to note that Rhode Island was the only New England settlement prior to 1650 that acknowledged the rights of all faiths.

Basic Facts

- By 1650 New England had five major English settlements. They were Massachusetts Bay, Plymouth.

- Separatists settled Plymouth in 1620. The Massachusetts Bay Company settled near Cape Cod in 1630. Connecticut, New Haven, and Rhode Island were settled in the 1630s.

- Massachusetts Bay was a royal colony which means that it was under the direct rule of the king, at least theoretically. Although the king had the right to choose the governor, though, the settlers in fact chose their first governor, John Winthrop. The other New England colonies were self-governing, meaning that they had the right to choose their own governor. Incidentally, by 1700 most of the self-governing colonies had been changed to royal colonies.

Constitutionalism (This choice is the toughest of the three and probably the best one to skip)

Your essay pretty much had to mention the following:

- The Mayflower Compact—This document is not a constitution in the strictest sense because it does not provide for an actual government. Still, it was an important forerunner to constitutional government in the New World. Those who signed it agreed to self-government and to abide by the laws they passed.

- The Fundamental Orders of Connecticut—While you may not know it by name, the Fundamental Orders of Connecticut is the formal constitution written by Connecticut settlers and enacted in 1639. (If you knew its name and date, give yourself bonus points.) You do have to know that this document was the first formal constitution in the New World and that it stated that the power of government rests in the consent of those being governed. In this assertion, the Connecticut settlers distinguished themselves from the royalists who often argued that the king, and therefore the government, ruled by Divine Right (that is, that the king's power came from God, who chose the king).

Give yourself extra credit for mentioning the following:

- The Massachusetts Bay charter—Acting as a constitution of sorts, it provided the mechanism for self-government. As mentioned above, Massachusetts Bay was technically ruled by the king, but actually it was governed by the company's general court, established in the company charter. All property holders—thus, nearly all the white males in the settlement— voted for deputies (representatives) to the general court. The charter also required the company's proprietors to seek the advice and consent of all freemen before making laws.

- English traditions—(1) The Magna Carta (1215) established a few fundamental, inalienable rights for property holders. (2) The concept of limited government—the idea that the king ruled by the people's consent, and not by Divine Right—was gaining wider acceptance in England at the time. (3) The existence of a bicameral legislature—the House of Lords and the House of Commons—gave the colonists a tradition in both representative government and constitutional government.

- The English Civil Wars—In the early 17th century, Parliament, backed by reform forces that included the Puritans, began to demand changes to make government more responsive to and representative of the people. King Charles responded by dissolving Parliament in 1629. When he finally recalled Parliament in 1640 (because his government was failing), Puritans demanded major constitutional reforms. Charles refused and a long, bloody war followed. When Puritan forces won in 1649, Charles lost his head and England, briefly, had a constitution. The whole episode demonstrates that the Puritans were strongly committed to constitutionalism.

- The New England Confederation—Founded in 1643, the confederation of New England colonies was mostly powerless because it had no executive power. However, it did settle some border disputes and it represented the people's willingness to create governmental agencies and to (sort of) abide by their decisions.

Democracy

Your essay pretty much had to mention the following:

- All the New England colonies had elected legislatures by 1650.

- Most had bicameral legislatures, with a lower house elected by all freemen and an upper house usually made up of appointees. Freemen also usually elected the governor.

- New England had a tradition of town meetings at which many of the decisions concerning local government were made.

- Women, indentured servants, and slaves could not vote.

- Except in Rhode Island, only Puritans had the right to vote.

- Otherwise, voting rights were extended to all property holders. Since most settlers were enticed to the New World by the prospect of owning land and because in the early years land was plentiful, nearly all the white male colonists could vote.

Give yourself extra credit for mentioning the following:

- The Massachusetts Bay Company, while technically controlled by the king, had little contact with England. It was empowered to make almost all important decisions. It set an early precedent for self-government in the New World.

- Although initially governed by the owners of the company, Massachusetts Bay's governors soon extended democratic rights to all Puritan property-owning settlers. The colony was ruled by a general court to which all towns were allowed to elect delegates.

- The Plymouth settlement formed a legislature as soon as the settlement expanded beyond a couple of towns.

- The Puritans valued the ideal of the covenant. They believed they had a covenant with God, and they used the covenant as a model for their secular behavior. Accordingly, the Puritans expected everyone to work for the communal good and that everyone would have a voice in how the community was run.

- When settlers moved into the Connecticut Valley, they had their first run-in with Native Americans. The settlers essentially tried to bully the natives out of their land. In the resulting Pequot War, settlers torched villages and killed women and children. You might mention this as evidence of the settlers' rather limited sense of fair play and justice, which are usually considered democratic ideals.

- English tradition—See "Constitutional government," above.

- The English Civil War—See "Constitutional government," above.

Freedom of religion

You had to mention the following:

- Even though the Puritans had fled England because of religious persecution, they did not allow freedom of religion in their colonies.

- Roger Williams—Williams came to the New World to teach in the Salem Bay settlement (part of the Massachusetts Bay colony). His writings and teachings advocated separation of church and state and the free practice of all religions in the New World. He also had some other radical ideas such as suggesting that the English had no right to take land away from Native American tribes. The Puritans banished Williams from the colony in 1636. He moved to modern-day Providence and in 1642 received a charter for the colony of Rhode Island. The charter specified that Rhode Island would protect the freedom of religion. By 1650 Rhode Island was still the only New England colony that allowed individuals to follow their religious faiths in freedom.

Give yourself extra points if you mentioned:

- Anne Hutchinson—Hutchinson fell from favor with the Puritans because of her ideas. She believed in the power of grace and also that God spoke directly to certain, chosen people. Those people, she argued, did not need Puritan ministers or the Church since God assured those He spoke to that they would be saved. Hutchinson's message appealed to many Puritans because of its assurances of salvation. She was considered dangerous, doubly so because she was becoming a powerful woman in a society in which women were definitely second-class citizens. The General Court of Massachusetts brought her up on charges of defaming the ministry, found her guilty, and banished her. She started a settlement in Portsmouth, Rhode Island.

- There was no separation of church and state as evidenced by the charges against Anne Hutchinson.

ABOUT THE STRUCTURE OF YOUR ESSAY

For this essay, you want a thesis statement that allows you to discuss both the basic characteristics of early American democracy. One way to achieve this is to discuss these developments in the context of their contribution to later developments in American self-governance. For example, you might phrase your thesis in the following manner: "Because of their distance from England, the English colonists in New England were in a situation which largely allowed them to govern themselves Other factors—English traditions, Puritan beliefs, the wide availability of land—helped create the communities that in many ways laid the foundation for American government. However, these communities also differed in significant ways from what we usually identify as the American ideal." This type of general statement allows you to write a "laundry list" essay in which you discuss as many pertinent facts and concepts as time allows with regard to your two chosen sub-themes (constitutionalism, democracy, or freedom of religion). A simple conclusion, perhaps mentioning the similarities and differences between Puritan society and the more pluralistic democratic societies that followed it, would be also be helpful.

Question 3—Hamilton v. Jefferson

> 3. Discuss the differences between Alexander Hamilton and Thomas Jefferson concerning the ideal relationship between the federal government and the states' governments.

This question presents a good, meaty issue as it allows you to talk about two fundamentally different interpretations of U.S. government—states' rights versus federalism—AND two fundamentally different interpretations of the Constitution—"strict constructionist" versus "broad constructionist."

Below is a list of concepts and events you might have included in your essay. The list is divided into to "sub-lists." The first sub-list contains that which you practically had to mention to get a decent grade, and the other sub-list consists of items, if mentioned, would definitely have raised your score. Of course, to get a very good score, your essay would also have to (1) make sense, and (2) demonstrate an understanding of the relationship between the facts and events you mention and your thesis statement.

Your essay pretty much had to mention the following:

- The fundamental difference between the two perspectives—Jefferson feared that a strong central government might look a lot like the British government, from which the colonists had just fought to liberate themselves. He favored a federal government empowered to defend the country and to regulate international commerce, but he wanted the states to maintain as much autonomy in all other affairs as possible This fear of a strong central government also led Jefferson to demand the inclusion of the Bill of Rights in the Constitution. Hamilton, on the contrary, wanted a very strong federal government. He viewed the states as a group of petty fiefdoms, and feared that their squabbles would prevent the United States from becoming a powerful country. Hamilton would have been happy with a Constitution that granted states little or no power independent of the central government.

- Jefferson and Hamilton during the Washington administration—Washington named Jefferson Secretary of State and Hamilton Secretary of the Treasury. The most noteworthy issue, as it pertains to this essay, was Hamilton's proposal for a national bank. Jefferson opposed it, both for practical reasons (he felt the bank benefited the wealthy elite in the Northeast at the expense of Southerners and Midwesterners) and on principle. Jefferson argued that because the Constitution did not empower the federal government to charter a bank, it could not legally do so. Jefferson's argument—that the federal government may only perform those actions permitted it by the Constitution—came to be known as the "strict constructionist" interpretation of the Constitution. This perspective also became identified with those who favored state power over federal power. Hamilton, on the other hand, argued that the federal government could do anything not prohibited by the Constitution. This argument is known as the "broad constructionist" interpretation of the Constitution and is associated with those who favor a strong central government. In the end, Washington agreed with Hamilton, and a national bank was created.

- Jefferson's presidency—As president, Jefferson tried to keep the federal government in check. In his inauguration speech, he promised "a wise and frugal government, which shall restrain men from injuring one another, and which shall leave them otherwise free to regulate their own pursuits." He also did his best to drive Federalist government appointees out of office and replace them with members of his party, the Democrat-Republicans. However, Jefferson's administration acted more broadly than its predecessors. While in office, Jefferson also signed the Embargo Act and made the Louisiana Purchase. It may therefore be best to conclude that Jefferson, while a states'-rights republican at heart, was also a political pragmatist.

Give yourself bonus points if you mentioned any of the following:

- Hamilton's proposals at the Constitutional Convention included a life term for the president and state governors appointed by the federal government and empowered with an absolute veto. These suggestions both strongly reflect his federalism.

- As Secretary of the Treasury, Hamilton argued that the federal government should assume the debts that the states had incurred during the Revolution. The plan, by centralizing the debt, strengthened the central government. Hamilton financed the debt with government bonds and land grants, thus giving the wealthy (who were the ones who bought the bonds) a motive for supporting a strong central government as they had invested in it.

- Other programs Hamilton supported as Secretary of the Treasury all required a powerful central government. These initiatives included incentive programs to attract immigrants with industrial skills, national investment in industry, protective tariffs, and the infamous whiskey tax (which instigated the Whiskey Rebellion).

- Jefferson supported the republican French Revolution and its motto, "Liberty, Brotherhood, Equality." As Secretary of State, he pushed for closer ties with the French. Hamilton hated the French Revolution; he viewed the revolutionaries as common rabble. He argued for closer ties with England whose parliamentary monarchy he openly admired. Note, however, that when the French asked for American assistance in their hostile conflicts with England, both Hamilton and Jefferson agreed that the U.S. should stay out of it, even though a treaty with France arguably obliged the U.S. to fight.

- Hamilton supported the Alien and Sedition Acts, which imposed strong federal restrictions on freedom of speech. The acts incensed Jefferson, who drew up the Virginia Resolution in response. (Madison, a political ally, wrote the Kentucky Resolution.) Both resolutions declared that the states had the right to review the constitutionality of federal laws and thus gave birth to the concept of nullification. (See p. 84 for more detail.)

- Even though both men disliked political parties, their disagreements gave rise to the first informal parties in the U.S. Jefferson led the group known as the Democrat-Republicans (because they favored as much democracy as possible and modeled their goals on the republican ideals of antiquity). Hamilton supported the Federalists (because they favored a strong federal government). Although these parties were neither as active nor organized as modern-day political parties, they served many of the same purposes. Party members usually voted as a bloc in Congress and ran on a party ticket.

About the Structure of Your Essay

Begin by defining the broad, fundamental differences between Jefferson and Hamilton. Spend the rest of your essay listing the events and concepts that illustrate that difference.

Question 4—Slavery and Political Parties

4. For the period between 1844 and the Civil War, evaluate the impact of slavery as a political issue on the history of any THREE of the following parties:

   Democratic Party
   Free-Soil Party
   Know-Nothings (American Party)
   Republican Party
   Whig Party

To do well on this essay, you must keep in mind that slavery was a regional issue. Parties that crossed regions were torn apart by the issue; parties that were isolated to particular region stayed together, but lacked a national mandate with which to lead the entire nation. Of course, you also have to remember at least one (and up to three) political parties that have not existed for 130 years.

There is a lot you can write about on this question. The grader will know that you will not have time to get to everything you could write about, and that is to your advantage. Make sure you get to the most important information, particularly the major historical events and issues that determined these parties' ultimate success or failure.

Here are the lists of what you might have mentioned in your essay:

Basic Facts and Events

You pretty much had to mention the following:

4. For the period between 1844 and the Civil War, evaluate the impact of slavery as a political issue on the history of any THREE of the following parties:

   Democratic Party
   Free-Soil Party
   Know-Nothings (American Party)
   Republican Party
   Whig Party

- Major land acquisitions during Polk's presidency—Slavery would eventually have torn the nation apart anyway, but U.S. expansion accounted for its becoming such a big political issue when it did. The acquisition of the Oregon territory and the annexation of territories in the Southwest led both Southerners and Northerners to fear that the balance of power in Congress would shift to one side or the other.

- Kansas-Nebraska Act (1854)—This legislation nullified the Missouri Compromise by allowing Kansas and Nebraska to determine the status of slavery in their territories.

- Dred Scott decision (1857)—This Supreme Court ruling rewrote the terms of the argument over slavery. It declared slaves to be property, consequently denying them the ability to sue in federal court, and the ruling also denied Congress the right to legislate the status of slavery in the territories.

Give yourself extra points if you figured out a way to mention the following:

- The Compromise of 1850—This legislation left the fate of slavery in the territories ambiguous, thus enforcing the notion of "popular sovereignty." The compromise also created a stricter fugitive slave law.

- "Bleeding Kansas"—After the Kansas-Nebraska Act of 1854 allowed the possibility of slavery in the Kansas territory, abolitionists and pro-slavery forces rushed into the area in order to dominate the political scene. Each side claimed victory, then attacked the other. Widespread violence ensued.

Democratic Party

You pretty much had to mention the following:

- The Democrats held the presidency during Polk's administration from 1844 to 1848, and then again during Pierce's and Buchanan's administrations from 1852 to 1860. As a national party, the Democrats tried their hardest to straddle both sides of the slavery issue. Polk's acquisition of new territory, however, heightened tensions on the slavery issue. (See "Major land acquisitions during Polk's presidency," above).

- The Democrats considered Pierce a "safe" nominee for president in 1852 because nobody knew who he was. Also, the Democrats hoped that the Compromise of 1850 had laid the slavery issue to rest for a while. In 1856 they chose Buchanan because he had been out of the country on diplomatic service and therefore had not been muddied by the slavery debate.

- By 1860 the party had split, literally. It held two conventions and nominated two candidates, one a Southerner (John C. Breckinridge), the other a Midwesterner (Stephen Douglas). Slavery had torn the party apart in regional divisions.

Give yourself extra points for mentioning:

- The Wilmot Proviso, authored by Democrat David Wilmot, would have banned slavery in the southwestern territories annexed from Mexico. John C. Calhoun, also a Democrat, fought the Wilmot Proviso strenuously. He argued that the federal government had no right to regulate slavery in the territories; most other Southern politicians soon picked up his argument.

- Anti-slavery Democrats called pro-slavery Democrats "hunkers," implying that they were so hungry for political power that they would court slave owners. Pro-slavery Democrats called anti-slavery Democrats "barn burners" because, they said, such folks would burn down the barn in order to kill the rats.

Free Soil Party

You pretty much had to mention:

- The party formed around a single issue—preventing slavery in the territories annexed from Mexico.

- The Compromise of 1850, and particularly its stricter fugitive slave law, helped the party gain support in the North. It attracted anti-slavery Democrats and "Conscience Whigs."

- The Republican Party eventually absorbed much of the Free Soil Party. The two parties had virtually identical policies on slavery. Because the Republicans appealed to a wider range of voters, many Free Soilers felt they could better accomplish their objectives in the larger Republican Party.

Give yourself extra points if you mentioned:

- The Free Soil Party elected nine congressmen in 1848.

- The Dred Scott decision killed the Free Soil Party once and for all by taking away its one issue. Free Soilers wanted the federal government to regulate slavery; Dred Scott ruled that it could not.

Know Nothings (American Party)

You pretty much had to mention the following:

- The Know Nothings formed around a single issue—anti-immigration. They hated Catholics, particularly the Irish and Roman Catholics.

- The movement started out in secret societies. Members would plan election strategies at private meetings and then vote en masse on election day, often swinging elections. Because they were so secretive about their agenda, they became known as the "Know Nothings."

- Events conspired to make slavery a more important issue than immigration during the 1850s. In the North, the Republicans eventually attracted most of the Know Nothings.

Give yourself extra points if you mentioned the following:

In 1854, the party did very well in state and congressional elections.

- The party ran Millard Fillmore for president in 1856. He received over 20 percent of the vote. Fillmore, a former Whig president, attracted many Whigs to the party.

- Know Nothings argued that Catholics were dangerous because they served the Pope, not the American government.

- The Republican Party had a nativist streak which also attracted the Know Nothings to the Republican Party. "Nativism" is defined as the favoring of citizens over immigrants, accompanied by general fear of those perceived as "outsiders."

Republican Party

You pretty much had to mention the following:

- Formed in 1854, the Republican Party organized around the effort to defeat the Kansas-Nebraska Act. The passage of Kansas-Nebraska and the ensuing turmoil (see "Bleeding Kansas," above) helped build the party's popular base.

- The Republican Party originated as the Whig Party, then the second most popular party, splintered over the issue of slavery. At the same time, Free Soilers, looking for a more powerful, broader anti-slavery program, found it in the Republican Party.

- The schism in the Democratic Party in 1860 practically guaranteed the election of the Republican candidate, Abraham Lincoln. The Republicans were considered a third party in that election; it is the only time a third-party candidate has ever won a United States presidential election.

- The Republican party was truly regional. Lincoln's name did not even appear on the ballot in any Southern states. He won with just under 40 percent of the popular vote.

Give yourself extra points if you mentioned the following:

- In 1856 the Republican presidential candidate was John C. Fremont. His campaign slogan, Free Soil, Free Labor, Free Speech, Free Men, Fremont, indicated the party's platform and its open courtship of Free Soilers.

- The disappearance of the Whigs and Know-Nothings by 1860 and the conversion of those parties' members to the Republican Party, provided the voters Lincoln needed to win.

Whig Party

You pretty much had to mention the following:

- The Whig Party was made up of disparate groups. However, the members of its coalition often had opposing political goals. Whigs drew their support from states' rights Southerners, former Federalists, anti-Masons, Eastern financial conservatives, and merchants. Consequently, their presidential candidates were usually military heroes who had loose political platforms. It was a party destined to fall apart; the only question was when, and over what issue.

- Slavery and the death of the party's great leaders, Henry Clay (from Kentucky) and Daniel Webster (from Massachusetts) caused its demise. (Note the cross-regionalism of the party leadership.) Clay and Webster worked out the Compromise of 1850, which became the Whig position on slavery. Both men died within two years of the compromise's enactment, leaving a leadership void in the party. Meanwhile, Southern Whigs sought more aggressive pro-slavery representation; anti-slavery Northern Whigs, often called "Conscience Whigs," drifted first into the Free Soil Party, then into the Republican Party.

Give yourself extra points if you mentioned:

- By 1856 so little endured of the Whig Party (just four years earlier one of the nation's two major parties) that the remaining members did not even bother to nominate a presidential candidate. At their convention they simply endorsed the American Party's nomination of Millard Fillmore.

ABOUT THE STRUCTURE OF YOUR ESSAY

How easy this essay was to write probably depended a lot on how you decided to structure your discussion of the subject. One effective way would have been to discuss the key events leading up to the Civil War in your first paragraph, then discuss how those events affected the three parties you chose to write about in your next three paragraphs. A concluding paragraph mentioning sectionalism would have been a nice touch.

A much less efficient method would have been to devote a paragraph to each major event, and describe how that event affected each of the three parties you chose. If you tried to write your essay this way, you probably found yourself experiencing a lot of stress. Since the main point of your essay should have been the history of these political parties, it would have been easier to focus all your attention on one party at a time.

Question 5—Progressivism

5. Analyze the reasons for the popularity of the Progressive movement during the first two decades of the twentieth century.

This essay gives you an opportunity to discuss the causes of the Progressive movement and its achievements. Below is a list of facts and concepts you might have included in your essay:
You pretty much had to mention the following:

- Public disenchantment with business practices—By 1900 many major businesses were controlled by virtual monopolies. Those who controlled the businesses were fabulously wealthy; those who worked for them were impoverished. Businesses had little regard for the welfare of their workers or their customers The government and judiciary proved to be shamelessly pro-business in their policies and rulings.

- Public horror at city conditions—Business' abuses adversely influenced the state of the cities. Urban dwellers lived under cramped, unsanitary conditions. Often entire families, including little children, worked in factories for sub-living wages. City governments were controlled by political machines, who helped their impoverished patrons survive but did nothing for their long-term welfare.

- Growth of the middle class—During this time, the U.S. middle class was growing. With their new-found comfort and respectability, many middle-class Americans wanted to increase their political power. They formed associations such as lawyers' American Bar Association and women's National Woman Suffrage Association. The groups served as interest groups that lobbied for progressive reform. Many in the middle class, outraged by the excesses of business and the corruption of government, fought to correct them.

- Progressivism built on the foundation laid by the Populist movement of the 1890s—Populism had fought for moral causes, sought to counter the trend toward monopoly, and worked to widen access to the democratic process. Progressivism picked up these traditions, and so inherited the farmers and clergy who had made up the Populist coalition.

- Journalists helped the spread of Progressivism—With magazine articles and books like Upton Sinclair's *The Jungle*, American "muckrakers" broadened public awareness of corporate excesses.

- Teddy Roosevelt's presidency—Roosevelt used the office of the presidency as a "bully pulpit" to popularize progressive ideals. During his tenure, he filed numerous antitrust suits against large corporations, tightened food and drug regulations, created national parks, and broadened the government's power to protect land from over-development.

Give yourself extra points if you mentioned the following:

- Other Progressive successes broadened the movement's appeal. On the state and local level, many new regulations were enacted, including child labor laws, limits on the lengths of the work day, minimum wage requirements, corrupt-practices acts, and housing codes. Many states adopted the initiative, referendum, and recall, thus empowering voters. Cities improved public transportation, adopted stricter health codes, and converted to a city-manager system. States introduced income taxes to redistribute wealth and provide public services.

- Wisconsin governor Robert La Follette led the way for many Progressive state leaders. He initiated such reforms as direct primaries, equitable tax structures, and the regulation of railways, all later adopted by many other states.

- Taft and Wilson continued the Progressive tradition in the White House. Taft strengthened antitrust law and expanded conservation efforts. During his term, two progressive amendments, the national income tax and the direct election of senators, were added to the Constitution. Wilson created the Federal Trade Commission, lobbied for and enforced the Clayton Antitrust Act, and helped create the Federal Reserve which gave the government greater control over the nation's finances. During his term, the 19th Amendment gave women the right to vote.

- The many successes of Progressivism actually helped bring about its downfall. Each success satisfied a portion of the Progressive coalition, and once satisfied, these people tended not to work as hard for Progressive goals. World War I also split the Progressive coalition. Some supported the war while others opposed it, but the feelings on both sides of the issue were strong. When the war ended and with Americans tired of crusading for justice, the Progressive movement petered out.

About the Structure of Your Essay

You really should have started this essay with a description of the social causes of Progressivism. Then you could have gone on to enumerate its achievements. Add bonus points if you got around to discussing why the Progressive movement came to an end.

12
BIBLIOGRAPHY

If you have not yet read enough about U.S. History or the AP History exam, here is a list of some of the resources I used to write this book. Your history teacher or your school's history department should have some of them; others should be at your local library; and others still are available for free on the Internet (free, that is, if you have unlimited Internet access).

First, here is a list of official College Board publications that your school should own:

- *A Student Guide to the AP U.S. History Course and Examination*—This booklet includes 25 questions that previously appeared on the AP U.S. History exam. Otherwise, it contains nothing that is not also in this book.

- *Teacher's Guide to Advanced Placement Courses in United States History*—Although it is called a "teacher's guide," anyone can buy it from The College Board, so there is no reason your teacher should not let you read it. It's written by Eric Rothschild, a New York state history teacher. The first 14 pages of the booklet are interesting and useful, and they provide insight into what history teachers are looking for from their students, both in the classroom and on tests. The four pages he devotes to the AP test are straightforward and honest, and I found them very helpful in writing this book.

- *Advanced Placement Course Description: History*—This booklet includes 35 questions that appeared on a previous AP U.S. History exam (all different from the 25 questions in *A Student Guide...*). It also describes the AP European History course and exam, in case you are interested.

- *Doing the DBQ*—This book contains every DBQ given between 1973 and 1994. Practice your DBQ skills with questions from this book. Work only on the questions from the 1982 through 1994 exams; earlier DBQs are in a different format and are more difficult, so they are not as helpful in preparing you for the exam.

- *Free-Response Questions Used in Recent Years*—This green booklet usually contains the last five sets of DBQs and free-response questions.

- *AP U.S. History Free-Response Questions, 1995*—This booklet contains the DBQ and the four free-response questions from the 1995 exam. It also contains copies of essays students wrote during the test and graders' notes concerning what was good or bad about those essays. Much of this booklet is posted at The College Board's AP website. (See below for more information.)

All of the above books can be purchased by calling The College Board's AP publications office at (609) 771-7300 or by writing to: Advanced Placement Program, P.O. Box 6670, Princeton, New Jersey, 08541-6670. Again, your school should own copies of them, so you should not have to buy them.

Here is a list of some short history overviews:

- *The Cartoon History of the United States* by Larry Gonick (Harper Perennial)—Fun and more thorough than you would expect. Do *not* rely solely on this book to prepare for the exam, or you will flunk. This book, however, provides an entertaining way to review an entire course, and you can read it in one sitting.

- *Don't Know Much About History* by Kenneth C. Davis (Avon Books)—Here is another fun book and an easy read. It is perfect for the bathroom or the bus because it can be read and enjoyed in small doses. Again, it is a nice supplement to your course textbook but it is *not* a substitute!

- *A People's History of the United States* by Howard Zinn (Harper Perennial)—Zinn's book provides a leftist/progressive perspective on American history. Unlike most history texts, it focuses on the history of those *not* in power: Native Americans, women, blacks, immigrants, and the poor. Sometimes this book preaches at you when it ought to just let the facts speak for themselves, but it is always interesting and is guaranteed to make you feel ashamed of America's past *at least* a couple of times.

Primary sources are writings by the people who made history. Here is where to find good primary source material:

- *Great Issues in American History* edited by Richard Hofstadter (Random House). Volumes I, II, and III. These pocket-sized paperbacks are thorough and cheap. Marvel at the *Mayflower Compact*! Thrill to excerpts from John Dickinson's *Letters from a Farmer*! Gasp in horror at the *Dred Scott Decision*! Get swept up in the war fervor with Wilson's *Speech for Declaration of War*! A very valuable series of books.

- *Witness to America* edited by Henry Steele Commager and Allan Nevins (Barnes and Noble Books). This book includes 250 excerpts from diaries, letters, books, government reports, and court proceedings. The sources run the gamut from presidents to privates on the battlefield. The selections are well-chosen, and this book makes for interesting reading at any time, not just when you are studying for a history exam.

Finally, if you have access to the Internet, you might want to look at the following websites:

http://cbweb1.collegeboard.org/index.html
College Board home page—This page links you to mountains of official College Board information about all college entrance exams and to lots of other interesting information for the college-bound student.

http://cbweb1.collegeboard.org/ap/history/html/indx001.html
AP U.S. History home page—This page links you to sample AP History questions, sample essays, an AP History FAQ sheet, and other information about the AP exam. The hints provided here concerning how to do well on the AP are only occasionally helpful and should be ignored; any worthwhile tips offered at the site is already in this book.

http://cbweb1.collegeboard.org/ap/history/html/link001.html
AP U.S. History page recommended links—A voluminous page of history links that will send you to archives, photo galleries, bibliographies, and pages full of still more links. The only way to begin to understand what's available is to go to the page and start pointing and clicking.

Here are some other, similar pages:

http://www.panix.com/~steel/
http://www.yahoo.com/Arts/Humanities/History/Indices/
http://www.fred.net/nhhs/html/urls.html
http://www.fred.net/nhhs/html3/bigbook.htm
http://grid.let.rug.nl/~welling/usa/
http://kuhttp.cc.ukans.edu/carrie/docs/docs_us.html
These are just a couple of the many pages of primary source documents on the Internet. You can find everything from the Magna Carta and the Constitution to obscure government memos on the Net if you look long enough. These pages will give you some idea of the scope of what is available.

http://lcweb.loc.gov/
This is the Library of Congress's home page. It links you to pages dedicated to historical events, databases, and the LIC catalogue. For example, the LIC home page has featured an exhibit of Civil War photographs and papers from the archives of George Washington and Theodore Roosevelt. Exhibits change, and they are always pretty good.

http://www.altavista.digital.com/
http://www.hotbot.com/index.html/
http://www.yahoo.com/
These are three great search engines. Go to these sites and enter a word or a phrase. The search engines will reply with a long list of Web pages—some interesting, some not. Not the most efficient way to do research, but a good way to waste lots of time. If you use search engines regularly, you occasionally stumble across something that is really great.

ABOUT THE AUTHOR

Tom Meltzer graduated from Columbia University in 1984. He is the author or co-author of *The Student Advantage Guide to the Best 310 Colleges*, *Cracking the CLEP*, and the forthcoming *Cracking the AP: U.S. Government*, and he has taught and developed materials for The Princeton Review for the past ten years. He is also a professional musician and performs with the band Five Chinese Brothers, whose three CDs are available at fine record stores everywhere. Tom lives in Brooklyn, New York, which is much nicer than you think.

NOTES

NOTES

NOTES

NOTES

e Princeton Review
gnostic Test Form ○ Side 1

NAME: _____
Last _____ First _____ M.I.

TURE: _____ DATE: ___/___/___

ADDRESS: _____
Number and Street

_____
City _____ State _____ Zip Code

NO.: _____

ST FORM

3. TEST CODE

4. REGISTRATION NUMBER

5. YOUR NAME

First 4 letters of last name				FIRST INIT	MID INIT
Ⓐ	Ⓐ	Ⓐ	Ⓐ	Ⓐ	Ⓐ
Ⓑ	Ⓑ	Ⓑ	Ⓑ	Ⓑ	Ⓑ
Ⓒ	Ⓒ	Ⓒ	Ⓒ	Ⓒ	Ⓒ
Ⓓ	Ⓓ	Ⓓ	Ⓓ	Ⓓ	Ⓓ
Ⓔ	Ⓔ	Ⓔ	Ⓔ	Ⓔ	Ⓔ
Ⓕ	Ⓕ	Ⓕ	Ⓕ	Ⓕ	Ⓕ
Ⓖ	Ⓖ	Ⓖ	Ⓖ	Ⓖ	Ⓖ
Ⓗ	Ⓗ	Ⓗ	Ⓗ	Ⓗ	Ⓗ
Ⓘ	Ⓘ	Ⓘ	Ⓘ	Ⓘ	Ⓘ
Ⓙ	Ⓙ	Ⓙ	Ⓙ	Ⓙ	Ⓙ
Ⓚ	Ⓚ	Ⓚ	Ⓚ	Ⓚ	Ⓚ
Ⓛ	Ⓛ	Ⓛ	Ⓛ	Ⓛ	Ⓛ
Ⓜ	Ⓜ	Ⓜ	Ⓜ	Ⓜ	Ⓜ
Ⓝ	Ⓝ	Ⓝ	Ⓝ	Ⓝ	Ⓝ
Ⓞ	Ⓞ	Ⓞ	Ⓞ	Ⓞ	Ⓞ
Ⓟ	Ⓟ	Ⓟ	Ⓟ	Ⓟ	Ⓟ
Ⓠ	Ⓠ	Ⓠ	Ⓠ	Ⓠ	Ⓠ
Ⓡ	Ⓡ	Ⓡ	Ⓡ	Ⓡ	Ⓡ
Ⓢ	Ⓢ	Ⓢ	Ⓢ	Ⓢ	Ⓢ
Ⓣ	Ⓣ	Ⓣ	Ⓣ	Ⓣ	Ⓣ
Ⓤ	Ⓤ	Ⓤ	Ⓤ	Ⓤ	Ⓤ
Ⓥ	Ⓥ	Ⓥ	Ⓥ	Ⓥ	Ⓥ
Ⓦ	Ⓦ	Ⓦ	Ⓦ	Ⓦ	Ⓦ
Ⓧ	Ⓧ	Ⓧ	Ⓧ	Ⓧ	Ⓧ
Ⓨ	Ⓨ	Ⓨ	Ⓨ	Ⓨ	Ⓨ
Ⓩ	Ⓩ	Ⓩ	Ⓩ	Ⓩ	Ⓩ

TEST CODE / REGISTRATION NUMBER bubbles

⓪ Ⓐ Ⓙ ⓪ ⓪ ⓪ | ⓪ ⓪ ⓪ ⓪ ⓪ ⓪
① Ⓑ Ⓚ ① ① ① | ① ① ① ① ① ①
② Ⓒ Ⓛ ② ② ② | ② ② ② ② ② ②
③ Ⓓ Ⓜ ③ ③ ③ | ③ ③ ③ ③ ③ ③
④ Ⓔ Ⓝ ④ ④ ④ | ④ ④ ④ ④ ④ ④
⑤ Ⓕ Ⓞ ⑤ ⑤ ⑤ | ⑤ ⑤ ⑤ ⑤ ⑤ ⑤
⑥ Ⓖ Ⓟ ⑥ ⑥ ⑥ | ⑥ ⑥ ⑥ ⑥ ⑥ ⑥
⑦ Ⓗ Ⓠ ⑦ ⑦ ⑦ | ⑦ ⑦ ⑦ ⑦ ⑦ ⑦
⑧ Ⓘ Ⓡ ⑧ ⑧ ⑧ | ⑧ ⑧ ⑧ ⑧ ⑧ ⑧
⑨ ⑨ ⑨ ⑨ | ⑨ ⑨ ⑨ ⑨ ⑨ ⑨

TE OF BIRTH

NTH	DAY		YEAR	
JAN				
FEB				
MAR	⓪	⓪	⓪	⓪
APR	①	①	①	①
MAY	②	②	②	②
JUN	③	③	③	③
JUL		④	④	④
AUG		⑤	⑤	⑤
SEP		⑥	⑥	⑥
OCT		⑦	⑦	⑦
NOV		⑧	⑧	⑧
DEC		⑨	⑨	⑨

7. SEX
○ MALE
○ FEMALE

◆ **SCANTRON**® FORM NO. F-592-KIN
© SCANTRON CORPORATION 1989 3289-C553-5 4 3
ALL RIGHTS RESERVED.

Begin with number 1 for each new section of the test. Leave blank any extra answer spaces.

SECTION 1

Ⓐ Ⓑ Ⓒ Ⓓ Ⓔ   26 Ⓐ Ⓑ Ⓒ Ⓓ Ⓔ   51 Ⓐ Ⓑ Ⓒ Ⓓ Ⓔ   76 Ⓐ Ⓑ Ⓒ Ⓓ Ⓔ
Ⓐ Ⓑ Ⓒ Ⓓ Ⓔ   27 Ⓐ Ⓑ Ⓒ Ⓓ Ⓔ   52 Ⓐ Ⓑ Ⓒ Ⓓ Ⓔ   77 Ⓐ Ⓑ Ⓒ Ⓓ Ⓔ
Ⓐ Ⓑ Ⓒ Ⓓ Ⓔ   28 Ⓐ Ⓑ Ⓒ Ⓓ Ⓔ   53 Ⓐ Ⓑ Ⓒ Ⓓ Ⓔ   78 Ⓐ Ⓑ Ⓒ Ⓓ Ⓔ
Ⓐ Ⓑ Ⓒ Ⓓ Ⓔ   29 Ⓐ Ⓑ Ⓒ Ⓓ Ⓔ   54 Ⓐ Ⓑ Ⓒ Ⓓ Ⓔ   79 Ⓐ Ⓑ Ⓒ Ⓓ Ⓔ
Ⓐ Ⓑ Ⓒ Ⓓ Ⓔ   30 Ⓐ Ⓑ Ⓒ Ⓓ Ⓔ   55 Ⓐ Ⓑ Ⓒ Ⓓ Ⓔ   80 Ⓐ Ⓑ Ⓒ Ⓓ Ⓔ
Ⓐ Ⓑ Ⓒ Ⓓ Ⓔ   31 Ⓐ Ⓑ Ⓒ Ⓓ Ⓔ   56 Ⓐ Ⓑ Ⓒ Ⓓ Ⓔ   81 Ⓐ Ⓑ Ⓒ Ⓓ Ⓔ
Ⓐ Ⓑ Ⓒ Ⓓ Ⓔ   32 Ⓐ Ⓑ Ⓒ Ⓓ Ⓔ   57 Ⓐ Ⓑ Ⓒ Ⓓ Ⓔ   82 Ⓐ Ⓑ Ⓒ Ⓓ Ⓔ
Ⓐ Ⓑ Ⓒ Ⓓ Ⓔ   33 Ⓐ Ⓑ Ⓒ Ⓓ Ⓔ   58 Ⓐ Ⓑ Ⓒ Ⓓ Ⓔ   83 Ⓐ Ⓑ Ⓒ Ⓓ Ⓔ
Ⓐ Ⓑ Ⓒ Ⓓ Ⓔ   34 Ⓐ Ⓑ Ⓒ Ⓓ Ⓔ   59 Ⓐ Ⓑ Ⓒ Ⓓ Ⓔ   84 Ⓐ Ⓑ Ⓒ Ⓓ Ⓔ
Ⓐ Ⓑ Ⓒ Ⓓ Ⓔ   35 Ⓐ Ⓑ Ⓒ Ⓓ Ⓔ   60 Ⓐ Ⓑ Ⓒ Ⓓ Ⓔ   85 Ⓐ Ⓑ Ⓒ Ⓓ Ⓔ
Ⓐ Ⓑ Ⓒ Ⓓ Ⓔ   36 Ⓐ Ⓑ Ⓒ Ⓓ Ⓔ   61 Ⓐ Ⓑ Ⓒ Ⓓ Ⓔ   86 Ⓐ Ⓑ Ⓒ Ⓓ Ⓔ
Ⓐ Ⓑ Ⓒ Ⓓ Ⓔ   37 Ⓐ Ⓑ Ⓒ Ⓓ Ⓔ   62 Ⓐ Ⓑ Ⓒ Ⓓ Ⓔ   87 Ⓐ Ⓑ Ⓒ Ⓓ Ⓔ
Ⓐ Ⓑ Ⓒ Ⓓ Ⓔ   38 Ⓐ Ⓑ Ⓒ Ⓓ Ⓔ   63 Ⓐ Ⓑ Ⓒ Ⓓ Ⓔ   88 Ⓐ Ⓑ Ⓒ Ⓓ Ⓔ
Ⓐ Ⓑ Ⓒ Ⓓ Ⓔ   39 Ⓐ Ⓑ Ⓒ Ⓓ Ⓔ   64 Ⓐ Ⓑ Ⓒ Ⓓ Ⓔ   89 Ⓐ Ⓑ Ⓒ Ⓓ Ⓔ
Ⓐ Ⓑ Ⓒ Ⓓ Ⓔ   40 Ⓐ Ⓑ Ⓒ Ⓓ Ⓔ   65 Ⓐ Ⓑ Ⓒ Ⓓ Ⓔ   90 Ⓐ Ⓑ Ⓒ Ⓓ Ⓔ
Ⓐ Ⓑ Ⓒ Ⓓ Ⓔ   41 Ⓐ Ⓑ Ⓒ Ⓓ Ⓔ   66 Ⓐ Ⓑ Ⓒ Ⓓ Ⓔ   91 Ⓐ Ⓑ Ⓒ Ⓓ Ⓔ
Ⓐ Ⓑ Ⓒ Ⓓ Ⓔ   42 Ⓐ Ⓑ Ⓒ Ⓓ Ⓔ   67 Ⓐ Ⓑ Ⓒ Ⓓ Ⓔ   92 Ⓐ Ⓑ Ⓒ Ⓓ Ⓔ
Ⓐ Ⓑ Ⓒ Ⓓ Ⓔ   43 Ⓐ Ⓑ Ⓒ Ⓓ Ⓔ   68 Ⓐ Ⓑ Ⓒ Ⓓ Ⓔ   93 Ⓐ Ⓑ Ⓒ Ⓓ Ⓔ
Ⓐ Ⓑ Ⓒ Ⓓ Ⓔ   44 Ⓐ Ⓑ Ⓒ Ⓓ Ⓔ   69 Ⓐ Ⓑ Ⓒ Ⓓ Ⓔ   94 Ⓐ Ⓑ Ⓒ Ⓓ Ⓔ
Ⓐ Ⓑ Ⓒ Ⓓ Ⓔ   45 Ⓐ Ⓑ Ⓒ Ⓓ Ⓔ   70 Ⓐ Ⓑ Ⓒ Ⓓ Ⓔ   95 Ⓐ Ⓑ Ⓒ Ⓓ Ⓔ
Ⓐ Ⓑ Ⓒ Ⓓ Ⓔ   46 Ⓐ Ⓑ Ⓒ Ⓓ Ⓔ   71 Ⓐ Ⓑ Ⓒ Ⓓ Ⓔ   96 Ⓐ Ⓑ Ⓒ Ⓓ Ⓔ
Ⓐ Ⓑ Ⓒ Ⓓ Ⓔ   47 Ⓐ Ⓑ Ⓒ Ⓓ Ⓔ   72 Ⓐ Ⓑ Ⓒ Ⓓ Ⓔ   97 Ⓐ Ⓑ Ⓒ Ⓓ Ⓔ
Ⓐ Ⓑ Ⓒ Ⓓ Ⓔ   48 Ⓐ Ⓑ Ⓒ Ⓓ Ⓔ   73 Ⓐ Ⓑ Ⓒ Ⓓ Ⓔ   98 Ⓐ Ⓑ Ⓒ Ⓓ Ⓔ
Ⓐ Ⓑ Ⓒ Ⓓ Ⓔ   49 Ⓐ Ⓑ Ⓒ Ⓓ Ⓔ   74 Ⓐ Ⓑ Ⓒ Ⓓ Ⓔ   99 Ⓐ Ⓑ Ⓒ Ⓓ Ⓔ
Ⓐ Ⓑ Ⓒ Ⓓ Ⓔ   50 Ⓐ Ⓑ Ⓒ Ⓓ Ⓔ   75 Ⓐ Ⓑ Ⓒ Ⓓ Ⓔ   100 Ⓐ Ⓑ Ⓒ Ⓓ Ⓔ

Completely darken bubbles with a No. 2 pencil. make a mistake, be sure to erase mark comp Erase all stray marks.

Begin with number 1 for each new section of the test. Leave blank any extra answer spaces.

SECTION 2

1 Ⓐ Ⓑ Ⓒ Ⓓ Ⓔ	26 Ⓐ Ⓑ Ⓒ Ⓓ Ⓔ	51 Ⓐ Ⓑ Ⓒ Ⓓ Ⓔ	76 Ⓐ Ⓑ Ⓒ Ⓓ
2 Ⓐ Ⓑ Ⓒ Ⓓ Ⓔ	27 Ⓐ Ⓑ Ⓒ Ⓓ Ⓔ	52 Ⓐ Ⓑ Ⓒ Ⓓ Ⓔ	77 Ⓐ Ⓑ Ⓒ Ⓓ
3 Ⓐ Ⓑ Ⓒ Ⓓ Ⓔ	28 Ⓐ Ⓑ Ⓒ Ⓓ Ⓔ	53 Ⓐ Ⓑ Ⓒ Ⓓ Ⓔ	78 Ⓐ Ⓑ Ⓒ Ⓓ
4 Ⓐ Ⓑ Ⓒ Ⓓ Ⓔ	29 Ⓐ Ⓑ Ⓒ Ⓓ Ⓔ	54 Ⓐ Ⓑ Ⓒ Ⓓ Ⓔ	79 Ⓐ Ⓑ Ⓒ Ⓓ
5 Ⓐ Ⓑ Ⓒ Ⓓ Ⓔ	30 Ⓐ Ⓑ Ⓒ Ⓓ Ⓔ	55 Ⓐ Ⓑ Ⓒ Ⓓ Ⓔ	80 Ⓐ Ⓑ Ⓒ Ⓓ
6 Ⓐ Ⓑ Ⓒ Ⓓ Ⓔ	31 Ⓐ Ⓑ Ⓒ Ⓓ Ⓔ	56 Ⓐ Ⓑ Ⓒ Ⓓ Ⓔ	81 Ⓐ Ⓑ Ⓒ Ⓓ
7 Ⓐ Ⓑ Ⓒ Ⓓ Ⓔ	32 Ⓐ Ⓑ Ⓒ Ⓓ Ⓔ	57 Ⓐ Ⓑ Ⓒ Ⓓ Ⓔ	82 Ⓐ Ⓑ Ⓒ Ⓓ
8 Ⓐ Ⓑ Ⓒ Ⓓ Ⓔ	33 Ⓐ Ⓑ Ⓒ Ⓓ Ⓔ	58 Ⓐ Ⓑ Ⓒ Ⓓ Ⓔ	83 Ⓐ Ⓑ Ⓒ Ⓓ
9 Ⓐ Ⓑ Ⓒ Ⓓ Ⓔ	34 Ⓐ Ⓑ Ⓒ Ⓓ Ⓔ	59 Ⓐ Ⓑ Ⓒ Ⓓ Ⓔ	84 Ⓐ Ⓑ Ⓒ Ⓓ
10 Ⓐ Ⓑ Ⓒ Ⓓ Ⓔ	35 Ⓐ Ⓑ Ⓒ Ⓓ Ⓔ	60 Ⓐ Ⓑ Ⓒ Ⓓ Ⓔ	85 Ⓐ Ⓑ Ⓒ Ⓓ
11 Ⓐ Ⓑ Ⓒ Ⓓ Ⓔ	36 Ⓐ Ⓑ Ⓒ Ⓓ Ⓔ	61 Ⓐ Ⓑ Ⓒ Ⓓ Ⓔ	86 Ⓐ Ⓑ Ⓒ Ⓓ
12 Ⓐ Ⓑ Ⓒ Ⓓ Ⓔ	37 Ⓐ Ⓑ Ⓒ Ⓓ Ⓔ	62 Ⓐ Ⓑ Ⓒ Ⓓ Ⓔ	87 Ⓐ Ⓑ Ⓒ Ⓓ
13 Ⓐ Ⓑ Ⓒ Ⓓ Ⓔ	38 Ⓐ Ⓑ Ⓒ Ⓓ Ⓔ	63 Ⓐ Ⓑ Ⓒ Ⓓ Ⓔ	88 Ⓐ Ⓑ Ⓒ Ⓓ
14 Ⓐ Ⓑ Ⓒ Ⓓ Ⓔ	39 Ⓐ Ⓑ Ⓒ Ⓓ Ⓔ	64 Ⓐ Ⓑ Ⓒ Ⓓ Ⓔ	89 Ⓐ Ⓑ Ⓒ Ⓓ
15 Ⓐ Ⓑ Ⓒ Ⓓ Ⓔ	40 Ⓐ Ⓑ Ⓒ Ⓓ Ⓔ	65 Ⓐ Ⓑ Ⓒ Ⓓ Ⓔ	90 Ⓐ Ⓑ Ⓒ Ⓓ
16 Ⓐ Ⓑ Ⓒ Ⓓ Ⓔ	41 Ⓐ Ⓑ Ⓒ Ⓓ Ⓔ	66 Ⓐ Ⓑ Ⓒ Ⓓ Ⓔ	91 Ⓐ Ⓑ Ⓒ Ⓓ
17 Ⓐ Ⓑ Ⓒ Ⓓ Ⓔ	42 Ⓐ Ⓑ Ⓒ Ⓓ Ⓔ	67 Ⓐ Ⓑ Ⓒ Ⓓ Ⓔ	92 Ⓐ Ⓑ Ⓒ Ⓓ
18 Ⓐ Ⓑ Ⓒ Ⓓ Ⓔ	43 Ⓐ Ⓑ Ⓒ Ⓓ Ⓔ	68 Ⓐ Ⓑ Ⓒ Ⓓ Ⓔ	93 Ⓐ Ⓑ Ⓒ Ⓓ
19 Ⓐ Ⓑ Ⓒ Ⓓ Ⓔ	44 Ⓐ Ⓑ Ⓒ Ⓓ Ⓔ	69 Ⓐ Ⓑ Ⓒ Ⓓ Ⓔ	94 Ⓐ Ⓑ Ⓒ Ⓓ
20 Ⓐ Ⓑ Ⓒ Ⓓ Ⓔ	45 Ⓐ Ⓑ Ⓒ Ⓓ Ⓔ	70 Ⓐ Ⓑ Ⓒ Ⓓ Ⓔ	95 Ⓐ Ⓑ Ⓒ Ⓓ
21 Ⓐ Ⓑ Ⓒ Ⓓ Ⓔ	46 Ⓐ Ⓑ Ⓒ Ⓓ Ⓔ	71 Ⓐ Ⓑ Ⓒ Ⓓ Ⓔ	96 Ⓐ Ⓑ Ⓒ Ⓓ
22 Ⓐ Ⓑ Ⓒ Ⓓ Ⓔ	47 Ⓐ Ⓑ Ⓒ Ⓓ Ⓔ	72 Ⓐ Ⓑ Ⓒ Ⓓ Ⓔ	97 Ⓐ Ⓑ Ⓒ Ⓓ
23 Ⓐ Ⓑ Ⓒ Ⓓ Ⓔ	48 Ⓐ Ⓑ Ⓒ Ⓓ Ⓔ	73 Ⓐ Ⓑ Ⓒ Ⓓ Ⓔ	98 Ⓐ Ⓑ Ⓒ Ⓓ
24 Ⓐ Ⓑ Ⓒ Ⓓ Ⓔ	49 Ⓐ Ⓑ Ⓒ Ⓓ Ⓔ	74 Ⓐ Ⓑ Ⓒ Ⓓ Ⓔ	99 Ⓐ Ⓑ Ⓒ Ⓓ
25 Ⓐ Ⓑ Ⓒ Ⓓ Ⓔ	50 Ⓐ Ⓑ Ⓒ Ⓓ Ⓔ	75 Ⓐ Ⓑ Ⓒ Ⓓ Ⓔ	100 Ⓐ Ⓑ Ⓒ Ⓓ

SECTION 3

1 Ⓐ Ⓑ Ⓒ Ⓓ Ⓔ	26 Ⓐ Ⓑ Ⓒ Ⓓ Ⓔ	51 Ⓐ Ⓑ Ⓒ Ⓓ Ⓔ	76 Ⓐ Ⓑ Ⓒ Ⓓ
2 Ⓐ Ⓑ Ⓒ Ⓓ Ⓔ	27 Ⓐ Ⓑ Ⓒ Ⓓ Ⓔ	52 Ⓐ Ⓑ Ⓒ Ⓓ Ⓔ	77 Ⓐ Ⓑ Ⓒ Ⓓ
3 Ⓐ Ⓑ Ⓒ Ⓓ Ⓔ	28 Ⓐ Ⓑ Ⓒ Ⓓ Ⓔ	53 Ⓐ Ⓑ Ⓒ Ⓓ Ⓔ	78 Ⓐ Ⓑ Ⓒ Ⓓ
4 Ⓐ Ⓑ Ⓒ Ⓓ Ⓔ	29 Ⓐ Ⓑ Ⓒ Ⓓ Ⓔ	54 Ⓐ Ⓑ Ⓒ Ⓓ Ⓔ	79 Ⓐ Ⓑ Ⓒ Ⓓ
5 Ⓐ Ⓑ Ⓒ Ⓓ Ⓔ	30 Ⓐ Ⓑ Ⓒ Ⓓ Ⓔ	55 Ⓐ Ⓑ Ⓒ Ⓓ Ⓔ	80 Ⓐ Ⓑ Ⓒ Ⓓ
6 Ⓐ Ⓑ Ⓒ Ⓓ Ⓔ	31 Ⓐ Ⓑ Ⓒ Ⓓ Ⓔ	56 Ⓐ Ⓑ Ⓒ Ⓓ Ⓔ	81 Ⓐ Ⓑ Ⓒ Ⓓ
7 Ⓐ Ⓑ Ⓒ Ⓓ Ⓔ	32 Ⓐ Ⓑ Ⓒ Ⓓ Ⓔ	57 Ⓐ Ⓑ Ⓒ Ⓓ Ⓔ	82 Ⓐ Ⓑ Ⓒ Ⓓ
8 Ⓐ Ⓑ Ⓒ Ⓓ Ⓔ	33 Ⓐ Ⓑ Ⓒ Ⓓ Ⓔ	58 Ⓐ Ⓑ Ⓒ Ⓓ Ⓔ	83 Ⓐ Ⓑ Ⓒ Ⓓ
9 Ⓐ Ⓑ Ⓒ Ⓓ Ⓔ	34 Ⓐ Ⓑ Ⓒ Ⓓ Ⓔ	59 Ⓐ Ⓑ Ⓒ Ⓓ Ⓔ	84 Ⓐ Ⓑ Ⓒ Ⓓ
10 Ⓐ Ⓑ Ⓒ Ⓓ Ⓔ	35 Ⓐ Ⓑ Ⓒ Ⓓ Ⓔ	60 Ⓐ Ⓑ Ⓒ Ⓓ Ⓔ	85 Ⓐ Ⓑ Ⓒ Ⓓ
11 Ⓐ Ⓑ Ⓒ Ⓓ Ⓔ	36 Ⓐ Ⓑ Ⓒ Ⓓ Ⓔ	61 Ⓐ Ⓑ Ⓒ Ⓓ Ⓔ	86 Ⓐ Ⓑ Ⓒ Ⓓ
12 Ⓐ Ⓑ Ⓒ Ⓓ Ⓔ	37 Ⓐ Ⓑ Ⓒ Ⓓ Ⓔ	62 Ⓐ Ⓑ Ⓒ Ⓓ Ⓔ	87 Ⓐ Ⓑ Ⓒ Ⓓ
13 Ⓐ Ⓑ Ⓒ Ⓓ Ⓔ	38 Ⓐ Ⓑ Ⓒ Ⓓ Ⓔ	63 Ⓐ Ⓑ Ⓒ Ⓓ Ⓔ	88 Ⓐ Ⓑ Ⓒ Ⓓ
14 Ⓐ Ⓑ Ⓒ Ⓓ Ⓔ	39 Ⓐ Ⓑ Ⓒ Ⓓ Ⓔ	64 Ⓐ Ⓑ Ⓒ Ⓓ Ⓔ	89 Ⓐ Ⓑ Ⓒ Ⓓ
15 Ⓐ Ⓑ Ⓒ Ⓓ Ⓔ	40 Ⓐ Ⓑ Ⓒ Ⓓ Ⓔ	65 Ⓐ Ⓑ Ⓒ Ⓓ Ⓔ	90 Ⓐ Ⓑ Ⓒ Ⓓ
16 Ⓐ Ⓑ Ⓒ Ⓓ Ⓔ	41 Ⓐ Ⓑ Ⓒ Ⓓ Ⓔ	66 Ⓐ Ⓑ Ⓒ Ⓓ Ⓔ	91 Ⓐ Ⓑ Ⓒ Ⓓ
17 Ⓐ Ⓑ Ⓒ Ⓓ Ⓔ	42 Ⓐ Ⓑ Ⓒ Ⓓ Ⓔ	67 Ⓐ Ⓑ Ⓒ Ⓓ Ⓔ	92 Ⓐ Ⓑ Ⓒ Ⓓ
18 Ⓐ Ⓑ Ⓒ Ⓓ Ⓔ	43 Ⓐ Ⓑ Ⓒ Ⓓ Ⓔ	68 Ⓐ Ⓑ Ⓒ Ⓓ Ⓔ	93 Ⓐ Ⓑ Ⓒ Ⓓ
19 Ⓐ Ⓑ Ⓒ Ⓓ Ⓔ	44 Ⓐ Ⓑ Ⓒ Ⓓ Ⓔ	69 Ⓐ Ⓑ Ⓒ Ⓓ Ⓔ	94 Ⓐ Ⓑ Ⓒ Ⓓ
20 Ⓐ Ⓑ Ⓒ Ⓓ Ⓔ	45 Ⓐ Ⓑ Ⓒ Ⓓ Ⓔ	70 Ⓐ Ⓑ Ⓒ Ⓓ Ⓔ	95 Ⓐ Ⓑ Ⓒ Ⓓ
21 Ⓐ Ⓑ Ⓒ Ⓓ Ⓔ	46 Ⓐ Ⓑ Ⓒ Ⓓ Ⓔ	71 Ⓐ Ⓑ Ⓒ Ⓓ Ⓔ	96 Ⓐ Ⓑ Ⓒ Ⓓ
22 Ⓐ Ⓑ Ⓒ Ⓓ Ⓔ	47 Ⓐ Ⓑ Ⓒ Ⓓ Ⓔ	72 Ⓐ Ⓑ Ⓒ Ⓓ Ⓔ	97 Ⓐ Ⓑ Ⓒ Ⓓ
23 Ⓐ Ⓑ Ⓒ Ⓓ Ⓔ	48 Ⓐ Ⓑ Ⓒ Ⓓ Ⓔ	73 Ⓐ Ⓑ Ⓒ Ⓓ Ⓔ	98 Ⓐ Ⓑ Ⓒ Ⓓ
24 Ⓐ Ⓑ Ⓒ Ⓓ Ⓔ	49 Ⓐ Ⓑ Ⓒ Ⓓ Ⓔ	74 Ⓐ Ⓑ Ⓒ Ⓓ Ⓔ	99 Ⓐ Ⓑ Ⓒ Ⓓ
25 Ⓐ Ⓑ Ⓒ Ⓓ Ⓔ	50 Ⓐ Ⓑ Ⓒ Ⓓ Ⓔ	75 Ⓐ Ⓑ Ⓒ Ⓓ Ⓔ	100 Ⓐ Ⓑ Ⓒ Ⓓ

FOR TPR USE ONLY	V1	V2	V3	V4	M1	M2	M3	M4	M5	M6	M7	M8

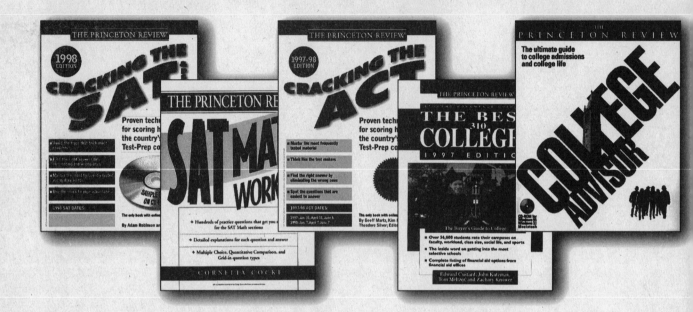

THE PRINCETON REVIEW WORLDWIDE

Each year, thousands of students from countries throughout the world prepare for the TOEFL and for U.S. college and graduate school admissions exams. Whether you plan to prepare for your exams in your home country or the United States, The Princeton Review is committed to your success.

INTERNATIONAL LOCATIONS: If you are using our books outside of the United States and have questions or comments, or want to know if our courses are being offered in your area, be sure to contact The Princeton Review office nearest you:

- CANADA (Montreal)   514-499-0870
- CANADA (Toronto)   800-495-7737
- HONG KONG   852-2517-3016
- JAPAN (Tokyo)   8133-463-1343
- KOREA (Seoul)   822-508-0081
- MEXICO (Mexico City)   525-564-9468
- PAKISTAN (Lahore)   92-42-571-2315
- SAUDI ARABIA   413-584-6849 (a U.S. based number)
- SPAIN (Madrid)   341-323-4212
- TAIWAN (Taipei)   886-27511293

U.S. STUDY ABROAD: *Review USA* offers international students many advantages and opportunities. In addition to helping you gain acceptance to the U.S. college or university of your choice, *Review USA* will help you acquire the knowledge and orientation you need to succeed once you get there.

Review USA is unique. It includes supplements to your test-preparation courses and a special series of *AmeriCulture* workshops to prepare you for the academic rigors and student life in the United States. Our workshops are designed to familiarize you with the different U.S. expressions, real-life vocabulary, and cultural challenges you will encounter as a study-abroad student. While studying with us, you'll make new friends and have the opportunity to personally visit college and university campuses to determine which school is right for you.

Whether you are planning to take the TOEFL, SAT, GRE, GMAT, LSAT, MCAT, or USMLE exam, The Princeton Review's test preparation courses, expert instructors, and dedicated International Student Advisors can help you achieve your goals.

For additional information about *Review USA*, admissions requirements, class schedules, F-1 visas, I-20 documentation, and course locations, write to:

The Princeton Review • Review USA
2315 Broadway, New York, NY 10024
Fax: 212/874-0775

TOURING COLLEGES VIA VIDEOTAPE

A critical part of choosing the right college to attend is visiting the campuses of those that you're considering. It's most likely that you'll apply to several colleges, which can send travel expenses soaring if you attempt to visit every one. And videos from the admissions office are far from the next best thing to being there—some of them are scripted and staged almost as elaborately as a Hollywood production! We've found an alternative.

The Klass Report College Video Tours can help to ease the hit on your parents' wallet and give you the chance to get a closer, objective look at the colleges you're considering. Their videos are full-length, unaffiliated, unbiased tours of major colleges and universities. Each tour includes the entire campus: academic and athletic buildings, housing, frats and sororities, the surrounding area, transportation, shopping and entertainment options, and student hangouts are all visited via the video lens. Candid interviews with students are also included to help clue you in on campus life. Once you've viewed Klass Report videos, you'll be better able to decide which campuses to put on your travel schedule.

The Klass Report College Video Tours cost $19.95 per school; if you order three or more you'll receive one free. To order, or to get more information, call 1-800-638-1330, write The Klass Report, 317 Madison Avenue, Suite 206, New York, NY 10017, or visit their web site at: http://www.klassreport.com/videos.